"A good story is worth its weight in gold! And the stories compiled by Lori and Mary are worth ten times the price of the book they have written. This is a true gift to all trainers and consultants. Thank you Lori and Mary."

—Elaine Biech, author,
The Business of Consulting

"Stories Trainers Tell *is full of fun, entertaining, and useful stories that help bring any training alive. Use it and watch people smile and learn!"*

—Ken Blanchard, coauthor,
The One Minute Manager® *and*
Whale Done!™

"This highly useful book is an immediate source of good stories to enrich training. But even more useful are the chapters on how to develop and present your own stories! A wonderful addition to any trainer's resource shelf."

—Barbara Benedict Bunker, Ph.D.,
professor of psychology emerita,
The University at Buffalo (SUNY)

"Stories Trainers Tell *is a 'must have' resource for any new or experienced trainer, speaker, or educator. It provides a wealth of 'real world' stories that you can use to help bring life, fun, and insight to a variety of learning situations and topics."*

—Richard Chang, CEO,
Richard Chang Associates, Inc.
and author, The Passion Plan
and The Passion Plan at Work

"I've forgotten most of everything I've ever learned, but I rarely forget a good story. This book will support you in telling stories that penetrate deep. Great storytelling will create magical links to the listener, resulting in sustained impact and transformation."

—Thomas Crum,
author of Journey to Center *and*
The Magic of Conflict

"Trainers and speakers from every discipline will create memorable presentations with use of this fine book. It explores the purposes for using stories, provides great stories that can be adapted for speaker presentations, discusses the elements of a successful story and even gives step-by-step guidance on creating new stories. This is a 'must have' book for speakers wanting to better relate to their audiences."

—Linda Ewing, vice president,
Marketing and Sales,
CUNA Credit Union

"As leaders and managers, we are all teachers within an organization and one of our most powerful tools in humanizing the mission of the organization is storytelling. This book serves as a comprehensive guide to unleashing that power to create a vivid picture of the organization's and people's potential."

—Jacquelyn Fredrick, president and CEO,
Blood Center of Southeastern Wisconsin
and former senior vice president,
American Red Cross

"For teachers, trainers, speakers, coaches and leaders at every level, this is the single most complete and useful resource I have seen for putting the power of storytelling to work for you immediately. It not only gives you stories to tell, it teaches you how to create and tell your own."

—Tom Hilgart, vice president,
Learning & Development,
CNA Insurance

"Bravo Mary and Lori! You've given your own profession a wonderful gift. Your contribution will be used by trainers for many years to come."

—Beverly Kaye, CEO,
Career Systems International, coeditor,
Learning Journeys: Top Management
Experts Share Hard-Earned Lessons
On Becoming Great Mentors and Leaders

"The most effective employee-development programs influence emotion, not just thought. Authors Silverman and Wacker understand this power of narrative to impact feelings, and provide a rich mine of insights and applications for using stories in the service of training."

—Peter Orton, Ph.D.,
chief learning designer,
IBM Center for Advanced Learning

"In my training experience, I have found storytelling to be one of the most powerful ways to deepen learning. This book provides trainers, consultants, and others with valuable tools and ideas to create and deliver engaging stories for any audience."

—Reggie Owens, manager,
Global Learning and Development,
Rockwell Automation

"Stories Trainers Tell *doesn't just give you powerful stories, it helps you turn your experiences into compelling narratives, people and teams into heroes worth emulating, and new changes into enduring traditions. It will help your own wisdom penetrate and be remembered through the stories you tell."*

—Terry Paulson, Ph.D., CSP, CPAE, past president,
National Speakers Association and author,
50 Tips for Speaking Like a Pro *and*
They Shoot Managers Don't They?

"People learn best through stories—something they can relate to and remember. Stories Trainers Tell *will provide me with a resource to help when I'm struggling to find just that right story. What a wonderful resource for all trainers and facilitators."*

—Kathy Zarr, director,
Management Training and Facilitation Services,
Fiserv, Inc.

Stories Trainers Tell

55 READY-TO-USE STORIES TO MAKE TRAINING STICK

Mary B. Wacker
Lori L. Silverman

JOSSEY-BASS/PFEIFFER
A Wiley Company
www.pfeiffer.com

Published by Pfeiffer
An Imprint of John Wiley & Sons, Inc.
989 Market Street, San Francisco, CA 94103-1741 www.pfeiffer.com

1640 King Street Box 1443
Alexandria, VA 22313-2043 USA
Tel 800.628.2783 703.683.8100
Fax 703.683.8103
www.astd.org

Page 398 constitutes a continuation of this copyright page.

Pfeiffer books and products are available through most bookstores. To contact Pfeiffer directly call our Customer Care Department within the U.S. at (800) 274-4434, outside the U.S. at (317) 572-3985 or fax (317) 572-4002. Substantial discounts on bulk quantities of Pfeiffer books are available to corporations, professional associations, and other organizations. For details and discount information, contact the Special Sales department at Pfeiffer.

Pfeiffer also publishes its books in a variety of electronic formats. Some content that appears in print may not be available in electronic books.

Printed in the United States of America

ISBN: 0-7879-6436-0

Library of Congress Cataloging-in-Publication Data

Wacker, Mary B., 1950-
Stories trainers tell : 55 ready-to-use stories to make training stick
/ By Mary B. Wacker and Lori L. Silverman.
p. cm.
Includes bibliographical references and index.
ISBN 0-7879-6436-0 (alk. paper)
1. Employees, Training of—Anecdotes. 2. Learning—Anecdotes.
3. Storytelling. I. Title: 55 ready-to-use stories to make training stick.
II. Silverman, Lori L., 1958- III. Title.
HF5549.5.T7 W314 2003
658.3'12404—dc21
2002154864

Acquiring Editor: Matthew Davis
Director of Development: Kathleen Dolan Davies
Senior Production Editor: Dawn Kilgore
Manufacturing Supervisor: Bill Matherly
Cover Design: Michael Cook
Printed in the United States of America
Printing 10 9 8 7 6 5 4 3 2

To trainers everywhere, in all walks of life—
storytellers, speakers, managers, facilitators,
consultants, and educators—
we applaud you for telling your stories
so that we may all continue to learn.

To my family—in appreciation for all the stories
we have lived together.

Mary

To Bob—whose incredible stories and love
have helped me blossom as a storyteller.

Lori

ABOUT ASTD

ASTD is the world's leading association of workplace learning and performance professionals, forming a world-class community of practice. ASTD's 70,000 members come from more than one hundred countries and 15,000 organizations, multinational corporations, medium-sized and small businesses, government, academia, consulting firms, and product and service suppliers.

Started in 1944 as the American Society of Training Directors, ASTD is now a global force, widening the industry's focus to connect learning and performance to measurable results, and is a sought-after voice on critical public policy issues.

For more information, visit www.astd.org or call 800.628.8723 (International, 703.683.8100).

CONTENTS

SECTION TWO

FOREWORD

Stories have long been used to teach. Probably the oldest recorded examples are Aesop's Fables. Was the story of a race between a tortoise and a hare about the facts, or were there deeper truths embedded in the story and transmitted to the listeners? Jesus taught in parables. Listeners learned on many levels depending on the degree of openness they had. However, learning always took place. Before history was recorded, stories were used to help people remember their past—where they came from. During the Dark Ages, minstrels went from town to town carrying the news, history, and legends in the form of song—stories put to music. In almost all of these settings stories were used to help people remember—and learn.

To use stories in training and other presentations there must always be a learning point, or perhaps more than one. The storyteller may provide it—or the listeners may come up with the point or points themselves.

"The Wise Man and the Baby Bird" is the story of a young boy who wanted to impress his friends (Chapter Four). An ancient mystic lived nearby who had never been known to give a wrong answer to any question he was asked. The boy said, "I will take a live bird in my hand to the wise one and ask him if the bird is alive or dead. If he answers, 'Alive,' I will crush the bird in my hands and throw it at his feet. If he answers, 'Dead,' I will let the bird go free."

The boys went to the place of the wise one and the brash boy asked his question. The ancient mystic pondered for a moment and then said, "The answer, my son, rests in your hands." A simple story, but how many truths are embedded within? At least three. See how many applications you can make from this story for yourself.

And that is what this book is all about. The authors, Mary Wacker and Lori Silverman, have drawn on the resources of many of the top trainers and consultants today, not simply to showcase their abilities as storytellers, but to get them to share with you the behind-the-scenes tips that will enable you to bring the power of stories to your own training, presentations, and consulting.

Some of us follow well the learning model of *experience, awareness,* and *theory.* What I mean by that, in the context of this book, is that you read or hear a story (experience), extrapolate all kinds of learning points (awareness), and then when you read the theory behind why a story is told in a certain way or used in a certain place, it cements everything for you. If this is you, you can go straight to the stories beginning with Chapter Seven.

For others, a better model is *theory, experience,* and *awareness.* You'll read the six chapters Mary and Lori have provided that relate how to choose stories, how to tell them, how to embed learning points, and so on. This is the *theory.* Then as you go on to the stories, you'll *experience* in practice all the theory they've shared with you. This will then deepen your *awareness* and allow you to start using these as well as your own stories in your work.

This book can be one of the most powerful learning tools you'll ever possess. The stories will ignite your imagination and enhance your own work. The how-to's will polish the stories you already tell to a greater degree than you perhaps ever imagined. Your audiences will be enriched by your expanded competence and confidence.

One final tip: As you go through this book, keep in mind these words—*modify, adjust, adapt,* and then *adopt.* The authors and storytellers in this volume are experts in what they do, but they are not experts in your situation, organization, or audience. So as you examine each idea, rather than thinking to yourself, "I could never use that," ask yourself, "How could I modify, adjust, and adapt this idea so that I could then adopt it for my work?" It's another way of saying, "I will look for ways things *can* be done, not reasons they *cannot.*"

And finally, a request—our storytellers have graciously shared stories that they have carefully crafted and polished over the years. If you choose to use one or more of these stories, please be sure to give them credit. For example you might say, "In talking about values, Ed Scannell shared a story that really makes a useful point here."

Regardless of whether you choose to start by reviewing the theory in the first six chapters and then diving into the stories in Section Two, or if you decide to go straight to the stories, please carefully read Chapter Six—it provides all the ethical and legal knowledge you need to know so that you will always be a storyteller of high integrity.

So, enjoy the book. I have.

Bob Pike CSP, CPAE, Speakers Hall of Fame
founder and editor of
The Creative Training Techniques newsletter
chairman and CEO of The Bob Pike Group

PREFACE

A child comes home from school. Her dad asks, "What did you do today?" At work, a staff member inquires of a colleague, "How are things?" Arriving home from a sales call, a husband asks his wife, "How did it go?" Each of these questions provides the opening for a story to be told and shared with others. Stories and storytelling are woven into the very fabric of our personal lives. Stories have the unique ability to engage our minds, our hearts, our physical beings, and our souls. In and of themselves, stories are able to move us and motivate us in ways that other forms of communication cannot.

Organizations spend significant dollars orienting new hires, providing on-the-job training, offering skill- and knowledge-based workshops, and fostering formal continuing education. While these endeavors may embrace an experiential approach to training and development—through the use of ice breakers, case studies, demonstrations, activities, and the like—those who facilitate them rarely use stories that are as well thought-out and planned as these other approaches. If stories are so powerful, what keeps us from using them more often in these settings? The opportunities to tell them are certainly plentiful. Our experience has been that trainers often do not see themselves as storytellers, incorporating them "in the moment" in their training sessions almost as an afterthought or in response to a participant's comment. One trainer and speaker, whom we highly value and have heard tell wonderful stories, took us by surprise with his response to the invitation to contribute to this book. He emailed, "But I'm not a storyteller! I don't think I have anything to contribute." For us as authors, this generated an insightful series of conversations about how trainers view themselves in relation to using stories in their work. It is our contention that those who provide training may not be fully aware of their own power and capability as storytellers. Nor are they fully aware of the purposes and benefits of stories in a training setting, how to find and create stories that have a powerful training impact, specific ways to incorporate them into a training session, and how to tell them in a memorable fashion.

HOW THE BOOK WAS DEVELOPED

This book was created using the expertise, wisdom, and stories from forty contributors who represent a variety of perspectives: professional storytellers, nationally known speakers, trainers, consultants, academics in higher education, and business executives and managers. During March and April 2002, thirty-one of them were interviewed on questions about the use of stories in their work, effective and ineffective storytellers, their own storytelling approaches, how they create stories, and using stories from other sources (see the Appendix for a list of the interview questions). The resulting responses were synthesized using an affinity diagram process. Along with our own insights and research, this material forms the basis for the first six chapters of the book. In addition, thirty-six of the participants elected to contribute one or more stories, which were either audiotaped or communicated to us in writing to ensure their content accuracy. Contributors were given guidelines that the stories had to be generally applicable to a wide variety of audiences, had to be easily retold by others, were to be no more than several minutes in length, and could be about real people and real situations or be allegorical or metaphorical in nature. The final story categories and their chapter titles emerged as the stories were compiled.

WHO WE ARE

We, as authors, collectively have more than forty years of experience in the training and development arena, as instructional designers, trainers, and managers. In addition, we present keynote talks, function as personal and executive coaches, provide organization development consulting, write for publication, and own our own businesses. The work for which people seek us out includes project management, business strategy, enterprise-wide change, customer service, teamwork and team facilitation, and leadership. In each and every one of these venues and niches, stories are a critical component of our work. In fact, we find that we cannot function without them as a part of our toolkit. Whether it is telling our own stories or those from other sources, or helping others to craft and convey their own experiences, stories form the basis by which we assist people and organizations in their lifelong learning journeys.

Our use of stories is both planned and spontaneous. When creating workshops or keynotes, we integrate stories into the design process before they are ever delivered. However, participant comments or non-verbal cues may trigger the need to communicate a story that was not a part of the original agenda. In our consulting and coaching work, stories give us the ability to easily express key points and enhance receptivity to change at all levels of the organization. When humorous and engaging, we have found that stories can also release tension and infuse energy into a situation.

We are continually on the lookout for new story additions to our existing repertoire. It is not unusual for our colleagues, friends, and family members to share stories with us that they believe will benefit others. We hope that you will do the same—information on how to contribute stories can be found in There Are More Stories to Tell.

It is our hope that we will instill in you the same passion we have for using stories in your work.

ACKNOWLEDGMENTS

Storytelling is, fundamentally, a collaboration between the teller and the listener(s). Thus, it is fitting that a book about stories is also, fundamentally, a collaborative effort. We celebrate here the many individuals whose insights, intelligence, energy, and generosity are woven into these pages and into our hearts. On behalf of all who use stories in their work, we appreciate you and your contributions.

The initial idea for this book was the brainchild of Laura V. Page of Page Consulting. Laura put forth the idea at a pre-Thanksgiving dinner in 2000 with friends that both Laura and Mary Wacker attended. Over the next several months, Laura and Mary expanded the general concept and submitted a proposal to Senior Editor Mark Morrow at ASTD Press. Mark's enthusiasm for the project led to approaching Jossey-Bass/Pfeiffer. When personal changes caused Laura to move in a different direction, Lori Silverman joined the project as co-author to help incorporate Laura's insights, guidance, and spirit throughout this work. We are extremely grateful for Laura's creative vision and insightful ideas.

The primary sources for this book were forty contributors who represent a variety of perspectives: professional storytellers, nationally known speakers, trainers, consultants, academics in higher education, and business executives and managers. Without these benevolent contributors, this book would not exist. We deeply appreciate their insights, humor, generosity, and willingness to share their personal experiences in print. We also appreciate their spirit of adventure to invest in this project. We have found them to be strong proponents of using stories in their work and extremely gracious with their time and knowledge. We honor this very special group of individuals: Merrill Anderson, Jean Barbazette, Joe Barnes, Paula Bartholome, Chip Bell, Geoff Bellman, William Austin Boone, Sharon L. Bowman, Karen D. L. Bryson, Chris Clarke-Epstein, Hortencia Delgadillo, Larry P. English, Marcy Fisher, Suzann Gardner, Joan Gillman, Steve Hanamura, Lunell Haught, Sandra Hoskins, Katherine M. Hudson, David Hutchens, Joan Lloyd, Kate Lutz, Robert McIlree, Maureen G. Mulvaney (MGM), Kathy A. Nielsen, Clare Novak, Julie O'Mara, Laura V. Page, Jonathan M. Preston, John Renesch, Shelley R. Robbins, Marcia Ruben, Sheriene Saadati, Edward E. Scannell, LG Shanklin-Flowers, Bob Shaver, Doug Stevenson, Ed Tate, Sivasailam "Thiagi" Thiagarajan, and David Zach. In addition to the many contributors who offered us referrals to other participants in this venture, we appreciate the suggestions from Sheila O'Shea, Molly Koranda, and Mary Hanneman. Please note that if a quotation that appears within the text is not attributed to a published source, it was taken from personal communications with the authors.

A special appreciation goes to Doug Stevenson who so generously allowed us to incorporate his models on story types and story structure into this book. Doug has influenced both our storywriting and storytelling styles and, in coaching the actors whose voices you hear on the CD-ROM, has greatly enhanced the value of this work. His unselfish support of this project is a model for all who create and yet are willing to share. Continuing in the spirit of sharing, we would like to acknowledge Ed Scannell, whose well-known *Games Trainers Play* series helped inspire the title of this work. He has been a wonderful collaborator.

Once we created the framework for each story, we greatly needed some objectivity. A group of colleagues and contributors kindly offered to review our stories and accompanying material. Their feedback helped shape the book you see today. We thank Cathy Alper, Merrill Anderson, Paula Bartholome, Marcy Fisher, Cheryl Lucas, Kate Lutz, Robert McIlree, Clare Novak, Laura V. Page, Sheriene Saadati, and Jennifer Stearns for their rigorous critiques and loyal support. Along with the story reviews, several blind reviewers offered many helpful suggestions and comments for our second draft.

When we first approached Bob Pike about writing a foreword for the book, we had to contact him by email as he was traveling in Kuala Lumpur. Despite an extremely busy international schedule, he most graciously contributed his thoughts on the history of storytelling and why stories are such an important resource for trainers. We appreciate his special words that so effectively set the tone for the book. His many contributions to the field, along with his extensive knowledge of the industry, are matched by his generous support of colleagues with new projects.

Our team of collaborators includes attorney Leslie F. Kramer whose knowledge of copyright and the publishing industry along with a healthy dose of goodwill continue to guide us and keep us legal. Steve Silverman, brand-marketing guru, helped create a brilliant list of title ideas reflected in the selected choice as well as cover ideas for the book. The hours he spent reading stories to get a true feel for the project were a sincere gift to us, one we deeply appreciate. Anita Johnson spent tireless hours transcribing audiotape interviews for us. Her humor and willingness to take on this monumental task enabled us to capture the wisdom of our contributors. We could not have done it without her. Among our valued supporters are our family and friends. Their willingness to serve as sounding boards, listeners, cheerleaders, problem solvers, and even cooks has been invaluable and reminded us once again how connected we all are in the ongoing stories of our lives.

Over the months, we have developed significant relationships with editors and staff at Jossey-Bass/Pfeiffer. Their continued support, willingness to consider our ideas and suggestions (of which we have many), and their follow-through on everything from copyright issues to formatting make them a terrific group with which to partner. Matt Davis, as senior editor, was our first connection on contracting and then marketing. His guidance, unfailing belief in this project, and unflappable goodwill have been a constant throughout. Kathleen Dolan Davies, director of development, is quick to respond to every request. Her intelligence, humor, and skill in juggling countless editorial decisions have helped the project immeasurably. Other key team members include Jeanenne Ray, Gabriela Bayardo, Jin Im, Samya Sattar, Laura Reizman, Dawn Kilgore, and Julie Matthews and her colleagues at ICC, along with the legal, marketing, and sales staff. Their judgment, faith, and talent helped bring this book into being. We also applaud Jill Tracy and Walt Anthony for their talent and expertise in recording the stories for the CD-ROM.

Finally, this book could not have been written without you, the reader, who shares our passion for making training, in any format, come alive. Your commitment to enliven your learning environments and deepen your participants' understanding has enabled this book to find its way to you. Your stories are some of your best resources in supporting you as a professional dedicated to developing others. Thank you for the opportunity to share a few more stories with you along the path we travel together.

Mary B. Wacker
Lori L. Silverman

INTRODUCTION

Discovering the Power of Stories (A)

Contributed by David Hutchens, principal, iconoclast communications

In the mid-1990s I worked as a freelance writer and training designer in Atlanta. For a long time I wanted to connect with a highly respected Fortune 100 corporation. Finally the opportunity arose. This organization was one of a handful that had a major initiative around what Peter Senge, author of *The Fifth Discipline* (1990) calls a "learning organization." The problem was that when key people talked about this concept nobody knew what they were talking about. Eyes would just glaze over. So I was brought in to write a communications piece to spread the word about being a learning organization.

I was thrilled. I went home and spent many, many hours summarizing the principles and the ideals and tools of a learning organization. I put them together in a graphically rich document that was attractive and pleasurable to read and illuminated what these models, tools, and ideals were all about.

I brought the document back to my client. She flipped through it one page at a time, nodding silently while I sat there. After the last page, she looked up and said, "What else have you got?" I gave her the standard consultant answer: "I really feel that this is our best option at this point." She said, "I want you to go home and take one more shot at this and see what you come up with." I gulped and said, "All right. I'll do that."

I felt *terrible.* I didn't know how to explain these models and tools and ideals any better or more clearly. After some long walks, I sat at my computer and wrote, "Once upon a time there was a sheep." What resulted was a story about a flock of sheep that outwitted a pack of wolves by becoming a learning organization and in the process modeled many of the principles. Then I sent an email to a buddy of mine in Dallas who illustrates children's books—he owed me a favor. I said, "Hey, Bobby, can you draw me a picture of a sheep and a wolf?" He said, "No problem." I finished it off by writing a few pages to connect the story to the concept: "Here's how the experience of the sheep mirrored that of a learning organization."

I went back for a second meeting with my client. I put the document in front of her and she opened it and began reading. I had built in some humor—it had a weird, *Saturday Night Live*-type irreverent vibe to it. So, I watched to see if she would laugh at the funny parts. She would kind of go, "A-ha." And I thought, "Is that a laugh or is it disgust?" I couldn't tell. As she finished the last page she said, "Thank you, David. I need some time to think about this." Just like that, the meeting was over. I went home and my wife asked how it went. I said, "I think I just lost the account."

Then, an interesting thing happened. My client made a photocopy of this story, which was called "Outlearning the Wolves," and gave it to one of her colleagues and said, "Tell me what you think about this." Well . . . her colleague read it, made a copy, and said to another colleague, "You've got to read this thing." Before you knew it there were underground black market copies of "Outlearning the Wolves" circulating everywhere. My client had to tell people to stop distributing it and collect all the copies.

This communications piece wasn't what the organization wanted but I did get some other work. I asked if I could retain the rights to the story and was told, "Sure. God bless you. We hope you can sell it." I sent it to a publisher called Pegasus Communications that does a lot of work in organizational learning. The firm called me within a week and said, "We want to buy this." It has since been published and translated into a bunch of different languages and has led to a series of four books that illustrate everything from mental models to system theory.

I frequently share this story with groups. When I get to the end, I'll say, "Notice what just happened. I just told you a story about storytelling. I did *not* start with a PowerPoint presentation. I did *not* have bullet points outlining what you need to know. Instead I simply *told* the story. It's interesting to watch all of you because you put your pens and pencils down, leaned back in your chairs, spread your arms, opened your postures, and just listened. If I had started with a bullet point list, you would have behaved differently. That's because when you hear statistics or information in list form you become very critical and evaluative. You start saying, 'Hmmm. That's a very interesting list. Are those points valuable for me and my organization? Yes, number one and number two are true. I don't know what he means by point number three. Point four . . . yeah, that's okay I guess.'"

Instead, when I told the story, you entered into a different orientation. You're no longer critical or evaluative. You aren't saying things like, "Hey, is that true? Does that apply to me?" Instead you're simply engaged and listening to me. I see you smile and nod and follow the story. You're participating. In fact, you're making your own connections. Like thinking about the times when you tried to land a big account and felt like you'd screwed it up. Or, identifying with how I was feeling or your own desire to write stories. Who knows? It's different with each person.

WHAT IS A STORY?

A parable. A myth. A fairy tale. Folklore. Legend. Life experience. Even gossip. All of these are examples of different forms that stories can take. David Hutchens defines a story as "a narrative that illustrates complex interconnections between agents, ideas, events, and even abstract concepts." Most of the contributors we interviewed for this book mentioned that every story at its core is about change—change in behavior, thinking, attitude, emotions, and the like. What is the converse? What types of communications do not qualify as a story? Facts, theory, brief examples, and lists of points to remember are not stories. In the workplace we often focus on this sort of communication—sharing facts and numbers, giving examples of what will and will not work, and providing information that describes the rationale for a decision. We use them because we feel pressured to be smart or come up with the "one correct answer."

Stories, on the other hand, are messier. One of our contributors, Chris Clarke-Epstein, suggests that there is a psychological change in brainwaves when we go into story mode—from left-brain judgment mode to right-brain experience mode.

When we hear a story, each of us creates our own sense of meaning from it. As David suggests, stories validate our experiences; they respect each person as being an expert in his or her own life. Often people do not even arrive at the same understanding or outcome—yet they collectively may be drawn closer together as a result of hearing it.

THE BENEFITS OF USING STORIES

What makes a story a unique form of communication? Contributor Doug Stevenson suggests that it is the only form that bridges all learning styles; that allows people to pick up information visually (by creating pictures in the mind's eye), auditorally (through hearing the story) and kinesthetically (through what one feels viscerally and/or emotionally); and touches one's mind, heart, soul, and physical being (for example, through laughter).

Both trainers and trainees know the long-term value of experiential or discovery learning. Consequently, those who provide training in this manner use techniques such as case studies, ice breakers, role-plays, large-group discussions, and small-group activities. Stories are another way of bringing discovery learning into a training situation. They are easier to listen to and are much more memorable and engaging than hearing a list of bulleted items that outline what to remember or how to behave in a specific situation. Think about it. When was the last time you told others about a checklist you received in training? Now, when was the last time you recounted a story that you heard in a training session? It is not unusual to find people retelling a story to their colleagues, rather than reciting specific content material, because it is the story that made a lasting impression.

STORYTELLING WISDOM

"Stories ground people to think differently—to be able to listen and hear things they haven't been able to in the past."

Paula Bartholome

Just by hearing a story, listeners have the opportunity to draw their own conclusions and decide what the story personally means to them. Chances are also good that they may email or talk about the story with their family and friends, thus reinforcing the message they gained from it. The impact of stories becomes even more powerful and much richer than other training techniques when trainees are given the opportunity to debrief them individually or in groups and engage in activities that encourage further reflection. In these ways, stories can accelerate learning.

As Steve Hanamura points out, stories are a way to bring "high touch" back into a "high tech" world—a world where people are starved for personal connections. Going further, Paula asserts that not only are people hungry for connections, they also hunger for things that are larger than themselves. She goes on to say, "Our work is fractured these days and people don't experience community and family in the same ways they have in the past. Stories allow emotions to come through and be honored." By using stories, including those based on personal experiences, trainers can more easily forge a connection with trainees and become more human in the process. Depending on the story, listeners may be more willing to be vulnerable if the main character was vulnerable as well, and yet still achieved success. Geoff Bellman's "Time Brings Perspective" (Chapter Twelve) is a good example of this; it demonstrates the power of teaching through our own life lessons.

Stories about the organization's products or services, past experiences, history, or industry can also help to personalize a workshop. In fact, the one learning technique that has withstood the test of time with various social and cultural groups is the communication of history and oral tradition through storytelling.

THE PITFALLS OF USING STORIES

Although we, as authors, are strong proponents of storytelling during training, we also recognize that there are several pitfalls associated with the story itself, how the story is told, and storytelling in general. Unless we carefully plan where to use stories, practice how to tell them, and think about the reason for telling them, we might encounter these pitfalls more than once.

What can go wrong with the story? A story will not be effective in a training session if it has no point or is not directly linked to the training. How many times have you had one of your learners tell a story that leaves the rest of the participants looking puzzled? Some stories ramble, or seem to head in a direction and then shift gears. While these stories may be humorous and take us on an enjoyable journey, without a clear link to the learning at hand they fall flat as a vehicle for increasing knowledge or understanding. A similar pitfall is telling a story with the *wrong* point. It may be a great story, but if it does not support participants' learning the particular material, save it for another time. These outcomes sometimes occur when a story is told as an afterthought by the trainer. While we encourage trainers to read their groups' needs and use stories as a way to spontaneously meet them, we caution you to make sure the stories have a clear connection to the information being taught and to the trainees' immediate needs.

A great story can also fall flat if it is poorly told. Trainers need to practice the stories they plan to incorporate into their teaching in order to convey them in a powerful way. Lack of confidence can hinder a trainer from venturing into the storytelling arena. Timing, pacing, vocal inflection, and creating a sense of drama through body movements all offer a richness of experience that a case study or example cannot. Without consideration for these elements, the story can miss the mark and reflect poorly on the trainer's skills. Trainers can miss the opportunity to build learners' interest and momentum by using a story as a brief example, revealing the point too early, and telling the rest of the story almost as an afterthought. Chapter Five offers a number of pointers on how to tell stories effectively in a training setting.

Finally, some pitfalls have to do with the relationship between the trainer and the concept of storytelling. For some, the very act of storytelling during training is seen as squishy, especially because stories forge a connection between the teller and the listener that is stronger and more emotional than other types of training techniques. Trainers may avoid using stories, believing that their participants will think the program is not credible if learning is linked to them. Having the appropriate balance between stories and other learning vehicles is important. Some trainers have been known to tell so many stories that while the participants may be entertained, they leave the session without having learned or practiced needed skills.

Numerous resources speak to the power of stories in enhancing learning. We encourage trainers to do their own research and to pay attention to the power of stories in programs and presentations they attend as participants. Letting these cautions influence a decision not to use stories can rob both trainers and their learners of enhanced skill development and enjoyment in the process of learning.

PURPOSE OF THE BOOK

Our main purpose is to provide fifty-five ready-to-use, scripted stories that anyone who provides training can tell to increase impact and make the training stick. The accompanying book chapters provide the framework for selecting, developing, and using stories in a training setting. As such, the book is a resource for those who want to know more about using stories in *training* to promote specific outcomes and instill long-term value. Woven throughout these chapters are additional stories that can also be shared orally with others. There are numerous books available on the topic of storytelling (see the Suggested Readings for titles). Because of this, *Stories Trainers Tell* is not intended to be an exhaustive resource on the topic.

Books of stories, such as the *Chicken Soup* series for the general public and the *Ready-to-Tell Tales* series for professional storytellers, have come to the forefront over the past decade. While these books present a variety of wonderful stories that can be told to others, the content of them has not been selected or designed for a training audience. What makes *Stories Trainers Tell* unique is that the stories within this book have been carefully chosen and specifically written to foster and enhance ongoing learning, behavior change, and skill development. In addition, the book also outlines the instructional design elements required to reap the stories' full benefit in a training setting.

WHO THIS BOOK IS FOR

This book is meant to be a resource for anyone who wants to increase his or her use of stories and their impact when providing training, whether it is one-on-one or in a small- or large-group setting. This includes training and development professionals, organization development and management consultants, personal and executive coaches, speakers, frontline employees, supervisors, managers, executives, business owners, teachers, and faculty at colleges and universities. All readers can benefit from identifying where stories can be beneficial in their training work, how to develop a story from real-life experiences or from other sources, and how and when to present them to others. The stories themselves are a wonderful vehicle for communicating challenging ideas, abstract concepts, appropriate or inappropriate behaviors, and enduring ideals.

Keep in mind that stories are not just for use in "soft skills" training programs. In fact, they can and need to play a critical role in technical training situations. Often these "hard skills" programs are very linear in design and instruction. They can benefit from stories that help participants to more fully grasp and recall key learning concepts, why a procedure needs to be done in a particular manner, and what can be the outcome of not following a specific policy or set of steps. Consider the following example. You have been asked to design and teach a course on the use of Microsoft Project software. The course covers the intricacies of using the software in planning, estimating, scheduling, and reporting projects. Stories that would be useful in this program include those that show what can happen when estimating does not precede scheduling, why it is necessary to collect data on actuals, and the impact on a project if certain controls are turned on versus turned off when information is input to the system.

STORYTELLING WISDOM

"Stories are the way we naturally think; the way we sort the natural information in our brain. They are also a way to remember—they cement ideas in our brain."

Kate Lutz

In general, full- and part-time training and development professionals, including instructional designers and developers of training materials, will find this book to be a complementary resource to the myriad of experiential training materials that are available. For individuals who provide training on an occasional basis, the stories and the information on how to discuss them will enhance their training delivery. Those who provide train-the-trainer workshops or more formal courses on developing trainers and their skills and knowledge will find the subjects covered in this book to be a valuable addition to their existing topics and course offerings. Individuals who are transitioning into the training and development field or who are adding training to their current skill set will be able to learn and practice their storytelling skills using this work.

Because the stories in this book often are examples of what or what not to do, they can be told by consultants and coaches to facilitate individual or group decision-making, to highlight the need to alter a particular behavior or skill, and to identify how to act in specific situations. Organizational leaders will find these stories help make enterprise-wide philosophies, values, and needed changes more visual, tangible, and real. For those who perform in a speaking capacity, these stories may serve as an addition to their existing repertoire.

HOW THE BOOK IS ORGANIZED

There are two distinct sections to this book. Section One is composed of six chapters. The question, "What makes a story a training story?" is the theme of Chapter One, which introduces seven types of stories based on the work of contributor Doug Stevenson. It also explores seven primary purposes of training stories and showcases several illustrative stories. In order to use stories in training, you need to identify how and where to find them, which is the topic of Chapter Two. For those of you who decide to use or create your own stories, Chapter Three gives you a step-by-step approach on crafting them for use in a training setting. The focus of Chapter Four is how to incorporate stories into training, both during the instructional design process and when the training is being presented. It also covers how to effectively use the contributor stories in this book during a training session. While selecting and crafting the perfect story to tell is key, the ability to tell it in a memorable fashion is just as important. Chapter Five highlights some tips and techniques that our contributors recommend for telling stories to others in a training setting. Rounding out this section is Chapter Six, which explores the ethical and legal issues associated with telling stories in a program.

At the beginning of Section Two, you will find two tables that will help you select the most appropriate stories, if the topic of your training program does not correspond with one of the story chapter titles. The tables also identify alternate uses, by topic, for each story. Following this introduction are fifty-five stories organized into ten different chapters by topic. Each story chapter begins with an overview of the stories housed within it. For each story you will find: a title, story contributor name and organization, story type and purpose(s), background on the author and/or story, presentation tips to help you deliver the story with impact, at least two lead-in (set-up) options, the story itself, sample debrief questions, key points, and one or more follow-up activities.

In the back pocket of the book, you will find an audio CD. Its primary intent is to provide you with a model for telling each story in a manner that captures your participants' interest. It also enables you to listen to the stories in a variety of settings: while driving, relaxing, or working at other tasks. In some training situations, you may decide it makes sense to play the CD version of the story for your audience, possibly to vary the media used during the training. However, the stories will be most powerful when you can tell them yourself and incorporate the visual aspects of storytelling.

HOW TO USE THIS BOOK

If using stories in your training efforts is fairly new for you, we suggest starting at the beginning of the book and scanning each of the chapters in Section One before selecting and telling a story. If you are familiar and comfortable with using stories in your work, we encourage you to first read Chapter Four to review how to incorporate stories into training and become acquainted with how each story and its accompanying material has been written and can be used. You can either recite the stories from memory or read them to others from the book itself. With the exception of the eleven previously copyrighted stories noted on the copyright continuation page (page 398) of this book, the rest of the book's stories may be duplicated for educational or training purposes (up to 100 copies per page per year) provided they include the designation noted on the copyright page.

It is not our intent for the stories in this book to replace other instructional design techniques that promote experiential learning, such as case studies, simulations, and group activities. We encourage you to use stories as an adjunct to these other methods, incorporating them before or after a case study or activity. To provide a more powerful training experience, however, they may replace a lecture, the presentation of a series of slides or overheads, or a handout discussion.

section **ONE**

Using Stories in Training

The first part of this book contains an introduction and six chapters providing information and suggestions on how to find, develop, organize, and tell stories in a training context. It also includes guidelines for the ethical and legal use of these stories. In these chapters, we introduce a story module framework and offer suggestions for incorporating stories into your training venues. The chapters in Section One each close with a segment—The Story Continues—that summarizes the chapter and includes Bringing Stories to Life, a checklist of questions to help you incorporate the information into your own storytelling.

While Section Two follows with fifty-five stories organized by topic and includes a story module for each, it is important to note that there are eighteen additional stories woven throughout the introduction and Section One chapters. These stories can also support your learning goals, and we encourage you to tell them in your training. Each of the stories noted here includes an identifying letter, which refers to the tables in Section Two providing story type, purpose, and potential uses. The eighteen stories include:

Introduction

"Discovering the Power of Stories" by David Hutchens (A)

Chapter 1: What Makes a Story a Training Story?

"Your Top Priorities" by R. Alec Mackenzie (B)

"On the Lookout for Body Art" by Lori L. Silverman (C)

"Keeping Your Cool" by Laura V. Page (D)

"The Camping Trip" by Mary B. Wacker (E)

"Why Can't We All Get Along?" by Hortencia Delgadillo (F)

"The Wake-Up Call" by Mary B. Wacker (G)

Chapter 2: Where Do Stories Come From?

"Right Under Your Nose" by Sharon L. Bowman (H)

"Follow the Leader" by John Renesch (I)

"My Mental Filing System" by Suzann Gardner (J)

Chapter 3: How to Craft a Story

"Losing the Sale" by Jonathan M. Preston (K)

"Seeing the Light" by Lori L. Silverman (L)

"7.1 on the Richter Scale" by Mary B. Wacker (M)

"Bun's Rush: Wienermobile Finds Route Near Pentagon No Picnic," adapted by Lori L. Silverman (N)

Chapter 4: Incorporating Stories into Training

"Prisoners, Vacationers, and Learners" by Steve Hanamura (O)

"The Wise Man and the Baby Bird" by Paula Bartholome (P)

Chapter 5: Tips on Storytelling

"Tuning-in to Trainees' Needs" by Jean Barbazette (Q)

Chapter 6: Legal and Ethical Use of Stories

"Whose Mother Was It?" by Chris Clarke-Epstein, CSP (R)

You will find the story modules for these stories at www.storiestrainerstell.com. Enjoy them and the storytelling information included in Section One. We encourage you to bring more stories to life.

chapter
ONE

What Makes a Story a Training Story?

Your Top Priorities (B)

By R. Alec Mackenzie

When Charles Schwab was president of Bethlehem Steel, he presented Ivy Lee, a consultant, with an unusual challenge. "Show me a way to get more things done with my time," he said, "and I'll pay you any fee within reason."

Handing Schwab a sheet of paper, Lee said, "Write down the most important tasks you have to do tomorrow and number them in order of importance. When you arrive in the morning, begin at once on No. 1 and stay on it till it's completed. Recheck your priorities; then begin with No. 2. If any task takes all day, never mind. Stick with it as long as it's the most important one. If you don't finish them all, you probably couldn't do so with any other method, and without some system you'd probably not even decide which one was most important. Make this a habit every working day. When it works for you, give it to your men. Try it as long as you like. Then send me your check for what you think it's worth."

Some weeks later, Schwab sent Lee a check for $25,000 with a note saying that the lesson was the most profitable he had ever learned. In five years this plan was largely responsible for turning Bethlehem Steel Corporation into the biggest independent steel producer in the world. And it helped make Charles Schwab $100 million and the best-known steel man in the world. Schwab's friends asked him later about the payment of so high a fee for such a simple idea. Schwab responded by asking, what ideas are not basically simple? He reminded them that for the first time not only he but his entire team were getting first things done first. On reflection, Schwab allowed that perhaps the expenditure was the most valuable investment Bethlehem Steel had made all year.

Mackenzie, R. Alec (1972). Taken from *The Time Trap.* New York: AMACOM, pp. 38–39.

This story is a classic in time-management training. In fact, it is written up in most books on the subject. It was Ed Scannell who first brought it to our attention in relation to this book. What makes this story a training story? From our perspective there are three criteria that need to be met in order to make a story viable in a training session: relevance, length, and learning. The story must be immediately relevant to the goal of the training program and one or more of its objectives. It also must be relevant to the trainee's own purpose or reason for attending the program. While story length is a subjective issue, the story must be short enough to hold trainee interest and long enough to make a point. Finally, the story must have the capability to deepen learning—either in the moment or soon after. What we mean is that the story must be able to support a follow-up discussion and/or applied learning activity.

In this chapter we discuss two topics pertinent to training stories: types of stories and the various purposes training stories can serve in a learning environment. These issues are key to selecting the appropriate story to tell and their placement within a training session.

TYPES OF STORIES

What types of stories do you tell in a training session? The individuals we interviewed most often use personal stories that explore a particular behavior, reinforce life lessons, or create an "a-ha." These stories tend to have two facets: *interest*—to be inspirational or motivational, and *learning*—to be educational or developmental in nature. Frequently, they also have another dimension in that they are entertaining, humorous, or funny in some way. Other types of stories contributors use are based on history, current events, fables, and traditional folktales. In any case, all of these stories have a key point or a moral associated with them.

STORYTELLING WISDOM

"If you are not using stories, you are missing the boat."

Sivasailam "Thiagi" Thiagarajan

Ed Tate uses what he calls "universal truth" stories. He defines these as "stories that exemplify that there is no relationship without trust and that there is no exception to this rule." Universal truth stories illustrate fundamental, deeply held values as opposed to stories whose purpose is more cursory in nature. Everyone who hears a universal truth story is able to relate to it, despite whatever differences they may have. The benefit of using this type of story is that the story itself does not need to change when it is told to different groups because the message it brings goes beyond culture, race, age, or geographic location. Chip Bell's "A Legacy of Generosity" (Chapter Twelve) or "The Bamboo Years" (Chapter Eleven), offered by Katherine Hudson, exemplify this type of story.

Doug Stevenson, in his audiotape series *Story Theater: The Science and Art of Storytelling and Humor in Business* (2001), provides a framework that outlines seven different types of stories that can be used in a speech. These story types also translate well to a training setting. They are:

1. **Crucible stories:** These are stories of great loss, hardship, or pain. They are survivor stories. They tell the tale of near-misses, of risking death and coming out alive. Kate Lutz's "In Search of Cappuccino . . . With a Little Chocolate on the Side" (Chapter Twelve) illustrates this type of story.
2. **Imbroglio stories:** An imbroglio is an acutely painful or embarrassing misunderstanding. They are stories in which we reveal our screw-ups and our vulnerability. Examples include Geoff Bellman's "Time Brings Perspective" (Chapter Twelve) and "The House Guest" (Chapter Eight) by Lunell Haught.
3. **Minerva stories:** Minerva was the Roman goddess of wisdom. Thus, these are stories that draw upon ancient wisdom. Examples include the parable of the good samaritan from the Bible; traditional Native American, African, and Celtic folk legends; and stories from Greek and Roman mythology or any religion. "A Family United" (Chapter Fifteen), contributed by Clare Novak, and Suzann Gardner's "The Porcupine and the Snake" (Chapter Fourteen) portray this type of story.
4. **Credibility stories:** These are any non-personal stories from an outside source such as the news or current events. Other types of credibility stories borrow from the expertise of a recognized authority or someone who has gained credibility through their celebrity or life experience. This story type is represented by Kathy Nielsen's "The Worth of a Contribution" (Chapter Eleven) and "The Bamboo Years" (Chapter Eleven) by Katherine Hudson.
5. **Pattern stories:** Some stories cover an expanse of time, in some cases months or years, with a plot structure that builds on a repetitive pattern. An example would be telling a story in which you compare your behavior over a period of time in different jobs or different relationships. These stories work well to illustrate change. Suzann Gardner's "How My Sons Learned to Dive" (Chapter Sixteen) is an example of a pattern story, as is "The Disapproving Neighbor" (Chapter Fourteen) shared by Kate Lutz.

6. **Instructional stories:** These are narratives that often contain many points. They move back and forth from the story to the lesson. They are more cerebral, the action is minimized, and the narrative is maximized. They exist to teach rather than entertain. In this category you will find Bill Boone's "A World Without Blacks" (Chapter Seven) and Joan Lloyd's "Isolate, Exaggerate, and Integrate" (Chapter Thirteen).
7. **Vignettes:** A vignette is a short illustration or a mini story. It is probably something that you use a lot to make a point but it only takes a minute or so to tell. It is really more of an anecdote. Stories such as Sheriene Saadati's "The Forest for the Trees" (Chapter Thirteen) and "For Lack of a System" (Chapter Fourteen) by Larry English fall into this classification.

Doug suggests that identifying the types of stories you are using influences your storytelling in two ways: where you "place" the story in your presentation (that is, the beginning, the middle, or the end of your training session) and the specifics of how you go about telling the story (see Chapters Four and Five for more information on both of these points). In addition to categorizing stories by topic, we have identified the story type for each contribution in Section Two of this book to aid you in appropriately incorporating them into training programs.

STORY PURPOSES IN TRAINING

In addition to knowing the type of story you are telling, it is essential to know *why*—the purpose or reason—you wish to tell a story at a particular point in your program. In our work, we have identified seven purposes that stories can have in training. They can:

- Entertain (or Energize)
- Educate
- Evaluate
- Engage
- Encourage
- Explore
- Evoke (Silverman, & Wacker, 2003, pp. 243–253).

Why is it important to know what purposes stories can serve in a training situation? Each of the seven purposes explored here has some type of relationship to the overall training: the topic, the trainees, the trainer, or the design of the training material. These purposes, in concert with the story types previously outlined, can help you to select or develop the most appropriate story to use at a particular point in a session. Knowing a story's purpose(s) can also help you determine how to best tell it and how to go about debriefing it with others. Keep in mind that a single story can have more than one purpose. For example, "The Roll of the Dice" (Chapter Thirteen), contributed by Sandra Hoskins, is a story that both entertains and explores what it means to set clear guidelines and to coach a new manager.

Stories That Entertain or Energize

There are a variety of reasons for using stories that entertain or energize in a training session. They can help to humanize the trainer, thus increasing the person's credibility and rapport with the audience. This is especially true if the trainer shares a situation that makes him or her appear to be a bit vulnerable. Stories that entertain can also be a way of remembering a concept that is to be applied in the workplace, such as "The Slingshot" (Chapter Fifteen), provided by Robert McIlree. While the story provokes quite a bit of laughter, it also demonstrates the fundamentals of teamwork: the team defined its membership, its reason for existence, its roles and responsibilities, and its ground rules. Stories can also set or reset the mood in a training session by changing the energy level in the room. Imagine being in a setting where the energy is low, such as after lunch, and hearing an instructor relate a situation that brings belly laughs to all who hear it. This type of story can also release pent-up tension on the part of trainees, such as during training that is preparing people to take a certification exam or that is addressing a serious organizational issue. Finally, entertaining stories can build group cohesiveness. Through shared laughter, a common bond is formed.

What about stories whose sole purpose is to entertain or energize? How do these sorts of stories qualify as training stories? While stories that energize an audience may not have a specific learning point inherent in them, they do help create an environment conducive to (or that sets the stage for) the trainee being more receptive to learning in the next phase of the program. Stories told for the chief purpose of entertaining or energizing a group can help trainees access a more flexible, resilient, and "teachable" mindset within themselves. They ready the learner for learning. They are relevant because they meet the needs of the participants at a particular point in the training. When told for the purpose of entertainment, these stories do not need to be debriefed. Their value is in the emotional and kinesthetic reaction that takes place. The story that follows is an example of one that can change energy and release tension. It has no other purpose. It is best told on a gorgeous day when participants are longing to be outdoors instead of in training.

On the Lookout for Body Art (C)

Contributed by Lori L. Silverman

On a day like this, who wouldn't want to be outdoors? Spending time with friends and family. Doing something really fun. Each Labor Day weekend in Madison, Wisconsin, there is a festival called A Taste of Madison. Many of the local restaurants set up booths around the Capitol Square and sell appetizer-size portions of their most famous dishes. Joining in are the local wineries and breweries and others who sponsor bands on four different music stages.

You can well imagine the crowds. Thousands and thousands of people flock to the downtown area for all the festivities. This time of year it's usually hot, so it's not unusual to find people sitting under large shade trees. That's what a close friend and I did one year, until we discovered a new pastime. Tattoo watching. Yes, you heard me right. Tattoo watching. We were people watching. Noticing all the scantily clothed men and women—and that's when we noticed all the tattoos. So, we decided to follow them and get a closer look. As we got bolder we started asking people about their tattoos. Everyone was eager to talk about them—why they chose a particular design, why it was located on a certain part of their body, and why it was important to them. We even learned who folks considered to be the best tattoo artists in town!

There was one, though, that stood out among all the others. It was truly unique. A man wore it in the center of his chest. As we got closer, the details became even more visible. It was a large tattoo of a genie coming out of a bottle. My friend and I both turned to each other in awe. That's when she whispered, ever so softly, "Do you think we'd get three wishes if we rubbed it?" I responded, "You better 'be careful what you wish for.'"

Stories That Educate

Stories that educate are meant to introduce new knowledge or increase existing knowledge. This knowledge may be in the form of philosophies, concepts, or theories. Consider situations—such as new employee orientation or a management development series—in which people need to learn the behaviors that exemplify the organization's values or philosophy of business. Instead of presenting a list that defines what they are, the trainer could tell a story that gets participants to identify the importance of one or more organizational values and how these values influence individual behavior. If, for example, the organization places a high value on customer service, "Ladies and Gentlemen Serving Ladies and Gentlemen" (Chapter Nine), provided by Chip Bell, would be an appropriate one to tell. This story brings to life specific behaviors that define exceptional service at The Ritz-Carlton Hotel, which can be used to help define service characteristics within the trainees' work environment.

When introducing theories or concepts, especially those that are complex or cumbersome to explain directly, using a story can make them easier to present. For example, a story that exemplifies special and common-cause variation involved in driving to work can be an effective way to initiate a conversation on the theory behind statistical variation. If you are trying to get people to act more collaboratively, "The Contest" (Chapter Fifteen) by Thiagi helps to make the transition between the concept of collaboration and actions that demonstrate collaborative behavior. Because training is often about imparting knowledge with a goal of application in the workplace, stories whose purpose is to educate are the bedrock of learning.

STORYTELLING WISDOM

"Stories make visible that which we would not otherwise understand."

Bob Shaver

Stories That Evaluate

Some stories allow trainees to evaluate the rightness or wrongness, goodness or badness, or appropriateness or inappropriateness of behaviors or options in a given situation. Evaluative stories are effective when speaking of policies and procedures, industry regulations, work practices, and customer requirements; and local, state, and federal guidelines. Consider the case of an employee who works in procurement who has been asked by a major customer to engage in a series of actions that have some ethical and legal implications. If the story surrounding the work situation is told without saying what the employee elected to do, trainees could brainstorm these options and the pros and cons of them. Used in this way, the story provides a context for discussing "right" and "wrong" behaviors. An example of a story whose purpose is to evaluate is "The Case of the Magician's Assistant" (Chapter Thirteen), contributed by Hortencia Delgadillo. It provides a scenario that leads to a discussion on fair employment practices.

Here is an evaluative story that showcases both appropriate and inappropriate behaviors. Its merit is that it addresses both sets of behaviors. Often, evaluative stories focus only on the negative.

Keeping Your Cool (D)

Contributed by Laura V. Page, managing principal, Page Consulting

One day, out of the blue, I hear this noticeable drumming coming from this gal, Sue, who lives below me. Every few minutes, I'd hear "boom, boom, boom," and then it would end. Now, I'm actually very tolerant of drumming—I used to be a drummer in a rock band. So I thought, "Okay, in the interest of being a good neighbor, I'm not saying a thing. Especially since this building has had some tension over typical condo issues—like what color the awnings should be." We were in conflict over that issue for months!

The drumming went on for months. Then, it started happening more frequently. One day, it happened in the morning, it happened around noon, and it happened again at 10:00 P.M. Boom. Boom. Boom. That's it. I've had it. This drumming had been going on far too long. So I storm out of my apartment in my pajamas, fly down the stairs, get to her door, and pound on it. Sue opens it and looks at me, startled. I say to her in no sweet way, "What the hell are you doing?" And she says, "Wow, you're really angry. Come in." So I walk in and continue attacking her with my comments. In the meantime, she is listening and restating what I am saying. Asking me questions like, "When do I do it?" and "How loud is it?" As I begin to answer her questions I find myself calming down. Then she says, "Well, I'm sorry. Is there a time I can do it that might be okay?" And, right there, at that moment, we negotiated. We agreed that she could drum during the day—just not real loud!

As I walked back upstairs I thought, "My goodness, I have just witnessed everything that I wished I could have done myself." About ten minutes after getting back to my apartment, I got a call and it's from Sue. And she says, "I just wanted you to know that it's really okay that you came down. I hope that we can always deal with things openly." I hung up the phone in disbelief and thought, "Oh my gosh, this woman really handled this well."

Let's face it. She could have attacked me for having pounded on her door and she didn't. She could've forcefully asserted her need to make noise and she didn't. Instead, she listened and actually reflected back to me some of the things that I was saying. She even kept her cool while I complained bitterly. She was amazing! Her ability to keep her cool, even through all my objections, changed my attitude. Under similar circumstances, what do you need to do to "keep your cool"?

After hearing this story, participants could discuss the positive and negative aspects of both Laura's and her neighbor's actions. A summary of the group's assessment of the incident can then be used as a lead-in to a conversation on conflict-management strategies. This can be followed by how Laura could have more constructively approached the situation—the specific strategy and the steps she could have employed and the use of non-defensive language.

Stories That Engage

Stories that engage participants help them move from being passive to being more invested in the training and their own learning. They allow trainees to access a deeper level of commitment within themselves during the training session and after, as they continue their lifelong learning. Stories that engage may be funny, as in "The Jock and His Wife Go Water Skiing" (Chapter Sixteen) by John Renesch. Or they may be more serious, as "In Pursuit of a Goal" (Chapter Sixteen) by Paula Bartholome, which depicts learning goals set by two very different students. Both of these stories are about discovery and personal change. John's story does this by getting trainees to think about whether they themselves are focused on knowing or on learning; Paula's story debrief accomplishes this by asking participants to reflect on their own learning goals. Hence, the story topics associated with this purpose are tailored to the demographics of the training audience, rather than being general in nature.

Imagine the following story being told to a health care audience at the beginning of a training session.

The Camping Trip (E)

Contributed by Mary B. Wacker

Much of the first eighteen months of Matt's life was spent in the hospital. Now, as a five-year-old with severe asthma, he was embarking on his first camping trip. When his family arrived at the campsite, he raced out of the car into the woods, shrieking with happiness.

His eyes opened wide when he discovered a nest of duck eggs at the edge of the campsite. Each morning he would get up and dash to the nest to check out the eggs. He would get very quiet and tiptoe around the nest whenever he saw Mama Duck sitting on the nest. He proclaimed to his family, "I'm not leaving until the baby ducks are born!"

Throughout the week, the family hiked, cooked out over a campfire, sang songs, and played catch. After each activity, Matt would return to the nest to see what, if anything, was happening. He desperately wanted the ducklings to hatch—soon!

On the last morning of the trip, Matt awoke and once again scrambled to the nest. To his sheer delight, he saw five newly hatched ducklings squirming in the nest. Ecstatic, he told his parents, "This is the best day of my life!"

Matt's hospital stays were here at this facility. He was served by some of you in this room. Being able to go on that trip was due to the wonderful medical care he has received. Thank you for the work you do and the inordinate care you take. You make a difference—to Matt, and to so many others. He could not have gone on that trip without you. As you go forward with the vital work you do remember how much "you make a difference."

This story acknowledges the result of investments in prior learning on behalf of the employees. If the story is positioned at the beginning of a training program, it can be used to promote individual participant investment in the current training opportunity. Wherever it is told within the program, trainees may be moved to revisit their commitment to their work and their customers. As a result, they will become more engaged in their own learning.

Stories That Encourage

Have you ever been in training situations when trainees did not appear motivated to change or take on new challenges? Stories can be used to encourage participants to demonstrate behaviors or take some sort of action they might not otherwise perform. Joan Gillman's "The Volunteer Job" (Chapter Ten) illustrates this when she relates the benefits of taking on new volunteer work simultaneous with starting a new job. Upon hearing this, listeners are encouraged to explore the opportunities in their lives that they might otherwise pass up. In this way, this type of story has a motivating effect on behavior.

STORYTELLING WISDOM

"Training is lifeless without stories."

Joan Lloyd

Stories that encourage may also offer ways to approach an uncomfortable situation, such as confronting a colleague on a sensitive issue or dealing with a long-standing problem. Consequently, they offer opportunity or options where none may have been visible before. As an example, LG Shanklin-Flowers shows us the power of "Fostering Full Potential" (Chapter Eleven) when, as a newly hired manager, she chooses to work with an employee she inherited and was asked to fire.

Stories of encouragement can be about an individual or organization that has overcome adversities similar to what participants are currently experiencing. Imagine a situation in which a large retail home improvement chain enters a small town that currently has a similar, locally owned and operated store. This competitive situation may at first appear negative because it may put the local store and its employees out of business. In a training session to explore ways to handle the new competition, the owner of the local business could relay stories about similar stores in other towns that have not only survived, but have thrived in the face of the same situation. Steve Hanamura contends that stories whose purpose is to encourage "motivate people to do things they would consider another's responsibility." As such, they are powerful tools to creating ownership. These stories inspire us to become our best.

"Spirit" and "transformation" often go hand-in-hand with the topic of adversity. Thus, stories with these themes are also considered to be stories that encourage. Both within organizations and our lives, stories that encourage are catalysts for us to appreciate our deep connections to others and to our own talents. "Preparing Yourself for the Unexpected" (Chapter Sixteen), by Larry English, is an example of the transformation of a trainer conducting a program into a spiritual advisor counseling his participants after the tragic events of September 11, 2001. Through his compassion and wisdom, participants were able to more fully access their connections to each other and to their nation.

Stories That Explore

Stories that explore a topic, concept, or behavior in more depth serve to enhance or expand upon knowledge and skills that participants already have. These types of stories may pick up on a nuance in a situation or explore it from a different angle. Consider the following situation that summarizes a story that could be told in an advanced coaching workshop. Keep in mind that participants who hear it would already have basic coaching skills as part of their repertoire:

> A new manager inherits a long-term employee with a history of significant performance problems. Unfortunately, the prior manager failed to coach this employee or document her poor performance. The employee has recently developed a serious chronic health problem and is now claiming this as the reason for her work problems.

After telling this story, the trainer could have participants identify actions the new manager could take given the sensitive nature of this circumstance. From there, the trainer might follow up with a discussion about the implications for effective coaching in a variety of difficult and unusual employee situations.

The following story is one that could be used to expand upon basic conflict resolution skills. It explores a situation involving multiple parties that does not appear immediately to be resolvable.

Why Can't We All Get Along? (F)

Contributed by Hortencia Delgadillo, attorney-at-law

There were a number of families who lived in a housing association. Two of them—the Johnsons and the Turners—were always at each other's throats, arguing, and accusing each other of all sorts of abuse. Over a period of weeks, things got progressively worse. It almost escalated into violence.

You ask, how did this all start? Mr. Johnson and Mr. Turner started criticizing the colors the other had painted his gate. Then the Johnson children told the manager of the association that the Turner kids had picked on them and had knocked down one of their bikes. It progressed from there to calling each other nasty names and saying things like, "Go back to where you came from." After that, the parents got into it and things really heated up. Being very protective of their children, Mr. and Mrs. Johnson went over to visit the Turners. They pounded and pounded on the door. The Turners had been eating dinner and having a quiet evening when suddenly they heard all of this pounding and shouting. Feeling threatened, they immediately called the police.

Of course, when the police showed up, everyone exaggerated what had happened—about how things had heated up and how the parties felt. Who knew what the true story was? The manager was ultimately called. He tried to talk to both the Johnsons and the Turners but to no avail. It had become a showdown—one family was going to have to leave.

You ask, "How did they resolve this?" They agreed to a time-out and found an outside mediator. Each party put together a list of all the things that disturbed them about the behavior of the other. Then they had a discussion about what each family meant by what they said, what they did that was bothersome, and what had happened between the kids. Both mutually agreed that they would have a discussion with their children about respect. They even signed a written contract to solidify their agreements. Conflicts escalate when we don't take time to reflect and cool down. Next time you're involved in a conflict, "take a time-out."

In this story, a complex series of interactions takes place with multiple viewpoints expressed at every step of the way. Taking each viewpoint, participants could explore the perspectives of each party to the conflict: the children, the parents, the police, the mediator. Participants in a session on mediation, negotiation, problem-solving, or conflict management would benefit from discussing the parameters of this situation. As a result, they would be able to explore the applications to their own work settings.

Stories That Evoke

Finally, there are some stories that when told, immediately call forth a response from trainees. These stories are wonderful lead-ins to large- and small-group discussions. Stories that evoke trigger strong reactions and emotions of all kinds on the part of the listener. They have an almost visceral feel to them and can build a cohesive bond between learners. They create a sense of unity among participants—a sense of being "in this together."

Stories that evoke are also a tribute to the nobility of spirit and may also highlight people's creative response to problems surrounding them. Stories that evoke strike a chord with listeners. Bill Boone's poignant "A World Without Blacks" (Chapter Seven) brings to forefront the largely overlooked contributions of people of African descent. In "The Contest" (Chapter Fifteen), Thiagi calls on us to examine our values regarding competition and collaboration, evoking strong response as to the strategy of the contest participants.

When telling stories whose purpose is to evoke, it is advantageous to have participants put themselves in the shoes of the person who is having the "experience." As you continue reading, imagine being the daughter of a man who has become gravely ill and is in the intensive care unit of a local hospital.

The Wake-Up Call (G)

Contributed by Mary B. Wacker

Exhausted and concerned, Cary arrived at the hospital to visit her father after he had had a day of urology tests. Her father had been ill this time around for six weeks. Three days earlier he had been moved to the intensive care unit. On the elevator ride to her father's room, Cary overheard two nurses talking about that "new case" in ICU. She was taken aback—they were so descriptive in their comments.
She thought to herself, "That's my father they're talking about. How dare they be so inconsiderate!" The nurses continued their chat

saying, "The doc is going to have to break some tough news to the family." Cary's heart almost stopped. "Tough news," she cried to herself. "What does that mean?" At that point, Cary broke into the nurses' conversation and demanded to know what was going on with her father. "I think you are talking about my father, Mr. Thompson. What do you know about him?" she cried in an anguished tone. The nurses were shocked into guilt-stricken silence and rushed to comfort Cary. They apologized profusely and escorted her to her father's urologist so they could talk. As they left Cary in the capable hands of her father's physician, one of the nurses commented, "I know we've always been told not to discuss patients in public areas, but I think I've just "learned my lesson" for all time. I never want to go through that again—or put a patient's family member through it either!"

We all receive wake-up calls in life. It doesn't really impact our lives until we follow through. Where have you learned a valuable lesson?

No doubt, when the trainer tells this story, participants will have a strong negative reaction. This energy can be used to fuel a discussion on what the participants would have done in the situation. This might also lead to a discussion on when trainees have been embarrassed when confronted by some action they themselves took and what they did to recover from it.

THE STORY CONTINUES

What makes a story viable in a training session? In this chapter, we review several elements that help answer this question. Doug Stevenson's seven types of stories—crucible, imbroglio, Minerva, credibility, pattern, instructional, and vignettes—provide us with one way to think about the stories we use and how they are structured. Knowing the story types encourages us to go beyond our comfortable collection of stories. It encourages us to broaden our range in seeking out new varieties of stories. In addition, in Chapter One, we look at the seven purposes for incorporating stories into your training—to entertain (or energize), educate, evaluate, engage, encourage, explore, and evoke. These purposes help us determine why and when we might wish to tell a particular story. Examples with specific purposes can be incorporated at a particular juncture within the program design to better meet learning objectives. Knowing the myriad types and purposes of stories deepens our understanding of the power of stories in our work. As an initial step, review how you currently use stories in your training sessions.

Bringing Stories to Life

- How would stories benefit my training programs?
- What types of stories do I currently use?
- What other types of stories might I tell in order to spice up my training style?
- What purposes are served by the stories I currently tell in training?
- For which purposes do I most frequently tell stories?
- How can I add more variety in my training by incorporating a wider range of story types and purposes?

Stories are a powerful vehicle for enhancing learning. With so many types of stories to choose from and so many purposes for telling them, they fit well into any training intervention, whether one-on-one or in a roomful of people.

chapter TWO

Where Do Stories Come From?

Right Under Your Nose (H)

Contributed by Sharon L. Bowman, director, The Lake Tahoe Trainers Group

A Cessna 172. Red and white. Four-seater. My first dual cross-country flight as a student pilot. All checked out to fly from the South Lake Tahoe Airport, high in the California Sierras, to Fallon, Nevada, a tiny airstrip in the middle of the Nevada desert.

My flight plan in my lap, the little plane droning loudly in the still morning air, I turned in the direction of Fallon and set the navigation instruments to guide me there. My instructor Gary sat in the right seat, quietly offering suggestions to polish my level flight skills.

An hour later, checking and rechecking my location, I proudly announced, "Here we are!" Then I looked around for the airstrip. To my consternation, I couldn't see it anywhere. I rechecked the instruments, looked over to the left and the right of the little plane, then said with panic in my voice, "But it *should* be here! The airstrip should be right here. But I don't see it and can't find it. What am I doing wrong?"

Gary sat in silence for about thirty seconds, until it became obvious that I didn't have a clue as to what to do next. Then he smiled, leaned forward, and whispered, "Look under your nose!"

I looked straight under the nose of the plane and sure enough, I was directly over the tiny airstrip. I had missed seeing it because it was under me and not in my line of vision.

Gary and I had a good laugh about it and I've remembered the lesson to this day: When you're looking for what you need most and can't seem to find it anywhere, it's often "right under your nose"!

Where can you find stories to share in training sessions? They are all around us—and are often right under our nose. We suggest you start with that which is closest to you—your own personal and professional life experiences and those of your family, close friends, and colleagues. From there you can branch out and explore print media, radio and television news programs, and the Internet. Do not wait to gather stories until you need to use them. We encourage you to collect them all the time so that you have a repertoire of stories on hand from which to choose. After you start to accumulate stories you would like to tell in training, you need to find a way to organize them so they are easily accessible when needed. Here, contributors share what they have found works for them.

FINDING STORIES IN YOUR OWN LIFE

The easiest place to find stories is within your own life experiences. These stories may arise out of conversations with your family members or significant others, observations of children or pets, meaningful experiences you encounter throughout the day at work, or something surprising that happened to you at home. It is not unusual for something very small that has happened to us to bring with it a story that has far-reaching significance. It might be a sentence that a grocery clerk said, a conversation you overheard while you were walking to lunch, a comment someone made at a conference, or what you observed when you sat down on a park bench.

Maybe you belong to a religious organization. Or engage in volunteer work. Perhaps you are a member of a civic or community organization, or a local theater group. Or maybe you are involved in a professional association. These outside activities are ripe opportunities for capturing stories. What insights did you gain? What did you learn about yourself or about others you met along the way? What special talents did you realize you had? Which talents did you develop? On a more global scale, what did you learn about humankind? Or about how people approach life? What do you now know about the strength of the human spirit? Each of these questions is meant to stimulate you to think of possible stories that you could use to help others grow and develop.

Turn on your story "ears" at special events such as holiday gatherings, birthday parties, weddings, anniversaries, graduations, and the like. These gatherings are places where people tend to recount humorous or life-altering stories and tales from the past. Ask questions or inquire about old photos to bring forth more story details. Do not ignore the more subdued occasions, such as funerals, hospital stays, and sick times. The circumstance itself may have stories inherent in it, or people involved in it may reminisce about the past. Family history is definitely a key source of stories for several contributors. Sandra Hoskins uses snippets from letters her mom received when she was younger as stories in her training. Maureen G. Mulvaney (MGM) uses personal and family history stories in her training and presentations; she has also documented them in her book, *Any Kid Can Be a Superstar* (1999).

STORYTELLING WISDOM

"I am a story and each of us is a story. We are each living out the story of our lives. We can only make sense of our earlier chapters by getting to later chapters. . . . Stories are a way to show your own vulnerability and they speak to the vulnerability in others. You, as the storyteller, are the one who makes it safe to be vulnerable and safe for others to tell their own stories."

Geoff Bellman

Your own thoughts, insights, hopes, fears, dreams, aspirations, and images are wonderful sources of inspiration for creating stories. Take a retrospective look at your own life and identify the patterns and themes that have occurred, your key successes and most challenging mistakes, and the significant turning points you have encountered on your life journey. Consider the following sorts of questions: What is the greatest life lesson you have learned? Which lessons have you yet to learn? How did you arrive at your most precious life value? Donald Davis's *Telling Your Own Stories* (1993) provides a wealth of trigger questions to help you create stories about "memorable people, places, or happenings" in your life. The *If*... series of books, including *If*... (*Questions for the Game of Life*) (1995), are also resources to get you to think about experiences you have been through or situations you might dream about.

COLLECTING STORIES FROM FRIENDS AND COLLEAGUES . . . EVEN STRANGERS

Friends and colleagues can be great resources for stories. They may tell you about situations they or others have experienced, or send you emails that trigger a story line. One of the authors received a series of daily emails from contributor, Joan Gillman, who was traveling on business through Eastern Europe. The following email was sent from Skopje, Macedonia. Embedded in the note, which is meant to keep in touch with family and close friends, are the beginnings of a wonderful story about the similarity between strategic plans and maps, for use (with Joan's permission) in planning workshops.

Interactive Map

Contributed by Joan Gillman, director, Special Industry Programs, University of Wisconsin-Madison, School of Business

Monday, February 04, 2002

Hi!!

Today was the first day with my new class. I had eight women in this class, four new and four that trained with me a year and a half ago. It was great to see old friends. This time they are staying in a less expensive hotel so the camaraderie is less with my class and greater with Fani (the coordinator) and my translators. They have been working on my schedule . . . I know I keep stressing it, but I feel really fortunate to be able to have this experience. Each trip really is a gift.

Today went well. . . . This is a great group, one works in tourism, two incubators, one works for our translator's company, several from the foundation and one business leader who does counseling on the side. It's an eclectic bunch but energetic. The hard part is people are going to come and go, so the group never really will solidify. One thing is for sure: one needs to be able to switch gears on a dime. Nothing goes as you planned.

I was talking about business planning today and talked about the plan being a map. I said there were so many ways to find one's direction. One could go on the computer and look at MapQuest, or buy a paper map at the bookstore, you could even have a mapping computer in your car, or you could use my Bulgarian colleague's method (Nick) and use an interactive map. Nick rarely read a map, although he has them. His method of finding his way is to stop and ask. If he doesn't like the first person's answer, he goes to the next person. After getting lost and taking the least direct way, he asked one man, the man used hand movements which I was able to follow, so I directed Nick, because the hand movements and the map (in Cyrillic, no less) made sense to me. . . . The moral of the story is you need to know where you are going, and asking everyone doesn't always get you where you want to go.

After class tonight the translators and I went out for a drink. They are a really great group.

Hugs and love,
Mom/Joan

To develop this analogy into a full-blown training story would require chatting with Joan to obtain more details about the time she and Nick were traveling together and she observed his use of what she calls "interactive maps." This additional information would help to add context, flavor, and color to the story, as well as the possibility of humor.

Consider querying friends and colleagues for stories on particular topics. One of the authors was asked to give a presentation on the do's and don't's of "schmoozing" to some attorneys who were going to be entertaining a large group of clients at a company-wide social event. Here is the letter she sent out to ten colleagues and friends.

> Hi,
> I am giving a talk in June on "schmoozing"—how to work a room—whether it be for socializing, networking, business, etc. What I am interested in are life's most embarrassing moments relative to this topic—something you've witnessed or been a part of. I promise not to share names. I have a client who wants to hear funny stories (but not about themselves!). Anything you can email me by Monday would be greatly appreciated! Thanks for helping me.
> Take Care,
> Lori

More than half of those individuals who were emailed responded with stories—all of them quite funny, some even outrageous. Their responses were the impetus for determining specific topics to include in the talk. In addition, these individuals supplied experiences that vividly brought out key points and related them to real-world behaviors.

Vacations. Business trips. Commuting to and from work. People you meet or overhear on buses, trains, boats, or airplanes may have interesting stories to share as well. Even your observations of their behaviors may hold nuggets for further exploring life lessons. For example, one of the authors had an interesting experience on a trip to Belize. Picture yourself riding around in an electric golf cart; everyone on Ambergris Cay does it. You pull up to a tranquil lagoon and see two men enacting a bizarre scene. About twenty feet offshore, an alligator lazily swims back and forth, swishing his tail about and periodically lifts his head above the water. And the two men, you ask? One of them is hopping about in the shallows, throwing chicken bones into the water and slapping the shallows with a branch. The second man is standing calmly by with a professional video camera. When you ask the man standing in the water, "What are you doing?" he says, "I want the alligator to swim closer so we can get some video footage of it." "Aren't you worried that the alligator might get *too* close?" you ask. "Nahhh, they don't swim very fast."

Well, you can see where *this* is going. Now, you had heard that an alligator could outrun a man in a short sprint, and you aren't about to test out this theory yourself. Just then the alligator makes a lunge closer in to shore and both the men jump, and nervously hop back into their golf cart and try to film the alligator from the safety of their completely open-air vehicle. As you drive away, you are thinking to yourself, be careful what you ask for!

This brief vacation episode can be crafted into a story to use in workshops on decision-making, the power of assumptions and expectations, or motivation. The only challenge with re-telling these stories is the ethical issue of attribution, which is explored in Chapter Six.

STORYTELLING WISDOM

"Be a life observer and then ask yourself, 'How can I teach this?'"

Suzann Gardner

STORIES IN THE PRINT MEDIA AND ON THE INTERNET

Print media—newspapers, magazines, industry trade journals, and so on—include a wealth of story ideas and possibilities. The stories that capture your attention may not be those that make the front page. In fact, some of the more interesting stories are often in the local or human interest sections of the newspaper. Access to online news services or having the headlines sent to you from major papers can make your search for stories on specific topics a lot easier to manage. Also look to organizations that publish regular online newsletters as a source for story ideas.

While a newsletter version of an article may not be as thorough as you would like, chances are there will be information available to lead you to other sources.

As is discussed later on in this chapter, keep the articles that interest you in paper or electronic files so you can access them in the future. It is best not to wait until you need a story to go and hunt it down. Constantly be on the lookout for personal interest articles and news reports that might be useful to you. Here is an example of the print and Internet media articles that one of the authors put aside during the course of a seventeen-day period:

June 26, 2002: *The Publicity Hound's Tips of the Week,* Issue 90—Highlights June 25, 2002, publisher: Joan Stewart, *The Wall Street Journal* article on the growing number of workers who are looking for spiritual involvement on the job.

June 22, 2002: "The Original Cheesehead has Aged Well," by William Wineke, *Wisconsin State Journal.*

June 20, 2002: "Bun's Rush: Wienermobile Finds Route Near Pentagon No Picnic" by Meg Jones, *Milwaukee Journal Sentinel.*

June 12, 2002; "Southern Pastor Works to Deliver His Flock From Credit Card Debt," by Ellen Graham, *The Wall Street Journal.*

June 12, 2002: "Herman Trend Alert: A Corporation of the Future—Here Today," by Roger Herman and Joyce Gioia, The Herman Group.

June 10, 2002: "How the [U.S.] Open Came to the People," by Bill Pennington, *The New York Times.*

You may be asking yourself: Why were these specific items kept? They either were very funny stories (the Cheesehead and the Wienermobile), they spoke to a trend (spirituality in the workplace and the changing nature of corporations), or they demonstrated the power of individuals to bring about change (the U.S. Open and the southern pastor). All of these are topics the author trains, speaks, or consults on—or are stories that have the potential to help energize a training group.

Other types of literature can also be a resource for stories and story ideas. These include professional and classical literature, science fiction, folklore, traditional folktales, Greek mythology, ancient parables, and so on. You can find stories similar to Aesop's Fables, such as "A Family United" (Chapter Fifteen), offered by Clare Novak, both in books and on Internet websites. There are also numerous resources that contain compilations of ethnic, folk, and fairy tales. When using creative literary works like these, be sure that they are in the public domain; otherwise, they may be protected by copyright. That generally means that at least seventy-five years has passed since the story was first published in print form.

One of the surprises we had when soliciting stories from contributors were the number of people who gave us stories that were being emailed around the Internet. In fact, we received the following story in one form or another (monkeys and gorillas) from three contributors. Here is the version of the story that is in John Renesch's book, *Getting to the Better Future.*

Follow the Leader (I)

Contributed by John Renesch, business futurist, www.renesch.com

Put five apes in a room. Hang a banana from the ceiling and place a ladder under the banana. The banana is only reachable by climbing the ladder. Have it set up so that any time an ape starts to climb the ladder, the whole room is sprayed with ice-cold water. In a short time all the apes will learn not to climb the ladder.

Now, take one ape out and replace him with another one (Ape 6). Then disable the sprayer. The new ape will start to climb the ladder and will be attacked unmercifully by the other four apes. He will have no idea why he was attacked.

Replace another of the original apes with a new one and the same thing will happen, with Ape 6 doing most of the hitting. Continue this pattern until all of the original apes have been replaced. Now all of the apes will stay off the ladder, attacking any ape that attempts to, and will have absolutely no idea why they are doing it.

This is how company policy and culture is formed.

Renesch, J. E. (2000). Taken from *Getting to the better future.* San Francisco: New Business Books, p. 91. Used with permission.

John notes that this is an unattributed story sent to him by a colleague who discovered it on the Internet. He claims no ownership of it and says he has no way of knowing the author. He also extends his gratitude to the author as he says it emphasizes the point made by Jerry Harvey in his book, *The Abilene Paradox and Other Meditations on Management* (1988)—that at times, individuals act collectively as a group, even though no one person in the group really wants to take the action that all are doing. From our perspective, any time you use an Internet story in your training, you still need to give attribution even if you alter the details. In addition, keep in mind that people may have already heard or seen it. Unless it is one of those "timeless" stories, its impact may be significantly reduced due to familiarity, unless you are able to connect it to your training in such a way that it deepens participants' understanding of a key learning point.

STORIES FROM RADIO TALK SHOWS AND TELEVISION NEWS PROGRAMS

STORYTELLING WISDOM

"There is a difference between current and timely stories and timeless stories."

Steve Hanamura

Steve notes that in every city he watches the local and national news the night before he trains or speaks to get up-to-the minute stories to use. In his travels, he has discovered that most news stories are only good for a short period of time. However, because of their real-time nature, they can lend significant credibility to a presentation. Ed Tate recalls pulling his car over to capture a radio story about what happened to the Arizona State football team after a game against Washington State University. Their plane was struck by lightning twice in ten minutes. He then followed up on the story he heard by searching through newspapers to uncover the rest of the details. To accurately recall facts and details, it is important to record notes during and/or immediately following what was heard and to find ways to verify them.

We suggest not telling stories based on movies and television shows, other than those that are relaying "hard news." While their use may not be a violation of copyright law, there is a possibility that their telling is an infringement of a state law. In general, even verbally *telling* the stories from the original creative work of others is surrounded by a complex and frequently updated set of laws.

STORIES BASED UPON HISTORY

The story describing a situation between President Franklin Delano Roosevelt and Harry Hopkins, his key economic advisor, called "The Worth of a Contribution" (Chapter Eleven, contributed by Kathy Nielsen), is an example of a story based on history, which can be local, regional, national, or worldwide in focus. It may also come from a particular cultural or social perspective. Often there are rich stories behind sports heroes, business executives, government officials, religious leaders, and others who have significantly impacted the course of history. These stories do not have to be "positive" in nature, although they may speak to overcoming adversities. In this way they may help training participants learn about the impact of a single decision or how a certain leadership style can influence the outcome of a situation. It is important that you select historical stories that are appropriate for your audience. Telling a story about a baseball hero such as Babe Ruth might not be relevant outside the United States.

Historical stories have a particular credibility about them that underscores the point a trainer is making. People *believe* historical stories and find them both wise and inspiring. Consider this summary example about First Lady Eleanor Roosevelt. She was reputed to be plagued with personal insecurities throughout her life. However, she never let it stop her from pursuing her ideals of equality and inclusion, as well as from encouraging her husband Franklin to pursue them as well. One of her oft-quoted sayings is, "No one can make you feel inferior without your consent" (Roosevelt, 1960). Despite any self-doubt, she has been an inspiration to millions throughout her lifetime and after. She lived her own words of wisdom.

To contributor Merrill Anderson, sharing the past means sharing a message; it legitimizes our heritage. Merrill has frequently worked with organizations that are eighty to 150 years old. He researches each company and digs into its early history to develop stories that make a point with groups and business leaders. His story, "A Culture Rooted in Gunpowder" (Chapter Eleven), is an example of this.

Think about your own organization. How did the organization begin? What transitions has it gone through? What contributions has it made to the industry of which it is a part? What events helped to shape its values and its overall culture? As you continue your reflections, think about how you might share this information and with whom it would be valuable to share.

STORIES FROM TRAINING SESSIONS OR KEYNOTE TALKS

Joan Lloyd once asked a group, "How many of you think you have job security?" One hand went up. Joan asked, "Would you mind sharing why you think you have job security?" The woman answered, "Oh, I don't mind. I'm a nun." Participants in training sessions can provide some of the best stories around—either through the stories they themselves voluntarily share or through the behavior they display during the session, as noted by Jean Barbazette in her story, "I Didn't Ask to Be Here" (Chapter Sixteen).

Often the experiences you yourself have as a trainer can be woven into a wonderful story to be used in future programs. For a train-the-trainer session or a seminar on stress management, consider referencing Clare Novak's experience. Clare was asked to do an evening session on coaching skills for an international group of pharmaceutical industry managers attending a multi-day management retreat. Clare asked the coordinator if the group was knowledgeable about basic coaching skills so she could do an advanced seminar for the group. "Yes, they all know how to coach," was the coordinator's response. When Clare arrived, she found a group of seminar participants who were all from other countries—because the managers from the United States had gone golfing. Also, the group had no coaching experience. They were exhausted from translating all day and were not looking forward to yet another workshop. Making massive adjustments in her original plans, she gave the group a brief definition of coaching and had them break into groups by country so they could discuss and practice in their own languages. The workshop got great reviews and the participants thanked Clare for her flexibility. Keep in mind that if you had had her experience and were to tell it again, that it would be best to do so in a situation where no one could identify the company or who the participants were.

Trainees may share stories in response to a question you ask, to elaborate on a key point, or as an example of something that happened to them. You also have the option of asking people to tell their own stories as a way of drawing out personal experiences and the learnings associated with them. However, remember that just because a participant shares a story during a workshop you are holding does not mean you have the right to tell it elsewhere without the person's expressed permission. It is always best to check with the person before sharing it with others, especially if you want to use it in similar training sessions throughout the organization.

Each of us in our lifetime will have the opportunity to hear keynote talks by well-known individuals. Often the stories these individuals share are those they consider to be their "signature" stories—stories around which they themselves have established notoriety. Once again, it is best to obtain permission from the speaker before using the story in a public setting. It is also important to give the person appropriate credit when you do share it.

ORGANIZING YOUR STORIES

With so many story ideas available on a daily basis, consider ways to log and organize them so they are handy when you want to develop a story. First and foremost, you need to find a method for tracking story possibilities. Consider keeping a personal journal and logging potential story situations in it. Or record items on index cards, in your daily planner, or on sticky notes so that you are able to remember the details of the circumstance. For example, Joe Barnes jots things down in a small notebook. Afterwards, he reflects on his experiences: How did life change? When did the light go on? These reflections help him to think about where these experiences may be valuable to training participants. Sandra Hoskins also logs her experiences and story ideas in her daily journal that she carries with her everywhere. She then gives titles to her stories and puts the titles into her computer database. Down the road she can type the title of the story into her computer system and it will pull up the day she had the experience or heard the story, which then allows her to go back to her journal for more details. The process Joan Lloyd uses goes beyond writing down funny events in her notebook. She follows up by categorizing and logging them based on a story checklist she has developed over time that contains a long list of key words. Then, when she is preparing a new program, she can scan the story list for material. It also helps her avoid repeating a story when she is invited back to speak.

In addition to logging story ideas, you will need a system to track them so you can remember them. How do those who tell stories organize them so they can easily be recalled?

My Mental Filing System (J)

Contributed by Suzann Gardner, associate professor, Alverno College

My husband took a position in Indianapolis right out of college. We'd been there a year and weren't sure if we were going to stay. So I thought, "Do I want to apply for a teaching job? I'd feel badly leaving my students on short notice." So I looked for another kind of job and found one full-time in retail. My husband was traveling a great deal so I thought I'd also pick up a part-time job, too. This little floral shop near our apartment hired me. I was terribly surprised. I didn't know *anything* about flowers.

I studied like crazy everything I could about plants. It was a small shop. Sometimes I was the only one there. People would ask me questions and I would have to know. I studied and studied and thought, "Oh my gosh. I'm just becoming a little dictionary of plant life." I was becoming obnoxious. I'd bring it into every conversation. "Do you know this about plants and that about plants?" I used to take all the little sick plants home with me and nurse them back to health, and then take them back to the store so they could be sold. I was so proud of my learning!

Then I had four sons, all a year apart in age. Between them and all the pets, I gave up gardening and all my plants. When we finally moved back to Milwaukee, a neighbor greeted me with a house-warming gift. She said, "This is my favorite plant and I thought you'd really like it." I replied, "Oh, thanks." And then I thought, "This is her favorite plant and I'm going to kill it!"

I put the plant on the table and thought of my young children and numerous pets. "I wonder if this a poisonous plant." I couldn't remember. Let me think. It was only fifteen years ago since I'd worked in a plant shop. I thought I knew everything. But I hadn't used those skills in years. I got furious with myself. Why can't I remember if this is a poisonous plant or not? At least I could come up with the name of the plant but I was frustrated. This was serious; the plant might be a killer.

So I looked in my memory. Now, when I try to remember something my children laugh at me because I put my right hand up with my index finger out pointing at the right side of my brain and I turn my hand like I'm searching through a Roladex. Actually, my mind *is* a Roladex and I'm turning it, trying to figure out where poisonous plants are located. I was so mad at myself. I thought, "I'm getting old and feeble and my memory is failing. It's like being in college and taking a test and knowing that you know something but you can't remember it. You just have to figure out where you filed it in your head." So I thought, "Relax and figure out where the file is. Do an association. Indianapolis. Plant. Dog. Cat. Children." I was getting madder. And the madder I got the less I could remember. I finally said, "Just focus." Voila. I found the file called "children," and sure enough I found a file called "Mr. Yuck"—that green sticker that you get from the poison control center with the face that has a tongue sticking out. And then I found the whole list of poisonous plants—right there in my brain.

I was so proud of myself because I was so very patient and so very persistent in finding the file in my mind.

We often have everything we need to know within us when it comes time to make an important decision. The secret is to persist until you "find the file."

Suzann puts stories she has fully developed onto a mental tape in her head and consciously connects them in her mind—she cross-indexes her brain based on the reasons she has told the stories. Clare Novak also keeps a large mental repertoire of stories so she can pull one out on a moment's notice—such as when she sees participants with blank looks on their faces. Chris Clarke-Epstein has a similar approach that she describes in the following way: "My mother volunteers in an art museum in Wausau. An Australian wildlife artist visited the museum and was asked if he went into the wild to see the animals. He replied, 'At first I took thousands of photos, but now I have an enormous repertoire so I no longer go out when I start a new painting. I review my slide carousel.'" Chris has a slide carousel full of stories in her head. When she selects a topic, the story drops down. With new stories, she suggests doing something to cement them—such as writing down key words or telling others the story soon after it is heard—or they can easily be lost.

For stories that she actually uses, Laura Page logs story titles along with key points on her computer, while Julie O'Mara writes them down in her client files. Doug Stevenson also names his stories and has two to three sentences about each of them to remind him of the details. He then electronically files these stories by category, such as "light versus heavy" topics. Steve Hanamura organizes his stories by one of three things: learning objectives for the training session, questions he wants the audience to respond to, or stories to emphasize a point. After titling her stories, Maureen G. Mulvaney (MGM) writes them out word for word so that she gets the same reaction or response from all her audiences. This way she knows exactly when they will laugh and cry and get the truth in it. However, MGM's presentation of her stories still looks spontaneous. Similarly, Ed Tate writes out his stories based on an outline that may have been put together from a combination of sources.

As mentioned earlier in this chapter, if you find articles you want to use, cut them out and save them in a file by topic area. If the story is one that is found online or is sent by email, keep electronic files of them either by topic or with the workshop to which they correspond. Unless you have the ability to easily and thoroughly recall stories logged in memory, or you have electronic or printed information on them, we encourage you to jot down the idea or key items in the story: the parties who are involved, what the issue or challenge or experience is, and highlights about what happens. To more easily recall the story, give it a title and put it in a paper or electronic file that has category titles that are familiar to you. When you get ready to use it, you can follow the steps outlined in Chapter Three, if it needs to be designed. If you have already written it up (in bullets or complete sentences), it is just a matter of finding this version of the story in whatever organizing system you are using.

THE STORY CONTINUES

To bring more stories to life in your training programs, you will need to develop your story discovery skills by seeking ideas from a variety of creative sources. These sources are almost limitless. From public events, to gatherings with family and friends; from overheard conversations to print media vignettes; while on vacation, at school, the grocery store, or the ball game, stories surround our lives. And do not forget training programs as a source of future stories. Becoming more observant will help you capture these creative possibilities. Once acquired, you then need to create a way to note these story ideas and keep track of them so they are easily accessible. Our contributors offer numerous suggestions about their own personal organizing methods.

Bringing Stories to Life

- Where do the stories you tell come from?
- What have been your favorite or most rewarding sources of stories?
- Which of the sources noted in this chapter are new to you?
- What questions might you explore that would lead to creating or discovering more of your own stories?
- How do you organize potential story ideas so you can easily access them?
- Which methods discussed here might add to your current organizational system?

Having a rich and varied collection of story ideas will support you when you need to find just the right story for a particular purpose. Setting up an organized bank of stories will also encourage you to build on your current use by drawing you into stories you just cannot resist sharing with others.

chapter THREE

How to Craft a Story

Losing the Sale (K)

Contributed by Jonathan M. Preston, senior manager of a major pharmaceutical firm

I was asked by a university to listen and grade the final sales presentation that three marketing students had prepared after a semester of learning the basics—how to determine needs, craft an initial benefit statement, probe for more information, and close a sale. The last presentation was by a gentleman who was very, very enthusiastic and really knew his product. Like the others, he was trying to sell me a cellular phone. This was when my sales staff and I really needed a new type of cellular phone because our sales region was expanding into Canada.

Early on, he asked me some great background and probing questions that made me enthusiastic about his particular product. We finally got to the point in his presentation where he was showing me a lot of phone features and extras and was converting the features into benefits, which peaked my interest even more. I told him, "You've got everything I need and the price is right." On my own, I was moving him to close the sale. He had covered all the basics and all the benefits. But he continued to sell me.

Then, he turned to a very wordy page in his sales materials that had something highlighted on it in order to find more information on a new type of security system called "thin air security." With this system, no one would be able to tap or hack into my employees' phone conversations. As he was reading, I looked down at the highlighted information at the bottom of the page. It clearly said that discussions were still going on with the Canadian satellite company to link his company's cell phone to its system. The cell phone company had anticipated that everything would be ironed out about one month after the release of the sales materials that this gentleman had brought with him. I said, "What is this?" He began to read the section with me. I said, "I told you that I need immediate service." He said, "It's only going to be delayed another month." I replied, "What if you don't get the approval? What if you can't make the link?" He immediately sat back in his chair, speechless. I said to him, "The two other people I talked to said their companies could give me immediate global service." At that moment he realized that closing a sale was all about getting "back to basics." Instead, he had allowed me, the prospective customer, to see too much information, which left me with a huge unknown. As a result, he knew he had lost the sale.

If you decide to develop stories on your own for use in training, they need to be carefully and thoughtfully crafted, just like the presentations sales or marketing professionals give to qualified prospects. If they are not, you may well encounter one or more of the pitfalls such as that experienced by the gentleman trying to sell Jon a new cell phone. Giving too much information—or not enough information, for that matter—can cause your story to fall flat on its face. Like a well-prepared sales presentation, storytelling is a process that actually begins *before* you stand in front of a group to relay your story. In this chapter we cover the basics of story construction, including Doug Stevenson's eight-step story structure model. You will see examples of how to create a story in three different ways—from a rough outline, from a mind map, and from a newspaper article—and learn how to hone your own story-writing skills.

There are some basic rules when it comes to story construction. In general, effective stories, according to Kate Lutz, have a beginning, a middle, and an end, which simply means they have a logical order that both the storyteller and the audience can follow. When it comes to the specific words that you tell within the story, Paula Bartholome suggests we use words that create vivid pictures in our minds while Joan Gillman goes a step further to suggest that stories must appeal to all five senses. Both Marcy Fisher and Karen Bryson caution trainers about the use of colloquialisms and analogies in stories, especially those told in cultures and countries that differ from the background of the trainer. Doug also encourages us to pick the "right" words and not "wing it," because there is often better language to use. He also mentions, for those who are curious about the appropriate length of stories used in training settings, that the length should match the importance of the point being made. For the main points of your training, four to seven minutes is appropriate. For secondary and minor points, less than four minutes is fine. The time you spend also depends on your ability to craft and present a story in a compelling manner. The longer the story, the more craft and rehearsal are needed.

Paula reminds trainers that stories need to be credible and believable in the context being used. Participants need to find the events of the story you are telling to be acceptable in order for them, as trainees, to be able to focus on the key point you are making. According to Kathy Nielsen, those who provide training also need to watch whether or not the story content presents a judgment, or evaluates participants' behaviors or attitudes. She offers the following example: "Most parents today are far too permissive" is a judgment that is outside of the role modeling trainers provide, whereas "good managers listen to their employees" is not.

Knowing the key point or moral of the story that you want to get across to others is critical to developing a story. From a participant's perspective, the "point" or the "moral" answers the questions, "So what are you trying to say?" or "What are you trying to communicate to me?" As a trainer, to ascertain the key point or the moral means, in Doug's words, "reflecting on the deeper meaning of the story and visualizing and developing it so it comes alive." It is important to note at this point that some stories, especially those that are instructive in nature, may have more than one key point.

STORYTELLING WISDOM

"Situation plus outcome equals a lesson for someone else."

Steve Hanamura

STORY STRUCTURE

Once you have identified the deeper meaning of a story, then you need to structure it in such a way that the appropriate moral, lesson, or key point is clearly brought out. Clare Novak develops stories so that each of them is its own mini-drama: there is an introduction, a build-up, and then denouement—that is, everything is made clear at the end and no questions or surprises remain. The story structure model that Chip Bell uses, which is described in his book, *Managers as Mentors* (1996), follows the same three steps: context—inviting the learner to listen and establishing and painting the background or scene in whatever amount of detail is required; challenge—a dilemma that people can identify with that creates the proper tension and a sense of anticipation; and climax—a punch line and a resolution paired with a lesson that produces realistic and relevant insights for trainees (pp. 115–120). Kate Lutz points out that stories need both action and tension. She recounts that Shakespeare's plays include light moments in even the most tragic works to provide the comic relief that ultimately heightens the dramatic tension. This means that along with structuring a story so that others can access the deeper meaning for themselves, it is also important to try to add levity—if not a laugh, at least a smile.

For stories that you consider to be at the core of your repertoire (what speakers call "signature" stories), Doug Stevenson's eight-step story structure model may be something you want to use to develop them. The eight steps summarized here are meant to be a working guide. They flesh out more detail and round out the three-part version of the model.

Step 1: Set the scene—Create the context for the story. Set time, location, weather, and conditions. What is going on emotionally, physically, or spiritually?

Step 2: Introduce the characters—Help me to see them with visual descriptions. Tell me about your relationship, their quirks. Become them. Add a character voice or physicalization to make them different from you. Do this with key characters only, not everyone.

Step 3: Begin the journey—What is the task, the goal, the journey? Where do you have to go? Who do you have to connect with? What is the challenge?

Step 4: Encounter the obstacle—Without conflict, the story will be boring. Something must happen to get in your way and make it interesting. The obstacle may be a person, a challenge to overcome, or a self-limiting belief. Exaggeration here will make it funny.

Step 5: Overcome the obstacle—What did you have to do to overcome it? What strength did you have to summon? Was there someone who helped you? Perhaps your helper is the hero; perhaps it is you. Be specific here. Break your solution down into a few steps in sequence. This is where the teaching happens.

Step 6: Resolve the story—Tie up any loose ends and make sure your audience knows how everything turns out. What happened to the other people, to your helper? Go back over your story for logic and hear it as the audience will hear it.

Step 7: Make the point—It is important that your story has one clear point. Too many points confuse the issue. Write out the point and memorize it. Work on the words. Make it simple and easy to remember.

Step 8: Ask the question—Make *your* story *their* story by asking the question. "Has that ever happened to you?" Turn the point into a question. Push their buttons. The question makes your story pertinent to them in the moment and adds power to your point (Stevenson, 2000, pp. 2–3).

This last step is critical when telling stories to groups where you will not be able to debrief with them or engage in a follow-up conversation. With stories used in an experiential training setting, this last step can function as the lead-in to a set of debriefing questions.

One of the added benefits of these story structure models is that they can also be used to critique and enhance your existing stories. Consider giving the story and the steps to a colleague and having that person do a critique for you. Sometimes our own biases about a story, especially if they are personal, can get in the way of clearly developing each part of the story. You may also find that a single story is better told as a series of shorter stories, in which the pieces unwind in a workshop over a period of time. Sandra Hoskins refers to these as chapter-by-chapter stories. She finds that she uses them more when she presents technical training topics. Or you may discover, as Maureen G. Mulvaney (MGM) has, that it is better to start the story out "backwards" and let the audience discover who you are talking about. She gives an example of beginning a story by saying, "Let me tell you the story of a young gal I once knew." She ends by saying, "Do you know who I might be speaking about? Yes, I've been talking about my *own* experiences. Therefore, what this young gal did must have worked, since I am here now. How did she get this way?" The structural enhancements described here will come over time, as you begin to develop and tell more stories in your training programs and become more practiced and skilled in creating your own stories.

THE WRITTEN VERSUS THE SPOKEN WORD

Keep in mind that writing a story versus telling it orally involves different sets of words. Your challenge will be to write out a story using the *spoken,* rather than the *written* word. If this is difficult for you to do, tape yourself telling the story and transcribe it verbatim. Then start to play around with the structure and specific wording until you are comfortable with the way it unfolds. Next, retell the story out loud several times to ensure you have continued to stay with the spoken word in your writing.

Here is how Kate Lutz, a professional storyteller, gets around the challenge of the written versus spoken word. She goes rollerblading to keep her body occupied in order to allow her brain to engage, and her thoughts to flow freely. Kate starts with a concept she wants to share with others and goes through what she calls a "tug and pull" process during the creative part of story development. She plays with different concepts, reworking them in her mind, tugging and pulling at them to bring out the ideas in new ways. This is why she does not use a computer to generate her stories. The four steps in her story creation process are:

1. Identify a sequential list of events, frequently chronological, but not always.
2. Draw a series of stick figures (pictures that create the characters and the primary action). Using colored pencils helps the memory process.

3. Tell the story again and again to family and friends, in person, and on the phone, testing for that "blank look" or confused silence that says, "Where are you coming from?"
4. Memorize beginning and ending lines and any dialogue—this is when Kate may create a "chorus" type of language—a repeated key phrase or scene (what is referred to as "patterning," evident in "The Disapproving Neighbor" [Chapter Fourteen]).

Kate has been using this method for years. It is a very right-brain approach to story development that taps into her creative spirit. The left brain gets engaged when she fine-tunes the story. Whatever method you use to craft your stories and however many steps you follow to structure them, your stories will benefit from both the creative and the logical abilities you bring to the process.

EXAMPLE: FROM ROUGH OUTLINE TO STORY

How can you begin to craft a story? The approach outlined in this section is one in which the trainer writes out the scenario in free-flow form—with no concern for structure, wording, punctuation, grammar, spelling, and so on. Once the initial draft has been written, reflect upon the deeper meaning of the story—its key point, moral, or lesson—until it becomes clear relative to the training topic in which you plan to incorporate the story. Then, go back to the rough draft and identify the context, challenge, and climax. Add details to them to flesh out parts that need more description and reorganize the story, if necessary, so that it clearly follows one of the story structure models presented earlier.

Here is the rough outline of a series of situations that happened to one of the authors. From this outline, determine what you think the key point, lesson, or moral of the story might be for others.

Week before 43rd birthday—I went for a routine eye exam. My vision had been 20/15 on my last visit two years ago in Spokane. Hadn't noticed any problems. Joked around a lot with the ophthalmologist; he was a cute, young guy. Suddenly he became quiet, almost introspective. I knew something was wrong. When done he told me I needed glasses, preferably bifocals. Then he told me I had a hole in my left retina and that I should have someone follow up on it. I go home and look up retinal holes on the Internet. Three days later, someone calls from Dr. S.'s office—he's a retinal specialist.

Tells me appointment has been scheduled for a day I have a client meeting, so I change it. She says plan on three hours. I hang up. Then it dawns on me—that's a lot of time. So I call back and ask why. She says because the doc might decide to do surgery. That Saturday I asked Gloria's fiancé about it—he's a neurologist. He says they might have to shoot dye into my body. So I call Dr. S.'s office again and ask what will happen. Get transferred to a nurse. She gets my records from other doc and says someone should drive me because I will not be able to see well even after going through only the exam. Karen takes me. Nurse does exam. Dr. S. does his exam. That bright light really bothered me when he dilated my eyes. Dr. S. says the hole is an atrophic hole—no need to fix it—don't worry about it. Should worry about cataracts instead. I ask if other doc should have told me. He hems and haws. I go home and call the ophthalmologist and ask why he didn't tell me I had cataracts.

From the story author's perspective, this entire situation signals three things about today's consumers—that they have access to more information, that they have become more knowledgeable over time, and that they often insert themselves into the work of others in order to ensure their own specific needs are met. In essence, consumers these days want immediate and complete answers and viable solutions to their problems. Here is the "retinal hole" story again, this time in the format in which it is told. See if you can pick out each portion of the three-part story structure model: context, challenge, and climax.

Seeing the Light (L)

Contributed by Lori L. Silverman

It's the week before my 43rd birthday. I'm in the exam room at the doctor's office . . . reading all the diplomas on the wall . . . waiting patiently for my routine eye exam to begin. My mind wanders. Huh. It's been two years since my last exam. I remember being told I have 20/15 vision. I awaken to reality when the ophthalmologist walks in. He's a young, good-looking guy. He shakes my hand and says "Hi, I'm Dr. B. Nice to meet you. Having any problems with your eyes?"

With my usual high intensity, I respond, "Nope. I'm just here 'cause it's time to have them checked!" He proceeds through all the tests, chatting non-stop with me as he goes. A real jovial sort of guy. Poof! Just like that, he goes silent. I just know something is wrong. After what seems an eternity, he pipes up, "You need glasses. Bifocals would be the best in your situation." As I'm thinking, "What's he talking about? I'm not having any problems seeing. . . ." I hear him say, "You also have a hole in your left retina that needs to be checked out. If it's okay with you, I'll have my nurse make an appointment with a specialist." He gives me a slip of paper with symptoms to watch for, which of course I can't read since my eyes are dilated, and says someone will call me at home. Stunned, I go downstairs to the optical center and buy a couple pairs of outrageous reading glasses—I pass on the bifocals—and drive myself home.

So . . . what do I do next? I phone my boyfriend at the same time I log on to my computer to search out everything there is to know about retinal holes. Did you know they could lead to detached retinas? And, that once diagnosed in one eye the other eye can get one, too? This is not looking too bright, if you ask me. Three days later, a woman calls from Dr. S.'s office—he's a retinal specialist. She tells me an appointment's been scheduled for a day I have a client meeting. No way! I change the appointment. She ends the call by saying, "Plan on spending three hours with us." I hang up. Then it dawns on me—three hours is a lot of time. She failed to give me what I needed to know. I immediately call back and ask why. She says, " 'Cause the doctor might have to do surgery."

So . . . what do I do next? Having exhausted the ears of all my friends, a few days later I ask my friend Gloria's fiancé what he knows about retinal holes—he's a neurologist. I figure brain . . . eyes . . . they're all in my head. He must know something. Demitri explains that the doctor might have to shoot dye into my body in order to see behind the eye.

So . . . what do I do next? I call Dr. S.'s office again and talk to his nurse. She gets my records and calls me back the next day. I hear, "Can you get someone to drive you? After the exam you won't be able to see very well. Especially if you have surgery."

So . . . what do I do next? I call Karen. She's a good mom and the wife of a doctor. At this point I need all the help I can get. She drives me. And gives me a bear hug before I enter the exam room. This doctor is different. Brusque. A man of few words. He dilates my eyes and shines this really bright light in them. "Ahhhh. It hurts," I scream out. He continues on as if he didn't hear me. When it's all over he hands me an eight-page pamphlet. Not a word can I see. Then I hear his voice, "The hole in your retina is atrophic—no need to fix it—it won't bother you. But you'll need to watch those cataracts." Now I've had it. "What? Cataracts? At my age? Is this typical? Should the other doctor have seen them?" He hems and haws, and says, "Don't *worry.* You'll have plenty of time to do *that* in a few years." Then he disappears. Poof! Just like that, he's gone.

But . . . I wasn't done yet. Over the next few days I called the ophthalmologist and drilled him mercilessly. I read everything about cataracts that I could get my hands on. Every person who was willing to listen heard my story and was quizzed for information. Finally . . . I was satisfied. You see, I'm a consumer who wants answers and solutions to my problems and I want them now. And, if I can't get them right away, I'll go hunt them down on my own. I'll even go so far as to stick myself in the middle of someone's work until I get what I need. Am I unusual? Not in today's world! I'm the new breed of consumer. Information hungry. Knowledgeable. And persistent! "Give me credit" for what I bring to the table. What about you?

What did you identify as the story's context, challenge, and climax? Here is how the story fits the structure. The context starts with the sentence, "It's the week before my 43rd birthday. I'm in the exam room at the doctor's office." The next several sentences continue to set the context for the story's challenge, which begins with, "Poof! Just like that, he went silent. I just know something is wrong," and continues through the next several paragraphs, building the tension as the medical details mount up. The climax occurs when Dr. S. tells Lori, "The hole in your retina is atrophic—no need to fix it—it won't bother you. But you'll need to watch those cataracts." From here forward, the story follows Lori's actions as a consumer.

You may have noticed in the story the use of a pattern phrase. "So . . . what do I do next?" is used four times to show Lori's specific actions as a consumer over a period of several weeks. This phrase was changed to, "But . . . I wasn't done yet" to signal a shift from climax to the key point of the story: "give me credit."

EXAMPLE: FROM MIND MAP TO STORY

Sometimes it is easier to draw a picture that typifies a situation, rather than to jot down an outline to describe it. A mind map is a fluid way to visually capture and represent a group of disorganized but connected ideas or pieces of information. You typically start a mind map by writing a central or core concept in a box or circle in the center of a piece of paper. Next, brainstorm key themes and depict them branching from the core concept. Subpoints—associations or related ideas—can then be added as branches to each theme as you brainstorm all the information related to the mind map topic. The resulting picture will be a free-flowing, well-organized representation of the entire concept.

When mapping a story idea, start by writing what you think may be the essence of the story—its core concept—in the center of a blank page. Then take the group of facts, impressions, emotions, intuitions, and experiences you would like to illustrate through your story, determine the key themes, and organize them around the core concept, as described earlier. Once you are finished, create an outline of the sequence of story events, which will help you in structuring the information into a full-fledged story. When creating a mind map, keep the momentum going while brainstorming, rather than concentrating on making the drawing look neat. Consider adding drawings or symbols to your mind map for added clarity and to enhance its visual impact.

Another potential use of a mind map is to work with an unformed story idea—to help you decide if you have the makings of a good story and to determine just what its essence is. You might start with a somewhat vague idea of where you wish your story to take you. Identify a potential title or working name for your idea—then add all the facts, impressions, emotions, and reactions to your chart, grouping related themes together. When you have finished brainstorming, review your themes in light of what the story's deeper meaning might be. Used in this way, mind mapping can help organize your thinking and lead you to your story's message. Once you have determined the story's essence, revisit how you have organized your information and make any changes to reflect the core concept or message around which the story will be built.

You might also create a mind map, as shown in Figure 3.1, by selecting a story structure model and making the structure elements the key themes of your mind map. Then, as you brainstorm story concepts, you can add them to the portion of the model in which they fit. For the story "7.1 on the Richter Scale," the author has chosen the three-step context, challenge, climax model described earlier in this chapter as the focus of her mind map. As you review the mind map, see what you can learn about the story and the way the author might develop it.

Notice how the details of the situation fit into the context, challenge, and climax parts of the story model. How might these be woven into a compelling story? What do you think the author intends as the story's deeper meaning? How might that point be made given this series of events? How could the story begin in a way that grabs the listener's attention? These are the types of questions you would ask yourself after completing a mind map to help you organize your own story ideas. Now let's look at how the author frames this story. The story not only follows the context, challenge, climax model, but Doug Stevenson's eight-step story structure model is also embedded in the story line. See if you can pick out these eight elements.

Figure 3.1: Mind Map of "7.1 on the Richter Scale"

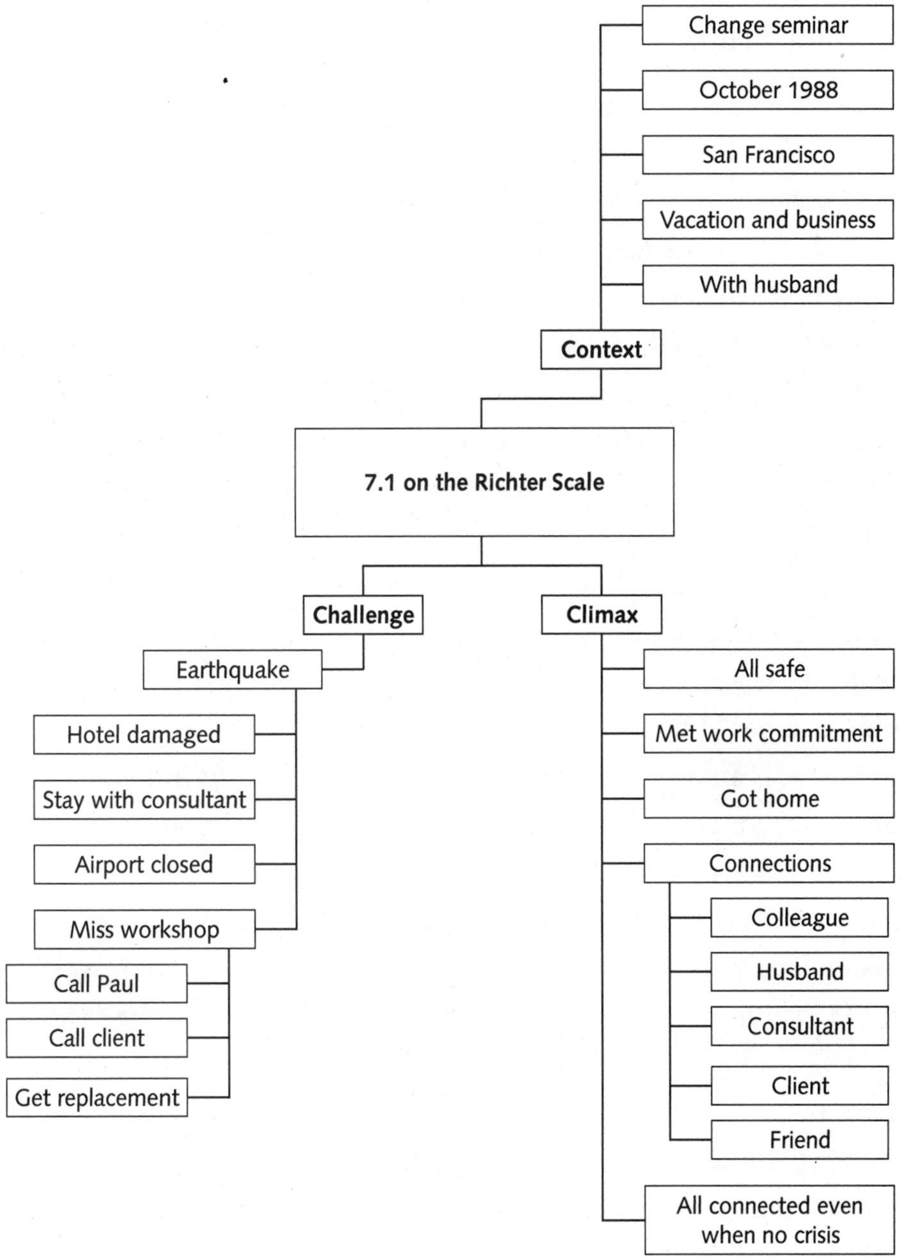

- **7.1 on the Richter Scale**
  - **Context**
    - Change seminar
    - October 1988
    - San Francisco
    - Vacation and business
    - With husband
  - **Challenge**
    - Earthquake
      - Hotel damaged
      - Stay with consultant
      - Airport closed
      - Miss workshop
        - Call Paul
        - Call client
        - Get replacement
  - **Climax**
    - All safe
    - Met work commitment
    - Got home
    - Connections
      - Colleague
      - Husband
      - Consultant
      - Client
      - Friend
    - All connected even when no crisis

7.1 on the Richter Scale (M)

Contributed by Mary B. Wacker

There was a low rumbling. I thought it was the garage door opening and wondered if Linda's husband was coming home. The noise didn't subside. In fact, the rumbling grew louder and louder! And suddenly the house began to rock on its foundation. I saw floor-to-ceiling plate glass windows move in a wavelike motion as plants and pottery crashed to the floor. "Earthquake!" Linda cried, "Everyone out of the house." This was easier said than done for Linda—our instructor—who was eight months pregnant with her first child and climbing two levels of steps from her business conference center. Just moments before we had all been meeting there for our seminar. We rushed to help her and our little group reassembled outside her home. I grabbed at my husband, Alan, who had just arrived to pick me up at the end of the day. "Whatever is happening, thank God we're together," I thought.

Linda was an organization development consultant in Berkeley, California, conducting a weeklong certification for six of us eager colleagues. This was the second-to-last day and we were an intimate group by this time, meeting in Linda's home conference center and making Peet's Coffee runs every morning. The seminar topic, you ask? Managing complex change. And boy, were we in for the case study of our lives! It was 5:00 P.M., October 17, 1989, and we were smack in the middle of one of the worst earthquakes this country had experienced in decades. Seven-point-one on the Richter scale! Our stricken group huddled around the car radio, and we heard the moment-by-moment breaking news. Several miles away, the World Series was being played at Candlestick Park with the Goodyear Blimp floating helplessly overhead. Chaos reigned as thousands upon thousands of fans poured out of the stadium. Only moments before, a section of the Bay Bridge had crashed, taking several cars along with it and stranding workers who were just leaving their downtown offices. Sirens pierced the air. The Marina District was in shambles. On the other side of the Bay, within minutes, the Oakland freeway had had become the world's largest parking lot.

Arriving back at our hotel, we found no power, no water, and a piece of ceiling occupying our bed. We remembered Linda saying, "you can count on me if you need a place to stay," and we decided to take her up on her generous offer. Fortunately, her home had been built to handle earthquakes! Several of us camped out on various levels and pulled tortellini out of the freezer to accommodate the crowd for dinner. It was immensely comforting to be together while we listened to the various news reports on the injuries and damage. We all hugged long and hard before going to bed that night. We were in this together.

The next morning, I was desperate to get home to Milwaukee for a speaking obligation I had early the next day. In my fifteen years in training, I'd never missed a seminar and I wasn't about to break my record. But the airports were still closed and it was painfully obvious I was stuck! Travel by any means—except horse or donkey—was completely out of the question. Options raced through my brain at the speed of light. Out of nowhere, Paul popped into my head. He owed me one! Paul was a fellow consultant and I had once taken over his university class when he'd had car trouble. Time to call Paul. Well, outgoing lines just weren't to be had. The world was trying to call San Francisco. It took two hours of continual dialing but I finally got through. "Paul, I'm stranded in San Francisco and I need help!" I cried. He responded, "You can count on me." After coaching Paul for an hour and going over the logistics, I knew my seminar was in good hands. Once again, I felt the gift of trust and being connected in times of crisis. Then I called my conference coordinator. "Lee," I said, "guess where I am? San Francisco!" Without missing a beat, Lee asked, "Mary, how is it in shake-and-bake land?" It was good to laugh. I again experienced the warmth of connecting to another person I could count on.

We finally made it home the day of the seminar by taking the red-eye flight out of San Francisco. As I fell into bed, too tired to sleep, I reflected on all the special people who had come together during this crisis, willing to step in to make whatever was needed happen: Linda, her husband, Alan, Paul, Lee, and the countless others who had supported me during this ordeal. More than a seminar on complex change could ever teach. I learned firsthand how a single experience can draw people together through a common bond. As I drifted off to sleep, I remembered all those who had said, "You can count on me." I wondered why it takes a catastrophic event for people to show their unconditional support and warmth for each other. I made a promise not to wait for the next crisis to show those who matter to me how much I care about them. They can "count on me."

Were you able to pick out Doug's story structure model? Within the first two paragraphs, Mary set the scene (Step 1)—a managing complex change certification seminar in October 1989 when an earthquake hit San Francisco; introduced the characters (Step 2)—the consultant, the other seminar participants, and her husband; and began the journey (Step 3)—trying to return home to facilitate a seminar the following day. In the ensuing paragraphs, she encountered the obstacles (Step 4)—the airports were closed and the phone lines were jammed. She then overcame these obstacles (Step 5)—by finding a colleague to fill in for her and coaching him over the phone. The author then resolved the story (Step 6)—by telling us that she communicated the change to her conference coordinator and then arrived safely home the following day. In one simple sentence, she made the point (Step 7)—that she learned firsthand how a single experience can draw people together through a common bond—that "you can count on me." She resolves not to wait for a crisis to show those who matter to her how much she cares about them. All that's missing is the final piece of the puzzle, to turn her story into their story by asking the question (Step 8). This can be accomplished with questions such as, "Whom do *you* feel most connected with? What can you do to show them how much they mean to you?"

The story structure is consciously chosen and relies on the author having a clear sense of the message to be relayed to her listeners. This is an example of a crucible story whose purpose is to encourage listeners to appreciate their deep connections with others and to evoke an immediate response. Who has not been through some type of crisis and reached out to connect with family, friends, and colleagues—even total strangers? The story has wide applicability and could be told in a program on collaboration, managing change, stress management, delegation, or juggling multiple priorities.

EXAMPLE: FROM NEWSPAPER ARTICLE TO STORY

As mentioned in Chapter Two, newspapers and other print materials are wonderful sources for training stories. Sometimes an article is short enough to be read out loud in a training situation exactly as it is written. Sometimes, even if the story is well-crafted, as the following example demonstrates, it may still need a few tweaks to make it one that is useful to learners. As you read through the article printed here, try to identify four items: the story type, its purpose(s), potential training programs in which to use this story, and the main point(s) of the story in these training situations.

Bun's Rush: Wienermobile Finds Route Near Pentagon No Picnic

By Meg Jones, *Milwaukee Journal Sentinel*

It's the most famous motorized sausage in the nation, but even the Oscar Mayer Wienermobile can't drive on a restricted road next to the Pentagon.

The crew of the 27-foot-long hot dog on wheels got grilled by police when it mistakenly traveled on a road closed to commercial traffic.

Ever since the terrorist attacks on Sept. 11, Route 110 has been off limits to vehicles with six wheels or more because of concerns that someone could drive a truck bomb close to the home of the nation's defense department.

So when the Wienermobile that departed from Madison lumbered down Route 110 Tuesday evening, a Virginia state trooper's eyes widened. Perhaps expecting the wurst, he flipped on his flashing lights and pulled over the lost dog.

Traffic on the busy road that runs along the Potomac River backed up for a short time as people craned their heads and gawked, obviously relishing the sight of the Wienermobile getting busted.

A passing motorist gave a frank appraisal of the sausage pilot's gaffe. "Everyone around here knows you don't bring trucks on that road, and it wasn't just any truck, it was the Oscar Mayer Wienermobile," said Carrie Witt, who was driving to her home in Alexandria, Va., after visiting a friend.

That stretch of Route 110 is lighted with large spotlights and staffed around the clock by armed officers in squad cars and Humvees at checkpoints, said Witt, who travels on the road several times a week.

"So here was this very serious (security) detail and they're pulling over a cartoon truck," said Witt. "It's probably the most benign truck on the road—that's why it's so funny."

At the Wienermobile wheel were Will Keller and Paula Pendleton, both 22 and recent college graduates from Illinois and California, who had just finished the two-week-long Hot Dog High at Oscar Mayer headquarters in Madison.

Packed in the back of the Wienermobile, which will travel throughout the East for a year, were boxes of Wienermobile whistles, Wienermobile Hot Wheels, Wienermobile-shaped bean bag toys and a karaoke machine featuring the Oscar Mayer wiener and bologna jingles.

After learning how to parallel park as well as boning up on the history of the company and Oscar Mayer jingles, Keller and Pendleton, who are called hot-doggers—like the drivers of the six other Wienermobiles—drove from Madison to Washington, D.C., for visits to a barbecue cook-off and charity events.

They didn't know Route 110 is verboten to Wienermobiles. "They were very apologetic," said Sarah Delea, Oscar Mayer spokeswoman. "They just did not realize. They were sorry for any sort of traffic delay."

Trooper Robert Stacy knew the Wienermobile drivers probably weren't casing the Pentagon. He knew it was also highly unlikely a terrorist would choose a 27-foot-long bright orange vehicle shaped like a hot dog to pack with explosives and commit mayhem.

So after checking them out, Stacy directed Keller and Pendleton to the nearest exit. He didn't give them a ticket either. "Obviously, this was a mistake," said Virginia State Police spokeswoman Lucy Caldwell. "This hot dog posed no threat to us."

Jones, M. (2002, June 21). Bun's rush: Wienermobile finds route near Pentagon no picnic. *Milwaukee Journal Sentinel,* 1B. © Copyright 2002, Journal Sentinel Inc. Reproduced with permission. This incident was first reported in the Reliable Source column of *The Washington Post.* This story may not be reprinted without the permission of the original copyright holder.

From our perspective, this is an imbroglio story because the situation brought on an embarrassing moment for the two hot-doggers, and no doubt to the organization and to Kraft Foods—the parent company of Oscar Mayer—as the story continues to be communicated in the media. The purposes this story serves in training are to entertain and evoke an immediate response from trainees. One place it could be used is in a marketing, sales, or customer service management program that covers the protocols of "representing" an organization to the public. Imagine the drivers' chagrin to have their actions reflect so visibly—and in such an embarrassing way—on their organization. The main points of this story in this context are twofold: (1) every action you take when representing an organization has the potential to reflect positively or negatively on the enterprise's credibility, and (2) seemingly innocent actions, when not thought through, can result in unintended consequences for your organization—consequences that may incur significant costs in pride and public image as well as dollars.

How the company responds to the drivers' actions could be another application of the story in a leadership development program—coaching your employees when their unintended actions have significant, visible consequences, or recouping lost credibility with the public. Consider your own coaching style when an employee of yours performs in a way that brings embarrassment to your organization. The main points that could be stressed in this type of training situation are: (1) how an organization responds to public scrutiny says a lot about its integrity and its sense of humor, and (2) performance management is full of challenges, especially when an inappropriate employee action is unintended but has significant negative consequences. Grace under pressure is a quality that helps organizations endure and rise above temporary setbacks.

Here is the story again, rewritten this time for presentation in a training situation, illustrating the first main point. The story's possible uses help to shape its conversion from a newspaper story to one that has application in learning.

Bun's Rush: Wienermobile Finds Route Near Pentagon No Picnic (N)

Used with permission from the *Milwaukee Journal Sentinel* and adapted by Lori L. Silverman

Many companies have an icon or image that represents what and who they are to the general public. Nike has its "swoosh," Coca-Cola has its trademark bottle, and Oscar Mayer has its Wienermobile—seven of them to be exact—the most famous motorized sausage in the nation. One hot, summer, Tuesday evening, one of those Wienermobiles found its way onto Route 110, a road next to the Pentagon. At the wheel were Will Keller and Paula Pendleton, both twenty-two and recent college grads, who'd just finished their two weeks of training at Hot Dog High. After boning up on the history of the company and the classic Oscar Mayer jingles—and learning how to parallel park a 27-foot-long hot dog on wheels—these two hot-doggers were in Washington, D.C., for a barbecue cook-off and several charity events.

Imagine their surprise when they saw the flashing lights behind them. Catching the attention of Virginia state trooper Robert Stacy who feared the "wurst," the Wienermobile was brought to a screeching halt, backing up traffic along the Potomac River as passing motorists gazed in disbelief. You see, Route 110 has been closed since 9/11 to commercial traffic with six wheels or more because of concerns that someone could drive a truck bomb close to the home of the nation's defense department. In fact, how the crew got the Wienermobile onto that stretch of Route 110 is quite the mystery since it's lit with large spotlights and staffed 'round the clock at checkpoints by armed officers in squad cars and Humvees.

Thinking that the hot-doggers might be casing the Pentagon, the crew was grilled by Trooper Stacy. And what do you think he found when he checked out the contents of the Wienermobile? Enough boxes of Wienermobile whistles, Wienermobile Hot Wheels, Wienermobile-shaped bean bag toys for a year's tour of the East Coast . . . and a karaoke machine featuring the Oscar Mayer wiener and bologna jingles. Once Trooper Stacy was convinced the 27-foot-long, bright-orange vehicle shaped like a hot dog wasn't packed with explosives, he directed Keller and Pendleton to the nearest exit without granting them a ticket. "Obviously, this was a mistake," said Virginia State Police spokeswoman Lucy Caldwell. "This hot dog posed no threat to us."

And how did the hot-doggers respond to the faux pas? According to Sarah Delea, an Oscar Mayer spokeswoman, they were very apologetic and sorry for the traffic delays. They had no idea Route 110 was verboten to Wienermobiles.

Major corporations like Oscar Mayer understand that "image is everything." The behaviors of each and every employee—intentional or not—can affect this image in a positive or negative way.

Jones, M. (2002, June 21). Bun's rush: Wienermobile finds route near Pentagon no picnic. Adapted by Lori L. Silverman from the *Milwaukee Journal Sentinel,* 1B. This incident was first reported in the Reliable Source column of *The Washington Post.*

What do you notice about this version of the story compared to the newspaper version? First, the training version hones in on the main characters—the two drivers and the state trooper. Second, the details of the story were rearranged to correspond to the context, challenge, and climax story structure model. Third, the first sentence of the story is new—it helps to set up its use in training. In this manner, any article, source, or idea can be translated into an interesting story customized to the intent of your training. Let yourself play with the ideas, the content, and the possible uses for the next interesting or humorous article you find and would like to share with others.

HONING YOUR CRAFTING SKILLS

Knowing the basics of story construction, and being able to recognize the various parts of story structure within a story that is already developed, can help you more easily develop your own well-constructed stories. To hone your skills in this area, practice identifying the deeper meaning and the story structure with stories you currently use in training as well as with the stories in this book.

Crafting training stories in a formal way may be new to you. How can you learn to develop these skills? The first step is to read. Numerous books offer stories that range from timeless fables to current events, from universal truths to highly personal experiences. As you read, notice the structure, content, and sequencing of the story information. How can you incorporate what you have noticed into your own writing?

Another way to hone your story-crafting abilities is to pay close attention to others who tell stories—in workshops, meetings, professional association gatherings, sales presentations, on television or the radio, and so forth. Rather than focusing on the presenter's technique, ask yourself a series of story structure questions. How are these stories constructed? What is it about this story that captures my interest? How does the story flow? Why am I having this particular emotional reaction? You can also apply the same process to stories that you read—in books (such as *Ready-to-Tell Tales* by Holt and Mooney [1994]), magazine articles, journals, and newsletters. Numerous organizations publish free online newsletters that include wonderful stories. Katherine Hudson's "The Bamboo Years" (Chapter Eleven) was originally published in Brady Corporation's 2001 Annual Report. Being the observer, both outwardly (to the story and its construction) as well as inwardly (to your reactions, thoughts, and feelings) will help you further develop your abilities to structure a story for meaningful impact.

What Sivasailam "Thiagi" Thiagarajan, a well-known trainer, has done to sharpen his skills is follow a writing method described in the book, *Fast Fiction: Creating Fiction in Five Minutes* (1997) by Roberta Allen. He has learned to take a situation and write a story about it in five minutes—no editing, no extra time. He practices this day after day. Then, after he has written ten stories, he goes back to the first one and evaluates it in terms of how energized he felt while writing it and its emotional impact on him.

THE STORY CONTINUES

Crafting a story that facilitates learning is a matter of design and construction. In this chapter we offer a number of ways to go about creating this design. To bring more stories to life in your training programs, we suggest you use a story structure model to help you develop your story into a compelling message to others. Craft your stories for telling once the ideas are crystallized. Chip Bell's context, challenge, and climax model as well as Doug Stevenson's story structure model are two such frameworks that can help you organize your story development process. Three specific examples provide ideas on how you can create your own stories from rough drafts, mind maps, or newspaper articles. We then provide tips on honing your story-crafting skills to develop a well-written story that can be told with confidence.

Bringing Stories to Life

- How do you currently go about developing an idea or incident into a compelling story?
- What structure or model do you currently use to develop your ideas into stories?
- What steps do you follow in taking a story idea and turning it into a finished story?
- How do you currently develop your story-writing skills?
- What other methods might you use to further enhance your story development skills?

A finely crafted *written* story is only a step away from a compelling story *told* to a rapt and appreciative group. It is worth investing both time and care to develop your story ideas into a powerful vehicle for learning.

chapter FOUR

Incorporating Stories into Training

Prisoners, Vacationers, and Learners (O)

Contributed by Steve Hanamura, president, Hanamura Consulting, Inc.

In the training my firm provides, we ask participants to put themselves in one of three categories—a prisoner, a vacationer, or a learner—based on how they view themselves relative to the session. A prisoner is someone who has been sent by management and personally doesn't see the need to attend. The vacationer is the person who says, "Boy, I can chill out in this class. I really don't need to work. I'll just come to the workshop and write a grocery list." The learner, on the other hand, is someone who truly desires to gain new skills and knowledge and grow personally and professionally.

There is one particular training session I will never forget. All the participants were prisoners; they did not want to be there. The first two days of training went horribly. So, on the third day I came to class and said to them, "It's clear to me you don't want to be here. I want to tell you where I am in this situation. At our firm we work from the mission to celebrate oneness. What celebrating oneness really means is that we develop people to their fullest potential. Right now, oneness also means to me that I'd rather be at home because you don't want to be here. So we have a choice today. We can sit and play cards, talk trivia, or we can work. Now I'm willing to work real hard but I need help and your cooperation. Quite frankly, if I get the behavior that I've gotten the last few days, I'm not going to work. I am going to sit here, play cards and talk with you. Which will it be?"

Well, the participants, to their credit, elected to roll up their sleeves and go to work. The work was so powerful that by the end of the day at five o'clock, a gentleman came up to me with tears in his eyes and said, "This is the best workshop that I've ever attended. I've gotten so much out of it and I want to thank you."

The point of the story is that sometimes when you have a resistant audience you need to name what's going on in the room and be truthful with them about how you are experiencing it. You also need to give people choices. Don't be surprised if they are willing to go to work, because they want to do what's right.

As leaders in any setting, our attitude affects those around us. In reality, when given a choice about applying themselves, most people are "willing to work."

Hanamura's experience provides several analogies for us as trainers who desire to incorporate stories into our work. While we may fear sharing parts of our personal lives with trainees and being truthful with them about our feelings and experiences, by doing so through stories they can benefit tremendously in their own learning. In addition, we cannot ignore the power of choice. Just like the trainees, who when given the choice to learn decided to do what was right, you, too, have a choice about using stories in your work. Consider how your choices support learning.

Making the choice means making a shift in our thinking, from trainer to storyteller. This shift in thinking is not about choosing between one role and another; it is about employing multiple roles in a training venue and using complementary, yet different skill sets to enhance the training experience for individuals and groups. Along with this shift in thinking comes the need to learn how to select stories to use in training—weeding out the bad from the good, determining when to use your own stories versus those from other sources, and selecting those that are most relevant to the audience. This chapter covers these topics as well as how to figure out the placement of stories in a training session. Rounding out this chapter is a discussion of the story framework we use in Section Two. We present this topic here because this framework was specifically developed to help you incorporate stories into your existing and future training.

SELECTING STORIES TO USE IN TRAINING

As much as possible, stories you plan to use in a training setting need to be selected and planned in advance—those that you know you want to tell and those that you may use spontaneously depending on which way the training discussion turns. Why do we encourage this level of planning and structure? This prevents stories from being mere afterthoughts, and prevents trainers from missing the powerful opportunity to touch people's minds, hearts, souls, and physical beings.

In general, the story selection process begins after you have outlined the overall goal of the training, created a skills hierarchy (a visual picture or diagram of all the things participants need to be able to do or know in order to meet the goal) and identified learning objectives. Chip Bell tries to tightly fit a story to the overall learning goal. He asks, "What do I want the learner to know, experience, and feel?" and "Is this the best story to illustrate this particular point?" Chip asks these questions because he has observed presenters (for example, purely motivational speakers) who get caught up in the fun of the story and forget about the learning. Kathy Nielsen also attends to the learning objectives in her four-step story selection process. First she thinks through training content. Next, she examines her life experience relative to the content. Then she recalls significant experiences that resulted in a-ha's for her. Finally, she reexamines the story to decide if it helps to achieve key learning objectives. Using an intuitive approach, Sivasailam "Thiagi" Thiagarajan says that he plans very obsessively for the program, and then throws out the plan, substituting it with an improvisational approach. He thinks of three to four stories on a topic and then during the program just goes with the flow. He has the experience to know that this method of story selection works well for him and his facilitative style. What this points out is that in addition to identifying and linking stories to the learning objectives, you also need to know yourself and your training style.

STORYTELLING WISDOM

"Stories are tools for conveying pictures that when we all see, we can act on collectively."

Chip Bell

Good versus Bad Stories

Let's face it. There are lots of really good stories and there are a few bad ones. There are stories that will hold special meaning for the person telling them and those who hear them, and there are some that will not move the storyteller or listener at all. There are stories that are more appropriate for a particular audience and then there are those that are less appropriate.

So, how do you identify and avoid "bad" stories? Here are a number of different types that stand out for others. Ed Tate offers an example of an ex-Marine secret service agent who presented extremely graphic scenes in his stories—such as cutting off someone's hands. While these images may stay with people for a long time, they do so in the wrong sort of way. If participants experience any emotion too strongly, except for sheer joy (or happiness) it makes for a bad story. Maureen G. Mulvaney (MGM) has found that people then become uncomfortable or angry that the emotion came out. It may erupt from the learner as, "You made me cry—I didn't come here for that."

Keep in mind that personal stories may be just one step away from gossip or complaining if they are not chosen with integrity and told within the guise of learning. Steve Hanamura encourages us to distinguish our public and private personal experiences from those that may be considered more intimate. Intimate experiences do not translate well to training or speaking engagements. Taking it a step further, as Doug Stevenson points out, "You don't get to do therapy in front of an audience." Stories that appear to be a confessional on the part of the storyteller are not appropriate for a training setting. Neither are stories where the trainer is still working through a situation. Chris Clarke-Epstein provides this example: You go through a customer service experience that made you angry and choose to gripe about it to trainees, openly showing your irritation, and asking how many people agree with you. As she points out, a training venue is not the time or place to garner allies to support your viewpoint; if you want to tell an emotional story, only do so after you are through processing it yourself.

Stories where the storyteller is the total fool, hero, or expert are not appropriate stories either. However, as Thiagi points out, if the story is going to have a fool, it is best for that person to be the teller of the story. On the topic of total experts, one of the authors attended an international conference and heard a workshop leader brag several times that he had won a training skills contest in which well-known author and training and development guru Malcolm Knowles had also been a participant. This individual kept saying to the group, "I won! Even over someone as famous as Malcolm Knowles!" Not surprisingly, the audience's reactions traveled a path from shock to dislike to complete disdain. Ed Tate also cautions trainers to avoid telling self-deprecating stories as well as those that brag or boast about their accomplishments. In his experience, if a story might make people feel ill at ease, then humor needs to accompany it. He gives an example of this from the introduction to his "Tate's Rules on Bullies" speech: "'Hey nigger—go back to the ghetto.' Those are the words of my first bully who greeted me at seven years of age at the playground. His name was Richard. I had another nickname for him." (People always laugh at this line.)

Good stories can come from a variety of sources, as outlined in Chapter Two. How do you choose those that are truly the best to use? Thiagi asserts that trainers need to tell stories that have personal meaning to them. While a trainer can read a story from another person or source, it has to *move you,* the trainer as storyteller, for it to work with the audience. As Joan Gillman points out, this is indeed the challenge with using "canned" stories, or stories that have been heard many, many times before. We, as authors, tell our own stories in front of audiences at least 50 percent of the time or more. This is because they "move" us at a very deep level or are tied to our own personal credibility. Kate Lutz tells personal stories when she needs authority, but views only telling her own stories as myopic. She goes on to state, "There is a whole wonderful world of experience out there with wonderful stories to tell. Don't lose the wisdom of the ages." Many of the stories she tells are ancient fables, stories, and folktales from other cultures.

Selecting Stories Based on the Audience

Knowing your audience and its composition can minimize the risk of embarrassment for both you and your training participants. Here are some worst-case scenarios as shared by contributors. Julie O'Mara was coaching an executive on modeling diversity behaviors. In a speech, the executive shared a story with a group of employees about his own experiences and interactions with people of color. He spoke about attending a cocktail party with well-known political leaders who were African American. Employees saw the story as elitist and hobnobbing—unfortunately, it backfired in the moment. The learning she took away from the situation is to listen to the stories others might tell *before* a training session—especially if they are using the stories to role model a particular behavior. In the same vein, Ed Scannell distinctly remembers hearing a speaker at a national conference tell several off-color stories. Ed watched the audience, as a result, turn off to the presenter who had missed the shift that had occurred in the audience's rapport with him. In another instance, it was only when Chris Clarke-Epstein was in the middle of a story about a friend whose wife was dying of cancer and how he brought her *Playgirl* magazines and posted the pictures on her hospital room wall that Chris realized her audience was primarily Catholic nuns—she says they handled it well! Both Ed and Chris stress the need for trainers who use stories to make a point of tuning in to trainees and their reactions to the stories in the moment. Trainers need to be able to immediately shift their approach if things are not working well. On a positive note, sharing the wrong kind of stories does not always turn out poorly. On one occasion, Kate Lutz picked all "girl" stories for what turned out to be an audience of teenager boys. She actually found that they were fascinated by the girl stories.

Being appropriate with overseas audiences and those whose culture and ethnicity do not match your own cannot be overlooked. Clare Novak recalls hearing a trainer make reference to Kahlil Gibran's *The Prophet* (1968)—and asking whether the audience knew "the Prophet." They all nodded yes and a bit later started arguing about interpretations of the Koran—they thought the trainer meant the prophet Mohammed. Her suggestion is to research the participant group and use stories that are meaningful for them—for example, Clare has learned that Egyptian people especially appreciate family stories, but generally do not have pets nor relate to stories about pets. Here is an ancient parable that is told by Paula Bartholome. See if you can pick out an uncomfortable reaction that someone might have to it.

The Wise Man and the Baby Bird (P)

Contributed by Paula Bartholome, principal and corporate jester, Parallax

Once upon a time there was a valley between two mountains. The people in the valley were very fortunate because a wise old man lived in a cave at the top of one of the mountains. He was *so* wise that he was able to give them all kinds of helpful information. He could tell them when it would rain so they knew when to plant their crops. He could tell them when the frost would come so they would know when to harvest. He could tell them what was wrong with them so they could get over their illnesses.

Unfortunately, there were some boys in the village who found the wise old man to be overbearing. He was always telling them what to do and people wouldn't listen to anyone else. So the boys decided to trick him and prove that he could make a mistake and that he really didn't know everything. They tried and they tried and they tried. But, every time they tried, the wise old man always knew the answer. He was always able to see through what they were doing.

One day, one of the boys ran up to the other boys. He had his hand cupped one over the other and said, "I've got it. I know how we are going to fool the old man. We'll prove that he doesn't know everything. Then people will listen to us." And the other boys said, "What is it? How are you going to do it?" The first boy replied, "Here in my hands, I have a baby bird. We are going to go up to the wise old man's cave and we are going to call him out. Then I am going to ask him two questions: 'What do I have in my hands?' and 'Is it alive or is it dead?' He'll know that I have a bird in my hands. He'll say, 'You have a baby bird.' But right when he answers the second question—if he says it's alive, I push my hands together and the bird will be dead—if he says that it's dead, I'll open my hands and the bird will be alive. We will have witnesses. We will be able to tell everyone he doesn't know everything and they should listen to us."

The boys thought about it. They all agreed. Absolutely it should work. So they ran up the mountain to the old man's cave and they called, "Old man, old man, come out." The wise old man came out into the sun and said, "Yes, my sons. What can I do for you?" And the boy with the bird in his hands holds them out and says, "Old man, we have two questions for you. What do I have in my hands? And is it alive or is it dead?" The old man looks at the boy and then at the boy's hands and says, "Why, you have a baby bird in your hands." The boy says, "Yes. Is it alive or is it dead?" The old man looks at the boy's hands and then at the boy and says, "My son, the answer is in your hands."

In daily life, when others ask you to make decisions on their behalf, you typically jump in and help. The wiser course may well be to convey to them, "The answer is in your hands."

In one of Paula's storytelling sessions, an Asian woman who was a cross-cultural trainer responded in the following manner to a debriefing question about the meaning of this story: "You need to have respect and listen to your elders. That was a wise man that helped; the boys were supposed to listen to him. In our culture we would never tell a story about young boys trying to trick a wise man. We respect our elders." Even though the woman was savvy and understood that the point of the story was about expectations of an organization around cultural change, she also realized that in her culture this point would be obscured because of the values and customs of her people. What is the lesson for us in this story? We need to pay careful attention to the ethnic, racial, and cultural implications of the stories we tell.

WHERE TO PLACE STORIES IN A TRAINING SESSION

You have written the learning goal. Created a skills hierarchy. Developed learning objectives. And selected stories—along with a variety of other experiential learning approaches—that will help trainees to realize the benefits of the training they are going through. Even if you are using stories to do one-on-one training or coaching, thinking through these elements is key to the learning process. Now you need to figure out where to specifically incorporate the stories you have chosen into the overall training plan.

STORYTELLING WISDOM

"Trainers need to start from the context of learning objectives. There needs to be a very pinpointed and overt connection to the learning points. I am not confident that there is any one recipe for including stories in training."

David Hutchens

Based on our experiences, there are a variety of places to put stories in a training session. You can use a story:

- To introduce a learning module.
- Between the introduction of a concept, theory, or model and an explanation or discussion on how to apply the concept, theory, or model.
- After a learning point has already been made, in order to reinforce it.
- As the response to a participant's question or a series of participant comments.
- Prior to asking participants to tell their own stories to help them feel more comfortable doing so.
- As the lead-in to a case study.

- As the actual content for a case study activity. You provide the background data and the participants play the "main character" in the case study. Their task is to develop the "story" about what this character needs to do next to handle the situation (usually a dilemma).

Ed Tate combines several of these story placement options in a single training module. He often wraps stories around the front and the back ends of a training piece. For example: first he tells a story about the need to be "change-skilled." Then he leads participants through an exercise that has them produce five comments about an innovative wheelbarrow design. In his experience, he knows that about 95 percent of the comments will be negative. So, Ed follows the exercise with a series of stories about businesses that were inflexible and what happened to them in the marketplace.

Here is another way to combine several of the story placement options. A series of stories can be connected together through a technique called "layering." This three-pronged approach builds on adult learning theory, advocating that repetition and practical application heighten learning. With this method, the point of the story is illustrated three times in three different settings: in a story from an outside source (such as this book), followed by the trainer's own personal application story, which is then followed by the participants' own personal application stories. Joan Lloyd's "Isolate, Exaggerate, and Integrate" (Chapter Thirteen) is an excellent example of this layering technique. While on a skiing trip, Joan learns a powerful model for coaching peak performance. She then goes back to her consulting firm and tells us how she successfully uses the model with a consultant who is doing work for her. Finally, she invites the participant group, through the follow-up activity, to design an application of the model to their own work situations. Similar to the age-old "tell them what you're going to say," "tell them," and "tell them what you just told them" speaker guideline, this layered approach deepens the learning experience and the likelihood that participants will use the information after the training session is over.

To employ this technique, share a story from this book—such as Shelley Robbins's "Who Called This Meeting?" (Chapter Ten)—with a training group. To further illustrate the story's key points, follow up with a story about your own experiences building collaboration between departments and what you did to create a positive outcome. Finally, invite participants to tell their own stories about interdepartmental cooperation in support of an organizational goal.

STORY FRAMEWORK

To help you incorporate the stories in Section Two of this book into your existing training or that which you may develop down the road, we have created a framework for each story. This framework—or story module—includes the following elements:

- Title
- Contributor
- Type and purpose(s)
- Background
- Presentation tips
- Set-up
- Story
- Debrief questions
- Key point options
- Follow-up activity

It is designed to help you present the story in both an interesting and meaningful way and to maximize the benefits of telling a story to an individual trainee or group of participants. This framework enables you to go beyond just *telling a story* by offering you—when you are training—a number of support tools to build on the key point you want to convey. Thus, each story has the ability to be inserted into a segment of your training program, complete with introduction, follow-up discussion, and application activity. Each element is outlined here so that you have a feel for how we created them for each story.

Title

The title of each story is a way for you to reference the stories in this book and in your training. They were developed to help you remember the stories so you can more easily recall them for use in your programs. Typically, you would *not* say the title out loud to your participants. In many cases, doing so would give away the punch line, thereby lessening the impact of the actual story. After each title is a story number, which refers to Table II.2 on page 116 of the Section Two Introduction. This table will help you identify alternate workshop uses for each story.

Contributor

The name of each story's contributor, along with the person's title and (in most cases) organizational affiliation, are listed here. For more information about a contributor, a brief biography and full contact information are available in the About the Contributors section on page 361. Most often, the events of the story happened to contributors themselves. However, some stories are fables or third-person accounts frequently told by the contributor during training and found to be useful in making a point.

Type and Purpose(s)

Knowing the type and purpose of the stories you select will help you effectively place them in the training session and assist you in achieving your learning goals. Use these elements as guides in addition to the story placement insights we presented earlier in this chapter. For quick reference, this data along with story and page numbers is summarized in Table II.1 on page 113 of the Section Two Introduction.

The story *type* that is noted is based on the framework created by Doug Stevenson as explained in Chapter One. His model identifies seven possible types of stories: crucible, imbroglio, Minerva, credibility, pattern, instructional, and vignettes (2000, pp. 2–3). Here are some examples of how a story's type can influence where you place it in your presentation. Crucible stories tend to be somber and serious. Thus, people need to warm up to the storyteller before hearing them. For example, "In Search of Cappuccino . . . With a Little Chocolate on the Side" (Chapter Twelve) provided by Kate Lutz, would not be a story to tell people immediately upon meeting them. Another type of story that is not ideal to share upfront is an imbroglio story. Because imbroglio stories such as "Time Brings Perspective" (Chapter Twelve) by Geoff Bellman are about life's most embarrassing moments, the audience first needs to get to know a bit about the trainer who is telling it. These stories work best in the middle of a presentation and can also be used to close a seminar as long as the story leaves people with a meaningful learning point.

A pattern story, such as Suzann Gardner's "How My Sons Learned to Dive" (Chapter Sixteen) can be used effectively at any point in a training program except to close the session. There are three story types that can be placed anywhere during training. Minerva stories, such as Clare Novak's "A Family United" (Chapter Fifteen), credibility stories such as Kathy Nielsen's "The Worth of a Contribution" (Chapter Eleven), and vignettes, such as Larry English's "For Lack of a System" (Chapter Fourteen), can be used at any time during a workshop. Why is this? Minerva stories draw upon ancient wisdom. Credibility stories bolster the credibility of the trainer and the subject matter being taught. Vignettes are short, usually funny, and easy to tell. Finally, instructional stories, which are exemplified by Bill Boone's story, "A World Without Blacks" (Chapter Seven) are best used in the middle of a training program because they tend to make multiple points that need to be processed fully by participants.

The story *purpose(s)* is also identified here based on the seven possible purposes outlined in Chapter One: to entertain (or energize), educate, evaluate, engage, encourage, explore, or evoke. Often a story can be used for more than one purpose; which one you elect to focus on can affect its placement in a training session and the way in which you debrief it. Making a conscious decision to include, for example, an energizing story after a meal—such as "The Customer Strikes Back" (Chapter Nine) by Bob McIlree—or a story that encourages your participants to take action, toward the end of your program—as with Chip Bell's "A Legacy of Generosity" (Chapter Twelve)—will help you design programs with impact.

Background

The background information we provide includes interesting or useful facts and details about the source for the story, the contributor, how the story came about, or its primary intent. This information is for you as the trainer, facilitator, or coach. However, you might decide to cull some of it to create a unique story set-up or to share it as part of your debrief discussion. This information is not intended to be told as part of the story itself.

Presentation Tips

Suggestions for maximizing the intellectual, physical, emotional, and spiritual impact of the story are contained in the presentation tips. Often the contributors themselves gave specific actions, gestures, or facial expressions they use while telling the story. In other cases, we offer suggestions about the tone of voice to use and when to adopt a voice change for different characters in the story. Thinking through and planning your presentation ahead of time will lend credibility to you as a storyteller and enable you to create an enriching experience for your participants. In general, when functioning as trainers or coaches, we can be more dramatic in telling these stories than we might be otherwise. Speakers and professional storytellers have much to offer us with their style of delivering a story. Chapter Five goes into greater depth on this subject and gives a number of pointers for presenting your stories in an appealing way.

Set-up

The story set-up provides several choices for introducing a story, if you elect to lead into the story in this manner. A set-up helps to create the context for participants so they begin to focus on your *reason* for telling the story. Set-ups can be dramatic, thought provoking, humorous, or inspiring. They set the tone and help participants to focus on what to expect from the story that follows. Two other elements factor in when introducing a story: how to give attribution to the story contributor, and the "voice" (that is, first-, second-, or third-person) you will use to tell the story. Both of these topics are discussed in more detail in Chapter Five.

Story

The stories in this book were provided by contributors either in writing or during an audiotaped interview. Each story has been edited to provide a short, interesting, *tellable* tale that makes an important point in a training setting. In each story, this point is illustrated through a powerful and memorable phrase, usually found at the end of the story. We have put the phrase in quotations to help it stand out. They have been written to be told orally and therefore include dialogue and slang in a conversational tone of voice.

The amount of detail included with each story reflects what we considered appropriate for a training setting as opposed to another type of venue. Often, speakers and storytellers include more detail in their stories, which aids them in bringing their audiences into the story in a visceral manner. Consultants and managers typically use less detail, relying on stories more as examples or illustrations, but they may spend more time discussing the story jointly with participants after telling it, which most speakers do not. We encourage you to experiment with telling the stories fully, as written here, and we recommend that you include all the details provided in the story. When you have tested a story several times, you will then be better able to determine what changes you might want to make to it.

Debrief Questions

The power of a story is unleashed through the application to our own lives. It is a major reason for including stories in training. A planned debrief discussion takes the learner on a continuing journey of discovery. It helps transfer the intended learning and provides a way for trainees to think through the meaning and apply it to their own situation. The debrief model we use in this book includes questions on three different levels, as noted by the symbol located in front of each question:

- The Story: What the story itself means—its moral or main lesson. What the story characters have experienced.
- The Learner: How the participant feels about the story and how it personally applies to the individual.
- The Organization or World: How the story applies to the participant's work group, department, business unit, division, organization, industry, or to society at large.

This model was designed to help facilitate change, which is a key aspect of every story. Questions at the story level help learners to talk about specific story content—what happened and why, what the main character(s) did or did not do, how these characters felt, and so on. It also guides them to the primary message of the story. The learner questions link people to their own feelings and life experiences. These questions explore what the trainee may need to do more or less of, what changes are required in their thinking, and attitudes they may need to adjust. The organization or world questions take learners beyond the story's application to themselves, to the broader context of the world that surrounds them. It is through the responses to these questions that they are able to focus on their interdependencies with others. In addition, these questions are a means of fostering group, organizational, and societal level changes.

To gain an appreciation for this model, let us look at Jon Preston's "Upstaged by a Rookie" (Chapter Ten). Jon, as the new district manager, intervenes with the physician client during a sales call in order to demonstrate to Bud, the salesperson, how to more appropriately close a sale. Here is how the model applies to the debrief questions that have been created for this particular story.

The Story Level

- Jon wanted to positively influence Bud's selling skills. As the new district manager, what risk did Jon take jumping into Bud's sales call?
- Why did Jon take *this* approach with his salesperson?
- We know how Bud and Dr. P. reacted. However, what *possible* reactions might Bud have had? What *possible* reactions might Dr. P. have had?
- How did Jon's coaching affect Bud's motivation to sell?

The Learner Level

- How did you feel as you listened to this story?
- When have you wanted to give feedback that you thought might not be appreciated? How have you gone about giving it? How did that work for you?
- Consider how influence and motivation work in organizations, especially in a sales culture. Jon was the new district manager and Bud was an experienced, high-profile salesperson. What organizational politics issues might be present in such a situation? What implications did Jon's actions have for their future working relationship?

The Organization or World Level

- What organizational influence and motivation issues exist in your workplace? How do they show up?
- How do you know if someone's actions are for the benefit of the organization or for the benefit of him- or herself? Are these two goals mutually exclusive? Why or why not?

As you can see, the debrief questions lead the participants from a discussion of the specific story implications, to the way in which these issues affect their own ability to give feedback, to an understanding of how influence and motivation work within organizations and how individual actions can help an organization meet its goals. Key points can be woven into this discussion as trainees bring up relevant responses. Following up a debrief discussion with an individual or group activity further solidifies the participants' learning and appreciation for the application of the story to their own lives.

The debrief questions included with each story reflect the particular topic chapter in which the story is placed. While there is no one best set of debriefing questions, the debrief questions included with each story are open-ended in order to elicit more than a cursory or obvious response and create the potential to call forth a variety of meanings. Consequently, they help participants deepen their awareness of key issues and lead to an "a-ha" or learning point. As you develop other uses for the stories in this book, you will need to adapt the debrief questions, to stay consistent with your new reasons for using them. Whether you use these stories in training, speaking, coaching, or managing, the intent of debriefing the experience is to draw in your learners and have them reflect on what the story means and how it applies to their own lives.

Key Point Options

The key point options provided in this book summarize the central learning associated with each story. They provide the message, lesson, or moral of the story. Often they reflect the work of noted educators and authors—such as Chris Argyris and Edgar Schein—whose work is respected and relevant to a particular story. The lesson you select should reflect your primary intent in telling the story. While several key points are listed for each story, they are by no means exhaustive. Add to or adapt a key point to match *your* purpose for using this story.

Follow-up Activity

A follow-up activity enhances the power of a story. Each activity included in Section Two is designed to provide a way for participants to work with the story's key point(s) in greater depth. Typically the activities relate to applying the key point(s) to participants' own lives, the department or organization in which they work, or the world at large. The activities presented with each story are only one option for follow-up applied learning. For additional ideas, there are numerous participative training activity books and kits available, such as the Jossey-Bass/Pfeiffer *Annuals* and the *Games Trainers Play* series by Edward E. Scannell and John W. Newstrom.

The story follow-up activities are varied and encompass:

- Individual reflection
- Paired discussion or activity

- Role plays
- Small-group discussion or activity
- Large-group discussion or activity

Often a single activity might draw upon several of these options in a sequence of steps. For example, in Sivasailam "Thiagi" Thiagarajan's "The Taxi Driver" (Chapter Nine), the follow-up activity includes small-group discussion—during which participants identify examples of their own experiences with making assumptions about customer service, and a large-group discussion—in which the examples identified in the small group are reported on and debriefed.

Some activities are reflective, asking participants to write about their personal reactions and some are active, such as having teams of co-workers design and demonstrate a dance based on an organizational value for their company after hearing "Doing the Packarena" (Chapter Fifteen) by Katherine M. Hudson. In each case, the activity reflects a way to apply the story more personally and more directly for participants so that they can walk away with deepened meaning.

THE STORY CONTINUES

Thus far, we have taken you along a story development path from story idea, to crafting a powerful story, to learning how and where to incorporate stories into your training environment. In this chapter we have focused on learning how to select stories to fit your particular training and participant needs. Recognizing both good and bad stories is key to successfully choosing the right story supporting your learning goals. When to use your own stories versus those from other sources, accommodating specific audience demographics or characteristics, and the many ways stories can be used to enhance training have all been discussed in depth. We highlighted numerous options for incorporating more stories in more creative ways in your programs and with individuals you train. In addition, we introduced the story framework that accompanies each story in Section Two and that provides complete story modules with introductions, debriefs, key point options, and follow-up activities.

Bringing Stories to Life

- What is your current approach to incorporating stories into your training programs?
- How might you become more aware in selecting appropriate stories and incorporating them into your sessions?
- Which stories will best fit the training topics you present? The individuals and groups you work with?
- Where do you currently place stories in your training workshops? What "missed opportunities" are there for incorporating stories more effectively during training?

Stories can serve as the link to learning at any place within your program: as an exciting attention-grabber, to illustrate key learning points throughout your seminar, as a way to shift the energy and focus within the group, in response to participant questions, and as a powerful closing statement. Stories are an amazingly flexible resource because they are universally understood and appreciated.

chapter
FIVE

Tips on Storytelling

Tuning-in to Trainees' Needs

Contributed by Jean Barbazette, president, The Training Clinic

Imagine you are a consultant who has been asked to visit a construction site. At the site, you ask the first person you meet, "What are you doing?" The person says, "I'm making $10 an hour." As you continue to walk around, you ask the second person you meet the same question, "What are you doing?" And he says, "Well, I'm a mason. I'm building a wall. I'm putting one brick on top of another, can't you see?" Then you come upon a third person and ask one more time, "What are you doing?" He says, "I'm building a cathedral for the greater glory of God."

Each of these people is performing the same physical work, yet in their own minds they have a totally different picture of what they are doing. The first person is being paid for his labor—he is just trying to make some money. The second person sees himself as someone who has a career—a craft, a trade—and takes pride in his work. The third person has a bigger picture of his job and what needs to be accomplished and how his labor is a significant part of the larger whole—he's building a cathedral.

Think about the employees who are coming to your training sessions. What view of their jobs do you think they have? How might this make it easier or more difficult for you to teach them the skills and the knowledge they need, to influence their attitudes toward their work and their job? How might you help them "build a cathedral"?

This story about building a cathedral has been around for many years. No doubt you have heard it before. Yet is has a message for us as storytellers that you may not have thought about previously. How we carry out our work as trainers can be in the same ways as the construction workers. To the point of this book, we can also tell stories in the same manner as the three workers view their jobs: as a necessary task to making an income, as part of our craft as a trainer, or as the means to achieving a greater good for the trainees who experience our storytelling. This chapter covers several aspects of storytelling: selecting a voice for your stories, how to effectively introduce a story, tips and techniques for presenting a story, and how to skillfully debrief a story. We offer these topics to you in the spirit of helping you become a storyteller who is able to reach beyond your income and career to having an impact on the lives of others.

THE INNER AND OUTER PROCESSES OF STORYTELLING

There is both an *inner* and an *outer* process to telling stories. The inner process focuses on how you are *being* in the world in that moment—what is going on within you, your frame of mind, and your sense of personal power and confidence. Marcy Fisher speaks to this when she says, "If I'm centered, my stories work really well; then my humility can come out—otherwise I'm forcing it." From Paula Bartholome's perspective, believability is a combination of knowing the story you are delivering and walking the talk. She says, "Groups tend to have radar for knowing whether you are being genuine or being slick." Stories, to Paula, are a tool—you can use this tool to do "good" or to achieve a negative end. To do "good," stories need to be used to increase knowledge, perception, and sharing; this implies that storytellers need to be risk takers.

The outer process focuses on what you are *doing*—your non-verbal gestures, facial expressions, the words you choose to say, tone of voice, actions, posture, and so on. For Kathy Nielsen, this outer process involves shifting into storytelling mode. She likens it to telling a story to kids—it engages a different kind of energy, the kind that is playful. Good storytellers always get caught up in their stories. It is the difference between reliving (living a story each time you tell it) versus relating the story; the more you can relive a story, the higher your perceived level of spontaneity, credibility, authenticity, and sincerity is with those who are listening to it. Thus, the delivery style that a storyteller uses must be such that the story comes organically from the storyteller's personality. Telling stories without props or slides aids in one's ability to relive a story with others. This, however, does not mean that visual aids cannot be used. It just means that they need to function as an adjunct to the story rather than the focal point. The dramatization of a story by a storyteller is the main visual aid.

There is a relationship between these inner and outer processes. In many ways, a storyteller, according to Clare Novak, is a one-person theater, conveying drama and making the story characters real and believable. Yet storytelling brings a special dimension. As Kate Lutz explains: "In acting, a stage allows the audience to view the action through what is commonly referred to as the fourth wall. I, as the audience, am allowed a peephole into the action—but I, as an observer, do not impact or change the acting or the action. Storytelling consistently eliminates the fourth wall—the interactive play of audience and action changes and impacts the story and the storyteller, who usually plays off the audience." Trainers who effectively tell stories help their trainees find ways to fully participate by allowing them to enter into the interactive elements of the story. It is also important to be aware of your learners' differing viewpoints because you never know with which characters in a story they might align themselves.

STORYTELLING WISDOM

"In many ways a storyteller is someone who tells their deepest darkest secrets to thousand of their closest friends."

Kate Lutz

SELECTING A VOICE FOR YOUR STORY

As part of preparing to tell your story, you need to select what *voice* you will use to tell it. You have three options for presenting any story:

First-person: This is a story that is told as a personal story; the trainer is the narrator and the main character. The trainer tells the story using the word "I" (for example: "I went to the store.").

Second-person: This is a story in which participants are asked to imagine being the main character. It is told using the word "you" (for example: "Imagine you are in this situation and a person says to you . . .").

Third-person: This is a story that is told from the perspective that it has happened to another person or "being" (for example, an animal, a tree, and so on.). The trainer uses the name of the main character or the words "he," "she," or "it" (for example: "Sandra went to lunch and saw a cup and a pair of dice.").

There are two types of stories that are best told using a first-person voice: those that have happened to you personally and those that have occurred to someone else but can be told more compellingly (with attribution, of course) in the first person. Whenever telling another's story as your own, Chris Clarke-Epstein suggests leading into the story by saying, "This story happened to Mary Smith, a colleague of mine. I would like to bring you the story as if it happened to me, personally." The participant group now understands that the story did not happen to you, but is prepared to hear you tell it as if it did. The story would then be phrased as follows: "It is 7:30 A.M. and I am driving to work. All of a sudden, a large, golden-haired dog leaps into the road right in front of my car. I slam on the brakes and . . ." When telling someone else's story in the first person, it is important to speak it from memory in a believable manner.

Use a second-person voice for stories in which you want the trainees to experience the story as though it is happening to them in the moment. This voice also works well for stories in which learners will be required to do some deep personal reflection afterwards and to apply the message to themselves. You can begin this type of story by saying, "Imagine that it is 7:30 A.M. and you are driving to work. All of a sudden, a large, golden-haired dog leaps into the road right in front of your car. You slam on your brakes and . . ." There is an immediacy that is created when stories are told in this voice that is not present when using other story voices. Stories told in this manner invite participants to get personally involved in the story and its outcomes. Often, participants become more vested in the discussion after the story than they might if it had been told in the first- or third-person.

Finally, relate stories in the third-person when the story is about a historical figure or a prominently known person, when a situation has been experienced by someone else (or a "being," such as an animal or a tree) in which it would not be conceivable for it to have occurred to you, or when it is your story but it is too personal to share in the current context. Keep in mind that historical and factual tales are best told in the third-person to preserve the accuracy of the story. In our example, your opening could be, "A friend of mine, Tom, was driving to work one morning at about 7:30 A.M. All of a sudden, a large, golden-haired dog leaped into the road in front of his car. Tom slammed on the brakes and . . ." While stories told in the third-person take on a narrative tone, they can achieve their impact through dramatic presentation.

The voice you select also affects your story lead-in sentence(s), as described in the next section. Specific examples of set-up options that illustrate each voice are also provided.

INTRODUCING A STORY

Maureen G. Mulvaney (MGM) reminds us that we, as storytellers, and the story itself must be gripping for the first thirty seconds to capture the attention of those in the room. The most dramatic way to open a story is with no set-up or introduction. This means that the first sentence or two of the story needs to be quite powerful, perhaps positioned after a long dramatic pause or a physical movement. Chris Clarke-Epstein offers one example that she uses to open a feedback training session: "I noticed right away his fly was open." Ed Tate also prefers to grab people's attention right away and dive into a story. One of his opening story lines is, "It was the day after Christmas and you could smell it through the house." While dramatic, David Hutchens points out that moving directly into the story without a set-up can be a bit unsettling for trainees because they do not know what to connect to yet. Therefore, the trainer needs to debrief a story introduced in this way to make these connections come alive.

If you elect to start with some sort of set-up or lead-in, the one opening to shy away from, according to Doug Stevenson, is, "Let me tell you a story." He believes the power of the story is in audience discovery, which is given away with this set-up option. The other type of set-up to avoid is giving away the punch line of the story—the moral, lesson, or key point. Chris prefers to take her listeners on the journey of discovery with her. She does not give away too many details up front unless the story needs this background, as demonstrated in the following example. "Let me tell you about when my daughter was born. There are three things you need to know for this story to make sense. I am near-sighted. There has been no girl in my husband's family for five generations. And English was not the physician's first language." From her perspective, this sort of background information for this specific story captures and engages people—now they want to know how this all comes together.

So what segues can you use to introduce a story? Chip Bell uses a thought-provoking point to lead into a story while Kate Lutz often uses a general lead-in that steers the audience towards a common experience and toward a point to look for in the story—for example; "You know, families have rules. Some are spoken and some are unspoken." You can also transition from a previous discussion on a topic into a story by saying, "We have been talking about 'x' and its effect on major corporations, but what about 'x' and its effect on our personal lives?" Examples of these types of oral set-ups can be found with the stories in Section Two of this book. Keep in mind that instead of using words, you can consciously select one location in the room from which you tell all your stories for a specific training session. After awhile, the trainees will know a story is coming when you move to that specific location.

Two other elements factor in when introducing a story: (1) how you will give attribution to the story contributor, and (2) what "voice" (that is, first-, second-, or third-person) you will use to tell the story. Set-up statements are a logical place to provide attribution to the contributor. As we discuss in Chapter Six, you are required to identify the source of the story for each story from this book that you tell. One option for doing this is to tell the story in the third-person voice, using the name of the contributor throughout the story. Consider the following examples that demonstrate several set-up options incorporating attribution and the third-person storytelling voice.

Example 1: "The Cobbler's Children" (Chapter Ten) by Geoff Bellman

Option 1:

"Have you ever wanted to change something about the way your organization works? Sometimes we try so hard to make an impact that we are blind to the implications of our efforts. Consider what occurred with Geoff Bellman in this story." In this set-up statement, you are creating an awareness that the story is about Geoff trying to make a change in his company and not achieving the goal he was hoping for.

Example 2: "A Fish Tale" (Chapter Eight) by John Renesch

Option 1:

"John Renesch, a business futurist, learned that sometimes situations are not what they seem to be." Here we have the story set-up apply directly to John and we introduce him through his relationship to the story.

or

Use background information as a story set-up option: "Some years ago, John Renesch, a business futurist, was the publisher of the New Leaders Press newsletter. One of his responsibilities was to interview executives for feature articles." In this example we chose not to use one of the stated lead-in options, but to create a different one using the background information as a way to introduce both John and the story in the third-person.

Example 3: "I Was Aching for a Fight" (Chapter Nine) by Marcy Fisher

Option 1:

"Imagine for a moment that you are a clerk in a department store. How do you prepare for the possibility of confrontation? One day, while fixing the garbage disposal, Marcy broke the allen wrench." In this instance, we use one of the stated set-up options, tell the story in the third-person using Marcy as the main character, and close with an attribution that explains who Marcy is.

Option 2 (with Attribution):

Another approach to positioning a story is to tell it in the second-person, as if the story happened to the participant. Notice how this can be applied to the same story.

"Imagine for a moment that you are a woman by the name of Marcy Fisher. One day, while fixing the garbage disposal, *you* broke your allen wrench." The use of the second-person voice throughout the story brings participants into the story in a compelling way, giving them the sense of having personally experienced the situation real time.

Option 3:

A third option for telling your story is to use the first-person voice as if the events in the story happened to you, the trainer. Using the same story to illustrate, consider the following.

"How do we prepare for the possibility of a confrontation? One day while fixing the garbage disposal, I broke the allen wrench." You would then provide attribution at the end of the story and may include the background information as a part of it. "This event happened to Marcy Fisher, a former vice president of Organization Development and Human Resources for Shell Technology Ventures, Inc. Prior to this incident, Marcy had had a series of negative customer service experiences with this department store. It was these experiences that led her to this response." After this, you can begin the debrief discussion with your group.

As mentioned earlier, using a set-up is optional. What is key is that your choice of opening statement(s) reflects the lesson or moral you are trying to make. At some point in the telling of a story that is not your own, you must link an attribution of the person who experienced the situation to the story itself.

STORY PRESENTATION TIPS AND TECHNIQUES

Before telling a story to a training group, the trainer must know the essence of the story, even if it is to be read from a prepared script. Assuming that the story has been written out verbatim, once you have a feel for its real meaning, then read it both silently *and* out loud several times. This allows you to pick up on the sequencing of the content and the pacing of the story. Then tell it out loud without your notes; this will help you discover ways to remember the flow and the details of the story.

Once you have a feel for the story content, you can then begin to add drama and voice alterations. As Clare Novak points out, you need to work with your own voice and body—you are the only instrument. The type of story you tell makes a difference in how you tell it. For stories that provide inspiration to others, Kathy Nielsen uses a softer tone and lower volume; with a humorous story, she may pump up her volume, energy, animation, and tempo. Several of the story types presented in

Chapter One lend themselves to specific presentation styles (Stevenson, 2001). Imbroglio stories lend themselves to comedy and exaggeration, while pattern stories benefit from the repetition of some physical gesture or movement. Because crucible stories are serious in nature, they need a somber tone and some humor, as well as silence. In these stories it is important to pause both for laughter that will come with the humor and to allow the depth of the story to make an impact.

Chris Clarke-Epstein is always aware of her gestures, facial expression, and body movements. She alters her voice to depict various characters. For example, in Sharon Bowman's "Are You Listening?" (Chapter Eight), consider using a moderately toned, feminine sounding voice for Sharon, and a deeper, more masculine sounding voice for her husband, Jim. Use your own voice for the narrated text. Try to avoid killer vocal inflections such as those that sound patronizing, arrogant, showy, or disinterested in the story. When telling a story with dialogue, Chris turns from side to side to represent each person who is speaking rather than saying, "he said, she said." As Laura Page states, it is critical to pay attention to your enunciation of words. She recalls a situation when a consultant used the word "brick" in a story to reference someone, and the audience heard the word "prick." Needless to say, the story was misunderstood.

When training people to become better storytellers, Doug Stevenson offers that sometimes there are short, strategic moments in a story when it is best to turn away from participants, figuratively speaking, and go into the moment—to "step in"—just like actors do in a play. During these moments, the teller of the story may present an inner monologue—what is going through his or her mind—or tell, in the present tense, what actually occurred in the situation. After these moments, the teller may go back to narrating the story. This technique, which Doug calls "stepping in" and "stepping out" narration, helps to make a story kinesthetic and experiential versus intellectual for the listeners. It is an effective technique for stories such as "I Never Noticed You Were Black" (Chapter Seven), by LG Shanklin-Flowers, Lunell Haught's "The House Guest" (Chapter Eight), and Marcia Ruben's "Thanks, I'll Do It Myself" (Chapter Thirteen). In each of these examples, the storyteller engages in an inner monologue that can be powerfully illustrated for participants by "stepping in."

Early in her use of storytelling, Sharon Bowman remembers rushing through stories. When she realized that stories are the *metaphor* for the learning point, she learned to dramatize and embellish them. Suzann Gardner adds the notion of pacing; your voice and body pacing need to vary to match the part of the story that is being told. She also mentions the need to control silence and offers the example of Martin Luther King, Jr., when he told his "I Have a Dream" speech. Each time he said "I have a dream," he paused; by the third time he said the phrase, people were anxious with anticipation, waiting to hear what came next.

STORYTELLING WISDOM

"Storytelling is a misnomer—it should be story living. We live our stories, we don't just tell them—consummate storytellers don't tell *you a story, they bring you into it."*

Chris Clarke-Epstein, CSP

It is one thing to tell a story out loud to others; it is another to practice it with all the physical movements and vocal inflections associated with it. Doing so, according to Doug Stevenson, "allows the story to be emotionalized." When storytellers practice with their body and rehearse on their feet, they work out the physical reality of the story and force congruence between the story content, their voice, and their nonverbal actions. He goes on to say it is important to practice timing—to take time to move and react and see how long it really takes to perform the story. Doug encourages trainers to practice in their living room—decide where to put your fictitious group and walk and talk in front of your "audience." Practicing in front of a mirror makes you stand still which does not match reality. After practicing in an empty room, you can next do what Julie O'Mara suggests, and rehearse in front of others who would not necessarily understand the subject matter. Practice in this manner to gauge potential participant reactions and decide if you need to make any changes in the story or your presentation of it. Kathy Nielsen even goes so far as to audiotape the story while she practices in order to critique her own vocal delivery. Why is all of this practice important? Chip Bell summarizes it with this comment: "Storytelling is theater, not improvisation."

Altering a Story

A story may need to be altered over time as you discover how to tell it more effectively. With one story, Maureen G. Mulvaney (MGM) tried fifteen different approaches before she found the right way to tell it, making the story better each time but keeping its integrity. Her rule of thumb with a good story is to tell it three times; if it does not work, she recommends getting rid of it or to keep working on it until you get the reaction you want. From her perspective, for it to be a great story, you must be able to get the same reaction from every single audience. For both MGM and Doug Stevenson, once a story is set, the story stays the same although its key point might change. Remember, Doug likens a story to a song—you want to be able to remember the *lyrics* for your chosen story.

For some contributors it is just a matter of selecting the best stories for the audience. For others there are a number of other considerations. Clare Novak tweaks stories when she uses them in another country. However, she prefers to take great care in choosing the right story rather than in changing the details because a story can lose its authenticity if its key elements are changed too frequently. Kathy Nielsen adapts her stories to mirror the audience (geographic region, organization, gender, ages, relationships, positions, and so on), such as telling a story from either the employee or manager point of view depending on the demographics of her group. She sometimes changes a story's outcomes and who it is about to avoid telling too many stories about herself. To better capture the attention of participants, Sivasailam "Thiagi" Thiagarajan will change the gender of the hero and the setting. He has found that audiences like stories that are more recent and immediate to their lives. As a result, he will tell a story about being stopped by the police for speeding when he was on his way to the airport as occurring within the past week or two, even though it may actually have happened several years ago. Kate Lutz cautions that when making changes to stories, you agree to "keep traditional frameworks—for example, you wouldn't tell the Cinderella story with a hat instead of a shoe." This counsel reminds us of the inherent nature of a story. We have a commitment to honor its foundation elements and its intent.

Highly practiced and professional storytellers will change a story as it is being told. Kate will make subtle changes depending on the audience's reaction. She likens a story to creating a series of pictures or incidents, which she can individually illuminate or dim in the process of telling depending on what she is seeing in the moment in the audience. Suzann Gardner uses what she calls a *constructivist* approach—she constructs a story with the listeners by relying on them to keep the story going. She pays attention to whether heads are nodding and bodies are engaged—if she wants people to buy into what she is saying, she will make the story's introduction longer to accomplish this outcome.

DEBRIEFING A STORY

How often do you find yourself debriefing a story you have just told in training? How much time do you spend discussing a story's key learning points? Laura Page points out that trainers "think the point is obvious so [they] shortcut the debriefing or think it isn't necessary." Going along with this statement, Doug Stevenson believes that too many trainers "don't think of a story as *content.* That is why they don't debrief it." He goes on to say, "A story is a content delivery vehicle."

So why take the time to debrief a story or engage your group in a follow-up activity based on the story? Steve Hanamura provides an answer: "Stories have business and personal outcomes. You must bring these out." Listeners often come to their own conclusions and draw their own meaning from a story. To strengthen these conclusions and meanings, along with any universal truths that might be exemplified by the story, it is both valuable and important to debrief a story in a training setting. In addition, because all stories at their core are about change, debriefing a story can identify or reinforce the need for individual and/or organization change, prompt the change to occur, or spell out the steps for making the change happen, thus making its occurrence more likely. Even your opening workshop story can benefit from a follow-up discussion relating the story to the purpose or goal and learning objectives of the program.

There are three exceptions to performing a story debrief: when the story is used solely to entertain or energize, when it is used to close a training program, and according to Chip Bell, "when a story is adequately powerful, people [can] debrief it on their own." In learning from master storytellers, Chris Clarke-Epstein adds to this last exception, "Jesus didn't stop to do a group activity after he gave the parables of the New Testament. Great stories can be self-sufficient." A compelling, well-told story that is positioned appropriately in a training session may make its strongest point without any follow-up conversation. Unless you are using a story in one of these three ways, we encourage you to debrief any story you tell.

Once you decide to debrief a story, what approach can you use? Questions are the most frequently used debriefing tool. Suzann Gardner actually begins to ask questions *during* the story itself. In the middle of a lengthy story in the college course she teaches, she might ask her students, "Have you ever had this happen to you? Turn to someone else and talk about your experiences." After a brief discussion, she will continue with the conclusion of the story. When the story is completed, a fundamental question Marcy Fisher employs is: "What is the point of this story?"

Paula Bartholome also uses the Socratic method—she asks a series of open-ended questions such as, "How does this relate to your situation? What did you hear? What does this mean? How can this be used?" She then summarizes at the end of the discussion, especially with cross-cultural groups, as they may have different interpretations. She asks us to "remember that meaning is made in the mind of the listener. If it is important that everyone walk away with the same shared meaning, then you *have* to ask questions to ascertain whether you accomplished this." Another question used by Marcia Ruben is, "What does this bring to mind for you?" This is followed by a request that participants tell their *own* stories. To further encourage trainees to apply the learning through their own stories, Laura Page asks, "What examples do you have of this in your life?" After trainees share several stories, she closes her debrief discussion with a reflection on the lessons learned, clarifies key learning points, and summarizes the application to trainees.

Lifting out the teaching points—that is, positioning the story to wrap around the teaching points—is the way Joan Lloyd approaches debriefing stories. She plans her debrief process before ever starting to tell her story and makes sure her story clearly leads to the important lessons. Ed Tate favors having participants take some kind of action. After a story on being change resilient, he might have participants move their wristwatches to the opposite arm. By checking in with participants throughout the workshop about their comfort level with this change, he continually reminds them about the story's key points through their own reactions. It is a form of ongoing debriefing of the story's main lesson.

How you incorporate a key point into the follow-up discussion can be done in several ways. You may choose to lead the entire debrief discussion and then summarize by stating the key point. Another approach is to weave a key point into the debrief discussion as it arises. Some debrief questions naturally lead participants to speak to one or more of the key points noted in a story. Take the story

"Expecting Too Little" (Chapter Eleven) by Paula Bartholome. Two of the debrief questions ask:

- Who are the people in your organization who may never have been asked to help with a project?
- What do you need to make clear to others so that they can choose whether or not to engage?

During this discussion with participants, it would make sense to bring out the following key points:

- Do not assume people will not be able to participate or volunteer because of their life or work circumstances.
- Clearly ask for and invite participation.

A third option is to open the debrief discussion with one of the key points and get a reaction from the group. Consider LG Shanklin-Flowers's "I Never Noticed You Were Black" (Chapter Seven). You could open the debrief discussion with the first key point: We all carry assumptions about others. Our early training and experiences have led us to create these assumptions. Then you could follow-up with the first debrief question: What were some of the stereotypes or assumptions that this man held?

STORYTELLING WISDOM

"Each trainer needs to be the judge of how, when, and if to debrief a story."

Joan Lloyd

As much as we use conversation and discussion as a primary debrief vehicle, Chris Clarke-Epstein reminds us to "consider the power of the pause. Pauses give transition time and help points sink in." When debriefing stories, Chris's rule of thumb for trainers is "to debrief twice as long as the story. For a three-minute story, you should have a six- to ten-minute debrief discussion."

If you are giving a short talk (around an hour or less) or if you are training in a large-group setting (over 100 people), then you may want to place a debrief question or statement into the story itself. Here are three ways to accomplish this, as demonstrated by Chip Bell's "A Legacy of Generosity" (Chapter Twelve).

1. End the story with a question: "Where has a legacy of generosity touched your life?"
2. End the story with a personal application statement following a summary comment at the end of the story: "Chip found generosity early in his life. I ask each of you to reflect on where you learned this fundamental value in your life."
3. End the story with the main lesson, key point, or moral and a personal application statement: "The moral of the story is that it is important to manage relationships, which are the foundation of our lives, with a sense of generosity—a sense of abundance. How can you build relationships with others so that the spirit of generosity flows within them?"

Each of the debriefing methods covered here takes planning on the part of the trainer as storyteller. Except when spontaneously telling a story in response to a participant's question or comment, we recommend that you take a thoughtful and organized approach to your debrief discussion. Ultimately, it becomes your decision as the manager of the workshop experience.

LEARNING TO BECOME A STORYTELLER

STORYTELLING WISDOM

"Trainers are becoming storytellers, more than in the past. This adds to their skills and to the value of the training."

Edward E. Scannell, CMP, CSP

Storytelling is a learned skill. While some of us may take to it naturally, each and every one of us can practice the tools of this trade until we become a skilled weaver of tales. Think about the powerful storytellers in your own life. Watch them—sit at their feet and learn from them. Chip Bell learned storytelling from his daddy growing up in South Georgia. Chris Clarke-Epstein grew up in a household of storytellers. She recounts for us that her parents courted during the first two years of World War II and were married during the last two years of the war. They spent four years corresponding—which is another way to describe telling stories. They *looked* for stories to tell each other in their letters and never grew away from that form of communicating. Kate Lutz studied with a renowned storyteller and attends conferences, such as the National Storytelling Network's annual conference in July and the National Storytelling Festival each October in Jonesboro, Tennessee. She also listens to tapes from storytelling performances and conferences. August House Publishers and Libraries Unlimited offer an extensive selection.

Taking a slightly different approach, Merrill Anderson studies basic acting techniques with a theater group in Des Moines, Iowa. He focuses on how to use these techniques to get his message across. Building on his acting experiences, Doug Stevenson provides private coaching and conducts two-day Story Theater™ retreats that teach business people and speakers how to maximize their messages through stories. Listening to books on tape can also give you a wealth of exposure to the power of different voices for different characters. They demonstrate how both male and female narrators handle voices for characters of differing genders or ages. Take note of your own reactions to a narrator's vocal flexibility. Notice how much this technique adds to your enjoyment of the story and how easily you can follow the story in part due to the vocal changes. Another way to learn from the "masters" of acting and vocal inflection are through videotapes of professional speakers telling their stories. The National Speakers Association is one means of accessing this type of resource.

HOW TO USE THE CD-ROM

The CD accompanying this book is another source for learning the specific stories included in this work and enhancing your skill as a storyteller. All except one of the stories in Section Two are recorded in either a male or female voice. Most of them are written in first-person voice as if told by the contributor. As trainers, you will most often tell these stories in the third-person with attribution. Therefore, several stories have been modified and recorded on the CD in third-person voice to provide examples of how to make these changes for your own use. Using both first- and third-person voice will give you a feel for how the stories sound and what types of adaptations you will make to tell the stories yourself.

While the CD's primary use is to provide a model for how the stories might be told and to support you in learning to tell the stories, there are times when you may wish to play a CD story for your group. You might consider playing the CD version of Sharon Bowman's "Are You Listening?" (Chapter Eight) in a workshop on listening skills, asking participants to practice their skills while listening to the CD story. You would then conduct the debrief and follow-up activity included in the book. Keep in mind that an audio format is never going to be quite as compelling as your in-person presentation that appeals to more than auditory senses. The visual and kinesthetic aspects of storytelling are powerful tools for getting your message across. Use the CD as an alternate medium of presentation but not as a substitute for developing your own storytelling skills. Your life as a trainer will be richer for learning the skill of storytelling.

THE STORY CONTINUES

As Chris Clarke-Epstein has commented, our challenge is to engage in story*living*, not just story*telling*. To assist you in meeting this goal, this chapter offers tools for effectively delivering your story to your audience. Storytelling is an art, but one that can be learned. We provide ideas on how to develop your skill as a storyteller through a number of presentation tips, suggestions for learning from experts in the field, and by accessing a variety of other media examples of storytellers. How to focus on both the inner and outer aspects of storytelling, how to select the voice in which you will relate your story, methods for introducing your stories in ways that heighten anticipation, methods for presenting stories in compelling ways, and guidelines for debriefing your stories are also included here.

Bringing Stories to Life

- What is your current story presentation style?
- How might you expand on your current storytelling expertise? How might you expand beyond your comfort zone?

- How can you convey a story's meaning in more than words? What gestures, facial expressions, and movements can you include in the telling?
- In what voice do you typically tell your stories? How might you vary the voice you select?
- What new ways might you introduce a story?
- How often do you currently debrief a story? What approach(es) do you use?
- How might you enhance your debrief discussions to create a deeper level of awareness and a greater commitment to change on the part of your trainees?

Storytelling is a noble calling. While it is not without its challenges, it is well worth learning to do it well. Maureen G. Mulvaney (MGM) would offer this guidance that she follows in her own life path, to encourage you on your journey:

- Toughen up and get to your goal.
- Face your fears and focus on the positive.
- Let go, stop resisting, and go with the flow.
- Open your heart to the joy and love around you (2002).

In other words, set a goal to develop your storytelling skills and go after it. Do not let anything get in your way. Reflect on what aspects of storytelling might make you fearful or uncomfortable and focus on your talents, strengths, and skills. You did not start out life knowing how to train and yet you learned how. In the same way, you can learn to become an expert storyteller. Make the decision to tell stories and see where this leads you. Finally, open your heart to the wealth of experience and depth of learning that storytelling will open for you and your learners. Storytelling will add immeasurably to the value of the work you do. Try it. People will be grateful for the opportunity to learn in a new way.

chapter SIX

Legal and Ethical Use of Stories

Whose Mother Was It? (R)

Contributed by Chris Clarke-Epstein, CSP, owner, SPEAKING!

I can't tell you how excited I was to get the brochure advertising the seminar I'd wanted to attend for a long time! A highly respected training company was presenting and I couldn't wait to learn from the "masters."

The program was everything I'd hoped for and more. At one point in the program, a trainer launched into a humorous story about his mother having attended one of his sessions and about the conversation they wound up having in front of the entire participant group. The program was magical and I left really charged up with all kinds of new ideas to put into use.

About three weeks later, I was speaking at a conference where this same training company was once again presenting, but on a slightly different topic. I thought to myself, "Great, now I get to see them twice in one month. It doesn't get any better than this!" I couldn't wait to go to another of the firm's programs. Once again, a different trainer was doing a masterful job. The program was wonderful until . . . he launched into a story about his mother having been in the audience in one of his sessions and about the humorous conversation they had had. At first, I just felt confused. "Wait a minute. I thought it was *the other guy* who had the mother in his training program. Whose mother was it? Was it the first guy's mother and this trainer 'borrowed' the story?" Suddenly, I realized I was "gone" from the training session and no longer paying attention. I felt betrayed by these wonderfully skillful trainers.

After the session, I thought about it further. You see, it wasn't that they *both* told the same story—it was the fact that each trainer told it as if it had happened personally to *him.* I couldn't understand why one of them didn't just say, "You know, this reminds me of a time when a buddy of mine was training and his mom was in the audience and here's what happened." Then he could've told the story—even told it in the first person—with enthusiasm and integrity and it would've been great. I caught him telling someone else's story as his own. His credibility suffered in my eyes. For all of us, when telling someone else's story, it is important to "give credit where credit is due."

"[T]he danger of telling somebody else's story as your own is enormous," Chris goes on to say, "[while] the benefit of telling somebody else's story as somebody else's story that you find valuable is also enormous. I learned a valuable lesson from attending both seminars—that it's okay to borrow stories from other people when you have permission, like the stories in this book. Just make sure that you put them into context."

How do you tell someone else's story in a training setting? What are the legal and ethical implications of doing this? Many trainers have circumvented this dilemma by only telling their own stories or those that are so time honored that they are already in the public domain. However, that limits us from accessing the rich opportunities that other people's stories provide. As with all work created by others, there are legal and ethical issues affecting your use of these stories. While we do not intend to fully explain the intricacies of copyright—a highly complex legal area—the guidelines offered here are intended to support you in making full and ethical use of the stories in your training, speaking, educating, consulting, or managing. It is important to note that these guidelines are not to be construed as legal advice; for that you will need to consult an attorney specializing in intellectual property issues.

COPYRIGHT

Contributors offered each of the stories in Section Two in the hope that you will use them to enhance your training programs. The stories are offered to you in written format. All except one story is on the audio CD.

Because copyright law protects the stories in this book (except when stories are already in public domain), they cannot be published in any future work without prior permission from the publisher. While the contributors own the oral version of their stories—except where cited as previously published in another source—John Wiley & Sons, Inc. owns the rights to each story in the specific format in which it is presented in this book. The publisher has granted permission to reproduce limited quantities (up to 100 copies per page per year) of the stories (those not previously copyrighted) for educational/training purposes for your organization. When reproducing stories for this purpose, they must contain the following copyright notice:

Reproduced from *Stories Trainers Tell* by Mary B. Wacker and Lori L. Silverman with permission of the publisher. Copyright © 2003 by John Wiley & Sons, Inc.

This permission does not allow for systematic or large-scale reproduction, distribution, transmission, electronic reproduction or inclusion in any publications offered for sale or used for commercial purposes. For any use other than limited reproduction for your organization, you will need to contact the publisher directly. Refer to the copyright page in the front of this book for information on how to contact the publisher and for a complete listing of the eleven previously published stories excluded from this reproduction permission. For permission to reuse the stories previously published, you will need to contact the original copyright holder that is cited at the end of each of them. Permission to reprint any information from the supporting chapters about storytelling or any of the story key points, debrief questions, or follow-up activities can also be done by contacting the publisher. Note that obtaining rights to reuse published material may incur fees. If you wish to communicate with a contributor about referencing his or her stories in a format other than that included in this work, you will find full biographic and contact information in About the Contributors at the end of the book.

What does all this mean for you as a trainer using the stories in this book? It means you have the right to use the stories in any of the following ways. You can:

- Tell a story orally in your own words.
- Memorize the stories and recount them to your group.
- Read the stories from the book to your group.
- Adapt the story to fit your specific purpose and relay it orally to your group.
- Provide an oral skit or role-play with the story content.
- Play the accompanying CD for your own development as a storyteller.
- Play a story from the CD (except for stories as noted) for your participant group (up to a total of 100 people per year).
- Reproduce up to 100 copies per page per year for educational or training events in your organization (except for stories as noted).
- Create a written form of the story (except as noted) in a handout, worksheet, overhead transparency, easel sheet, or slide.

Memorizing or telling the story orally in your own words keeps the immediacy of the story intact and allows you to use physical movement and gestures for dramatic effect. Reading a story can be used to create the feel of a "story circle" with participants gathered around the reader, hanging on his or her words. While physical movement can be limited by this method, you can still take on voices and facial expressions to represent characters in the story. Better yet, role-play the story with another trainer or participant or develop a skit using the story events as the basis for it. We encourage you to listen to the CD as a way to develop your own storytelling skills. While there may be times when you wish to play a recorded story for your participants, we encourage you not to substitute the audio version for your own more visually oriented storytelling style. As you can see, there are numerous ways to share the stories with your participants and still respect the rights of each contributor and the publisher.

What you are not able to do, without prior written legal permission, is:

- Photocopy a story for large-scale use (over 100 copies per page per year).
- Distribute any of the stories in written or electronic form.

- Videotape or audiotape yourself telling one of these stories that will then be shown to others. This has particular ramifications for telling these stories during training sessions that an organization wishes to videotape or audiotape.
- Include a story in participant training manuals and facilitator or leader guides.

STORYTELLING WISDOM

"Good stories are really a reflection of their authors. Telling them without credit is a form of cheating them of what they have created and what they have put into the story of themselves."

Hortencia Delgadillo

ETHICS OF SELECTING AND TELLING STORIES

If Sandra Hoskins is training in a small town where everyone knows each other, she uses her own stories, not those from other sources, so there is no opportunity for participants to identify who the story is about. Respecting the privacy of your participants is paramount, according to Jonathan Preston and Marcy Fisher. Jon once heard a senior manager in a training class try to tell another person's story—the only problem was Jon knew the actual story. The manager not only miscommunicated how the situation had happened, he also completely missed the mark on stating its moral. Marcy relayed an experience when a presenter told a story about a person and the individual just happened to be in the room, although the trainer did not know it. The trainer introduced the story by saying, "I picked up this story but don't know who it is about." The person got up and ran out in tears; the trainer was not able to recover during the session. When you select a story to tell and it is not your own story, you have an ethical responsibility to be thoughtful about the topic, the source, and the ramifications of telling the story in a particular locale to a participant group.

Attribution

Giving credit for borrowed work is an issue of morality as well as being legally and ethically correct. In order to tell a story from this book, you are agreeing to provide attribution. What this means is that you are agreeing to identify the source of the story by contributor name either *just before* or *just after* telling the story. There are numerous ways to incorporate attribution into the flow of telling a story so that it becomes a natural and comfortable part of the experience. In Chapter Five, we gave numerous examples of incorporating attribution into the set-up or lead-in comments at the beginning of a story. If you do not include the attribution in the story set-up, you will need to mention the source immediately following the story.

STORYTELLING WISDOM

"People have taken others' signature stories and used them without attribution. Plain and simple, it is wrong to do this!"

Edward E. Scannell, CMP, CSP

VERIFYING SOURCES IN STORIES THAT YOU CREATE

As trainers, facilitators, and coaches, we encourage you to take "facts" and other pieces of information and create stories from them that you can then incorporate into your training sessions. Think for a minute. How often do you stop and actually verify the source of these items? You might be surprised if you did. Ed Scannell shares this account in the National Speakers Association journal article, "A Look at Some 'Myth' Information":

How many times in the past few years have you heard or (heaven forbid) told the story about the now-famous Yale University "study" that supposedly documents the importance of personal goal-setting? In this popular and oft-quoted study, we are told that over forty years ago—1953 to be exact—the graduating class of Yale University was queried as to how many members of that class actually had written down their own personal goals for the future. Not surprisingly, only 3 percent of that class had done so.

As the story goes, this same group was surveyed some twenty years later, and the research team found that the 3 percent who had written out their life's goals had gathered more personal financial wealth than the rest of that class combined!

Although this makes for a great story and really fortifies the importance of goal-setting, it has to rank among one of the best fables ever told! In a recent issue of the excellent magazine, *Fast Company*, their staff went to great lengths to substantiate the study, but to no avail. Their work was most thorough and followed every possible lead that might have had even a remote connection to the supposed research. They even checked with a research associate at Yale who personally searched through the university's archives. Their response? "We are quite confident that the 'study' did not take place. We suspect it is a myth" (1997, p. 20).

This story illustrates how easy it is to fall into the trap of passing on inaccurate "truths" in training programs. Our best advice is to have known sources for anything you are using in your stories and to provide full attribution for anything that is the work of others.

THE STORY CONTINUES

Great stories are everywhere and they often originate with someone else. Add to that the speed and variety of information transfer vehicles available to us today—such as the Internet—and the number of available stories multiplies exponentially. At the same time, the sources for these stories may be obscure or even untraceable. While the temptation to go ahead and use these stories is powerful, as storytellers, we have some decisions to make about how to uphold the ethical integrity of this growing profession. In this chapter, we have highlighted some of the key ethical and legal issues facing anyone who tells someone else's stories or creates their own stories from other sources. This brief overview, while by no means exhaustive, serves to point out the most important pitfalls to avoid when ethically using stories in your work.

Bringing Stories to Life

- How does copyright law affect your actions and the choices you make to incorporate audio, video, or written stories into your training?
- How can you ensure that the stories you choose to tell respect the privacy of your participant group?
- How do you give attribution when you tell stories from other sources?
- What research do you do to identify the sources of your story ideas?

Sharing stories is a way to connect us to each other as well as a way to explore our own humanity. Shared experiences validate us. The unusual pushes our boundaries. In all ways, stories help us grow. Our contributors encourage you to use their stories and have offered them as a way to support your growth and development as trainers. Tell the stories with energy, joy, and integrity. Follow the ethical guidelines. Explore your own best uses for your favorites. Each of these stories is a gift—offered with love—and to be treated with care.

section
TWO

The Stories

Each of the following ten chapters contains four to seven stories. The stories in each chapter are presented in alphabetical order, by the contributors' last names. To determine the chapter topics, we reviewed the stories and identified common themes among them. These themes gave rise to the chapter titles. While these topics are by no means inclusive, we believe they provide a good cross-section of stories with broad applicability. The topics represented here reflect contemporary training themes.

An introductory paragraph opens each story chapter. It describes the topic, identifies the specific stories we included, along with a brief description of each, and relates the common themes that weave these stories together.

As discussed more thoroughly in Chapter Four, each story is presented within a story framework that includes: title, contributor, type and purpose(s), background, presentation tips, set-up options, the story itself, debrief questions, key point options, and one or more follow-up activities. We strongly recommend that you review the story framework information beginning on page 75 in order to have a good understanding of how the framework can support your use of these stories. Note that the debrief questions provided here are set-up in three levels, each with its own symbol: the story—what occurred, what the story means; the learner—how the participant feels about the story, how it applies personally to the learner; and the organization or world—how the story applies to the participant's work or the world at large. For each story, select the most relevant key point and debrief questions that fit with your purpose for telling the story. You do not need to use all the debrief options provided. Typically, in telling a story, you will want to emphasize one key learning, moral, or lesson, so select or create the one that best delivers your point. Also note that each of the fifty-five stories is numbered sequentially throughout the story chapters. The numbers are referenced in Tables II.1 and II.2 that provide summary information about the stories and ideas for alternate topic uses.

To select an appropriate story, start with the chapter that most closely reflects your topic area. After reviewing the stories in that chapter, search other chapters that might have stories that are applicable to points you wish to make in your particular program. Keep in mind that you might need to alter the key point, debrief questions, and the follow-up activity to fit this new use. While individual stories have been categorized in a particular manner, they can typically be used with many other training topics. To identify alternate uses for a story, refer to Table II.2.

To assist you in using these stories easily and effectively in your work, we have provided two tools:

Table II.1: *Story Information* provides the title, number, page on which the story is located within the book, the story type as defined by Doug Stevenson, and the purpose(s) for which it might be employed. This summary data will help you quickly access the story you are looking for. It will also help you identify stories that would fit a particular purpose—to entertain, or to encourage participants to make a commitment, for example.

Table II.2: *Stories by Training Topic* provides an extensive, alphabetical list of training topics. For each topic, the numbers of the stories that fit within that topic area are listed. The matrix will enable you to use the stories in this book in a variety of program settings.

In addition to the fifty-five stories contained in these ten chapters, eighteen stories from the Introduction through Chapter Six are also included in the tables. These Section One stories are labeled sequentially with letters of the alphabet A through R on page 115. While they are not accompanied in this book by the story framework that the Section Two stories include, the frameworks for these front of chapter stories are available at www.storiestrainerstell.com.

We hope you enjoy the stories and find a wealth of ideas for using them in your training.

Table II.1: Story Information

Number	Title	Chapter/ Page	Type	Purpose
1	"A World Without Blacks"	7 / 120	Instructional	Educate, evoke
2	"Look at Me!"	7 / 125	Imbroglio	Evaluate, explore
3	"When in Egypt, Do What?"	7 / 128	Vignette	Explore
4	"Catching an Unconscious Bias"	7 / 132	Imbroglio	Evaluate
5	"I Never Noticed You Were Black"	7 / 135	Imbroglio	Evaluate, evoke
6	"The Scratch-and-Sniff Test"	7 / 139	Imbroglio	Evaluate, engage
7	"Are You Listening?"	8 / 145	Vignette	Evaluate
8	"If You're Not Asked, Keep Your Mouth Shut?"	8 / 149	Vignette	Evaluate, encourage
9	"The House Guest"	8 / 152	Imbroglio	Evaluate, explore
10	"How Far is Far?"	8 / 156	Vignette	Educate
11	"A Fish Tale"	8 / 159	Vignette	Entertain, explore
12	"It's the Little Things That Count"	9 / 165	Vignette	Evaluate
13	"Ladies and Gentleman Serving Ladies and Gentlemen"	9 / 168	Credibility	Explore
14	"I Was Aching for a Fight"	9 / 172	Imbroglio	Evaluate, explore
15	"The Customer Strikes Back"	9 / 176	Vignette	Entertain, evaluate
16	"You Don't Qualify for the Senior Discount"	9 / 180	Vignette	Explore, evaluate
17	"Sorry, We Can't Do It"	9 / 184	Vignette	Explore, evoke
18	"The Taxi Driver"	9 / 187	Vignette	Encourage
19	"The Cobbler's Children"	10 / 193	Imbroglio	Evaluate, evoke
20	"I Haven't Worn My Hat in a Long Time"	10 / 198	Vignette	Evaluate
21	"The Volunteer Job"	10 / 202	Vignette	Engage, encourage
22	"Missing a Golden Opportunity"	10 / 206	Vignette	Educate, evaluate
23	"Upstaged by a Rookie"	10 / 210	Imbroglio	Educate, explore
24	"Who Called This Meeting?"	10 / 215	Vignette	Explore, evoke

(*Continued*)

Table II.1: Story Information (Continued)

Number	Title	Chapter/ Page	Type	Purpose
25	"A Culture Rooted in Gunpowder"	11 / 221	Credibility	Educate
26	"Expecting Too Little"	11 / 225	Vignette	Encourage
27	"The Bamboo Years"	11 / 229	Credibility	Educate, encourage
28	"The Worth of a Contribution"	11 / 232	Credibility	Encourage
29	"Fostering Full Potential"	11 / 235	Instructional	Educate, encourage
30	"A Legacy of Generosity"	12 / 241	Vignette	Encourage
31	"Time Brings Perspective"	12 / 244	Imbroglio	Engage, explore
32	"In Search of Cappuccino . . . With a Little Chocolate on the Side"	12 / 248	Crucible	Encourage, evoke
33	"Values Aren't Accidental"	12 / 252	Vignette	Explore
34	"A Nation's Values Connect Us"	12 / 255	Credibility	Educate, explore
35	"The Case of the Magician's Assistant"	13 / 261	Instructional	Evaluate, evoke
36	"The Roll of the Dice"	13 / 265	Vignette	Entertain, explore
37	"Isolate, Exaggerate, and Integrate"	13 / 269	Instructional	Educate, encourage
38	"Thanks, I'll Do It Myself"	13 / 273	Vignette	Evaluate
39	"The Forest for the Trees"	13 / 277	Vignette	Evaluate
40	"Is He Qualified?"	13 / 280	Instructional	Educate, evaluate
41	"For Lack of a System"	14 / 287	Vignette	Entertain, explore
42	"The Porcupine and the Snake"	14 / 290	Minerva	Explore
43	"Viewing the Problem Through a Different Lens"	14 / 294	Vignette	Explore
44	"The Disapproving Neighbor"	14 / 298	Minerva, pattern	Entertain, evaluate
45	"The Road to Peoria"	14 / 302	Imbroglio	Explore
46	"Doing the Packarena"	15 / 309	Credibility	Entertain, evoke
47	"The Slingshot"	15 / 313	Imbroglio	Entertain, explore
48	"A Family United"	15 / 318	Minerva	Explore

Table II.1: (Continued)

Number	Title	Chapter/ Page	Type	Purpose
49	"The Contest"	15 / 321	Minerva	Explore, evoke
50	"I Didn't Ask to Be Here"	16 / 329	Instructional	Educate, explore
51	"In Pursuit of a Goal"	16 / 335	Vignette	Engage, explore
52	"Teaching a Dog to Whistle"	16 / 339	Vignette	Entertain, engage
53	"Preparing Yourself for the Unexpected"	16 / 342	Crucible	Encourage, explore
54	"How My Sons Learned to Dive"	16 / 346	Pattern	Educate, engage
55	"The Jock and His Wife Go Water Skiing"	16 / 352	Vignette	Evaluate, engage
A	"Discovering the Power of Stories"	Intro / 1	Instructional	Educate, engage
B	"Your Top Priorities"	1 / 3	Instructional	Educate, encourage
C	"On the Lookout for Body Art"	1 / 9	Vignette	Entertain
D	"Keeping Your Cool"	1 / 12	Imbroglio	Evaluate, explore
E	"The Camping Trip"	1 / 14	Vignette	Engage, evoke
F	"Why Can't We All Get Along?"	1 / 17	Vignette	Evaluate, explore
G	"The Wake-up Call"	1 / 19	Imbroglio	Evaluate, evoke
H	"Right Under Your Nose"	2 / 23	Vignette	Entertain, engage
I	"Follow the Leader"	2 / 31	Instructional	Educate, explore
J	"My Mental Filing System"	2 / 36	Instructional	Educate, engage
K	"Losing the Sale"	3 / 41	Vignette	Educate, evaluate
L	"Seeing the Light"	3 / 48	Vignette, pattern	Educate, evaluate
M	"7.1 on the Richter Scale"	3 / 54	Crucible	Encourage, evoke
N	"Bun's Rush: Wienermobile Finds Route Near Pentagon No Picnic"	3 / 61	Imbroglio	Entertain, evoke
O	"Prisoners, Vacationers, and Learners"	4 / 65	Vignette	Engage, encourage
P	"The Wise Man and the Baby Bird"	4 / 71	Minerva	Evaluate, evoke
Q	"Tuning-in to Trainees' Needs"	5 / 85	Instructional	Educate, engage
R	"Whose Mother Was It?"	6 / 103	Vignette	Evaluate, evoke

Table II.2: Stories by Training Topic

Training Topic	Story Number
Appreciating differences (Chapter 7)	1, 2, 3, 4, 5, 6, 18, 26, 32, P
Business strategy	16, 17, 19, 20, 22, 23, 24, 25, 27, B
Career development	21, 22, 23, 29, 38
Change: Individual	2, 3, 5, 6, 7, 9, 18, 22, 23, 29, 32, 37, 40, 44, 45, 49, 53, I, M
Change: Organizational	19, 20, 24, 31, 39, 40, I
Coaching (Chapter 13)	19, 22, 23, 29, 35, 36, 37, 38, 39, 40, 50, 54, 55
Collaboration (Chapter 15)	3, 15, 17, 24, 46, 47, 48, 49, M
Communication (Chapter 8)	2, 3, 7, 8, 9, 10, 11, 13, 14, 17, 52, D, F
Conflict management	7, 14, 16, 17, 19, 29, 31, 50, D, F
Creativity	15, 36, 39, 43, 46, 47, C
Customer service (Chapter 9)	10, 12, 13, 14, 15, 16, 17, 18, 24, 41, E, G, L, N
Decision making	21, 47, B
Delegation	38, M
Difficult people	14, 15, 16, 24, 31, 44, 50, D, F
Discipline	25, 29, 50
Diversity	1, 2, 3, 4, 5, 6, 18, P
Employee involvement	19, 20, 24, 46
Ethics	29, 31, 35, G, R
Feedback (Chapter 8)	5, 7, 8, 9, 10, 11, 14, 19, 22, 23, 35, 40, 50, 54, D, F, G
Financial management	26, 36
Followership	6
Goal setting	3, 9, 10, 21, 26, 29, 39, 47, 51, B, H
Group facilitation	24, 31, 50, O, Q, R
Influence (Chapter 10)	6, 14, 18, 19, 20, 21, 22, 23, 24, 28, 31, 48, 49, I
Innovation	43
Interviewing	40

Table II.2: (Continued)

Training Topic	Story Number
Leadership (Chapter 11)	13, 16, 20, 23, 25, 26, 27, 28, 29, 31, 35, 37, 38, 40, 46, 53, N
Learning	2, 22, 37, 40, 49, 52, A, J, O, Q
Learning styles	51, 54, 55, J
Listening	7, 8, 9, 23, 31, D
Marketing	46, G, N
Meeting management	11, 24, 31, 39, 50, O
Motivation (Chapter 10)	3, 17, 19, 20, 21, 22, 23, 24, 29, 31, 32, 38, 46, 48, I, L, O, Q
Negotiation	F, D
New employee orientation	28, 30, 49
Organizational culture	12, 13, 16, 19, 20, 24, 25, 27, 36, 39, 53
Performance (Chapter 13)	7, 17, 22, 23, 25, 29, 35, 36, 37, 38, 39, 40, 45, 50, 54, 55, O
Personal development	1, 4, 5, 6, 7, 9, 21, 26, 30, 31, 32, 33, 34, 44, 53, 54, C, E
Policy compliance	13, 16, 17, 25, 39, G
Power or politics	19, 24, 26, 28, 31, 49, 50
Presentation skills	50, K, Q, R
Problem-solving (Chapter 14)	3, 22, 41, 42, 43, 44, 45, 47, H, J
Process improvement	40, 41, 43, H
Project management	24, 43
Risk management	18, 25, 35
Safety	25, 35
Sales	15, 16, 22, 23, K
Strategic planning	27, 34
Statistical analysis	41, 43
Stress management	9, 32, M
Teamwork (Chapter 15)	15, 17, 24, 46, 47, 48, 49

(Continued)

Table II.2: (Continued)

Training Topic	Story Number
Technology	11, 43
Time management	9, 28, B, J, M
Training fundamentals (Chapter 16)	2, 22, 37, 50, 51, 52, 53, 54, 55, A, O, Q, R
Trust	5, 6, 8, 9, 16, 19, 20, 23, 27, 29, 31, 38, F, P, R
Value creation	13, 16, 17, 27, N
Values (Chapter 12)	1, 2, 4, 5, 6, 9, 12, 19, 20, 25, 26, 30, 31, 32, 33, 34, 35, 48, 49, C, E, P, R
Volunteerism	21, 26
Writing skills	38

Appreciating Differences

chapter **SEVEN**

Welcoming and respecting the diverse aspects of our world is key to living in a global society. What brings us together is often through what we have in common. Yet how we grow and develop beyond a narrow perspective is through appreciating the ways in which we are different from each other. Creating a common bond can create uncommon others who are then excluded from our shared experiences. It is through our own commitment to learning that we seek out both our internal and external biases and act on behalf of our connectedness.

The six stories in this chapter are about noticing the times in our lives that cause us to reflect and expand on our perspectives on the world. Both LG Shanklin-Flowers's experience in "I Never Noticed You Were Black" and Bob Shaver's "The Scratch-and-Sniff Test" make us stop and catch ourselves when we form a judgment based on someone's appearance. Steve Hanamura's "Look at Me" and Clare Novak's "When in Egypt, Do What?" address cultural differences—Steve comments on the differing ways cultures define respect and Clare raises what can happen when one follows directions in another country. In "Catching an Unconscious Bias," Julie O'Mara, a noted diversity consultant, shares a time when her unconscious assumptions arose almost without her recognizing them. Bill Boone brings us a heartfelt narrative on what we would miss in "A World Without Blacks."

These stories help us examine how our attitudes are formed and all the ways in which they influence our actions. They encourage us to expand beyond our limits and consider new ways of looking at our world. The stories evoke both smiles and tears and they make us think. Together, they celebrate our unique humanity.

A WORLD WITHOUT BLACKS (1)

Contributor

William Austin Boone, senior associate, MARTIN, BOONE ASSOCIATES

Type and Purpose(s)

Instructional; educate and evoke

Background

William Boone created this story in the mid-1970s with the imagination and input from numerous trainees and friends along the way. He has revised and added to it over the years. It has since been circulated on the Internet. This story speaks to the universality of the creative spirit—the inventiveness in all people even under debilitating circumstances or extreme duress, such as slavery and low expectations by others of black people's humanness, ability, and intelligence. It also speaks of America's miseducation about and purposeful omission of the contributions of people of color to America, especially from those of African descent.

Presentation Tips

This story can be narrated to participants as though you were reading a book out loud to a group gathered around you.

Set-up

Option 1—Reflect on what your life would be like today if the following contributions had not been made.

Option 2—In our daily lives, it is easy to overlook the contributions of others.

A World Without Blacks

Once upon a time there was a group of Americans that was "fed up" with African Americans, so they joined hands together and wished themselves away to the New America that *should have been*—an America without black people.

Almost instantly, they passed through a deep, dark tunnel and emerged into a twilight zone where there was an America of whites only! They breathed a deep sigh of relief.

"At last!" spoke one. "No more demands for equality, affirmative action, blacks on street corners begging for money, violence, drugs, and welfare! They're all *gone*!

"Yes!" screamed another. "Who *needs* them, anyway?"

Their gleeful cheers and laughter soon turned to quiet amazement as they looked around at an almost barren America.

First, they noticed only a few crops growing. (The other America was built on a *slave-supported system,* where crops were bountiful, and with a wide variety coming from Africa, the Caribbean, and South America—where slaves were also imported—and attended to by the *enslaved Africans.*)

Then they noticed that there were no cities with tall skyscrapers . . . because Alexander Mills, a black man, invented the *elevator,* and without it one finds great difficulty reaching high floors.

There are few if any cars because Richard Spikes, a black man, invented the *automatic gearshift,* Joseph Gammell, also black, invented the *Super Charge system* for internal combustion engines, and Garrett A. Morgan, one of America's most prolific inventors, invented *traffic signals.* Furthermore, one could not use the rapid transit system because another black man, Elbert R. Robinson, invented its precursor, the *electric trolley.*

But, even if there were streets on which cars and a rapid transit system could operate, they were cluttered with paper because an African American, Charles Brooks, invented the *street sweeper.*

The group noticed that there are few if any newspapers, magazines, and books because John Love invented the *pencil sharpener,* William Purvis, the *fountain pen,* Lee Burridge, the *type writing machine,* and W. A. Lovette's inventions advanced the *printing press.* They all were (you guessed it) black.

But even if these Americans could write their letters, articles, and books, they would not have been transported by mail because William Barry invented the *postmarking and canceling machine,* William Purvis, the *hand stamp,* and Phillip Downing, the *letter drop.*

As the group continued walking, their faces obviously perplexed by this unexpected turn of events, they noticed that the lawns were brown and wilted. (Two black men, Joseph Smith and John Burr, respectively, invented the *lawn sprinkler* and the *lawn mower.*)

They entered a home in this new America and found it to be poorly ventilated and poorly heated. You see, Frederick Jones invented the *air conditioner* and Alice Parker, the *heating furnace.* Their homes were also dim . . . but of course! Lewis Latimer invented the *electric lamp,* Michael Harvey, *the lantern,* and Granville T. Woods, the *automatic cutoff switch.* (Their homes were also filthy because Thomas W. Steward, who invented the *mop,* and Lloyd P. Ray, the *dustpan,* never lived in this new America.)

Their children met them at the door . . . barefooted, shabby, and unkempt. But what could one expect? Jan E. Matzeliger invented the *shoe lasting machine,* Walter Sammons invented the *comb,* Sara Boone invented the *ironing board,* and George T. Samon invented the *clothes dryer.*

Finally, they resigned to have dinner amidst all of this turmoil. But, alas, the food had spoiled because another black man, John Standard, invented the *refrigerator*!

In noting the historical proliferation of inventions and other creative endeavors by diverse people, Martin Luther King, Jr., once remarked: "By the time we leave for work we . . . will have been dependent on half the world. Modern America is created by dependencies on inventions from the minds of Black folks and other (diverse) people." It is clear that "contributions shape society." And the contributions of African Americans are at the heart of this nation.

Boone, W. A. (1972). "A world without blacks." Unpublished story, Chicago, Ill. Used with permission. This story may not be reprinted without permission of the original copyright holder.

Debrief Questions

- What was the point of this story?
- Which of these inventions were you aware of prior to hearing about them today?
- What were your reactions to this story? How did this story affect you?
- How does having this knowledge about these contributions change your perspective?
- How does this story relate to the assumptions we make about groups of people?
- What are the probable consequences or results of excluding the contributions to America made by people of color? How has this omission impacted whites? People of color?

Key Point Options

1. No one knows how many other inventions, artistic creations, and ideas were stolen, borrowed, imitated, and/or adapted from those of slaves, Native Americans, freed men and women, and their ancestors.
2. The notions of black *non*-contributors and *only* white contributors to America are erroneous. At their worst, such notions give a false sense of white superiority and, for African Americans, a tragic sense of black inferiority. Both notions maintain myths that feed racism.
3. Knowledge and education can replace the bias and prejudice that come from assumptions based on limited information or exclusionary upbringing.
4. We all have much to be proud of in our unique heritages and cultures. We need to celebrate each other's contributions.

Follow-up Activity

Step 1—Individually: Identify your own ethnic and racial heritage(s).

Step 2—Small-Group Discussion: Each person takes several minutes to talk about his or her own heritage and what he or she is most proud of in that heritage.

Step 3—Large-Group Discussion: What similarities and differences did you notice in your conversation?

LOOK AT ME! (2)

Contributor

Steve Hanamura, president, Hanamura Consulting, Inc.

Type and Purpose(s)

Imbroglio; evaluate and explore

Background

This is a powerful story because we often say, “let’s build respect,” yet we have very little understanding of the cultural differences that may impact a person’s perception of respect.

Presentation Tips

Use three different voices to depict the narrator, teacher, and the little boy. Consider acting out Thomas’s actions after he is screamed at by the teacher—drop to your hands and knees as you narrate that portion of the story.

Set-up

Option 1—Where do our expectations come from?

Option 2—How explicit do we need to be when defining behaviors in the workplace?

Option 3—Just because people use the exact same words when they talk to each other doesn’t mean that they are in agreement.

Look at Me!

A teacher in an elementary school in California was having a problem with Thomas, a Native American student. Thomas wouldn't look at her! This problem had persisted for quite some time. Every single day she kept encouraging him to look at her. Every single day she kept saying, a little more intensely each time, "Look at me . . . *look at me*."

By the fourth week of the term, the teacher got so frustrated that she hollered, "LOOK AT ME!" Surprised and scared, Thomas got down on his hands and knees and crawled under his desk. When he finally got back up, he looked at her and thought, "Well, if this is so important maybe I should go home and practice." So he went home and immediately started practicing eye contact with his parents. The result? He was promptly sent to his room!

When my firm came in to address the problem, it was painfully obvious to us that the teacher wanted Thomas to show her some respect. From her perspective, eye contact is a way to show this. Unbeknown to her, in the Native American culture, respect is shown by looking down.

Picture how confused Thomas must have been about the word "respect." How was he supposed to act? Which behavior was going to be acceptable to his teacher *and* to his parents?

We brought the parents and the teacher together to talk about the concept of respect and what respect "looks" like in their respective cultures. The outcome? Together they were able to come up with an agreement about how they wanted Thomas to act. Imagine Thomas's relief! He now knew exactly how to demonstrate respect in a way that pleased both his parents and his teacher.

Each of us has our own definition of what it means to "show some respect." What does it look like in your world?

Debrief Questions

- What dilemma did Thomas face with his teacher?
- How did the expectations of his teacher and his parents differ?
- How do you define respect?
- In what ways would you like respect to be given to you?
- In what ways do you show respect toward others? How do you know it is perceived that way?
- How can we promote the concept of respect in our organization?

Key Point Options

1. Diverse cultures interpret behaviors, especially non-verbal behaviors, differently. When we impose our interpretation of behavior on someone from another culture, we may be creating misunderstandings.
2. Respect means being willing to ask others for their perspective and for workable solutions to problems that do not impose a culture's set of values on another culture.
3. People typically do their best to meet expectations. When those expectations are confusing, unclear, or place them in conflict, their actions can often be viewed as performance problems. It takes a skillful person to uncover these conflicting messages that can reduce clear communication and mutual understanding.

Follow-up Activity

Step 1—Individually: Write down at least five behaviors that you believe show respect in your workplace (for example, to listen until someone is finished speaking without interruption).

Step 2—Large-Group Discussion: Compare lists and create a "group norm" for respect in the team, department, or organization. Identify the most significant behaviors. Consider posting these in the workplace.

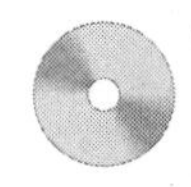

WHEN IN EGYPT, DO WHAT? (3)

Contributor

Clare Novak, president, Novak and Associates

Type and Purpose(s)

Vignette; explore

Background

This story brings into focus how our expectations shape our experiences, especially when traveling in other countries and cultures.

Presentation Tips

Tell this story in a conversational tone of voice.

Set-up

Option 1—Wherever we go, our mental models accompany us.

Option 2—Being in unfamiliar territory can alert us to our blind spots.

When in Egypt, Do What?

While I was in Egypt, I read a great review about a restaurant in a local magazine called *Egypt Today*. From the address, I knew it would be across from the Marriott Hotel.

One afternoon I went to the area to check out the restaurant and was unable to find it. There was no sign for it anywhere. Eventually I found the address on what appeared to be an apartment building. I entered and searched the premises. I searched the lobby. I searched the stairwells. I even searched the floor tile markings for signs of the restaurant. Amazing! Nowhere was I able to find any indication of it. It ought to be easier to find.

Not being one to give up, my colleagues and I returned that evening to the Marriott Hotel and asked about the restaurant. No one knew anything about it. Unsure of what to do next, we went outside and surveyed the situation. Soon after, someone came out from the apartment building and gave us directions to a lovely restaurant on the second floor. Being ever observant, I noticed that there was no signage anywhere for the establishment! True to the magazine review, the restaurant, which overlooked the Nile River, had terrific food.

Over time, my colleagues and I became more savvy about finding our way around the city. Whenever we discovered a restaurant we wanted to visit, we got directions to the *exact* location and checked out all the floors of the building. We even scoped out the location after dark so we could look through the windows for people who were dining! Our success in finding the spot each time was rewarded with a wonderful meal. As I reflect back, I realize we learned something. We learned that our "oughts" and our "shoulds" get in the way.

They "ought" to have better signage. They "ought" to give clearer directions. We "should" be able to locate a restaurant without making two trips!

At the same time, we learned that expecting things to be different in another country goes a long way towards dispelling those "oughts and shoulds."

Debrief Questions

- What mental models kept the storyteller from seeing the restaurant?
- What changes did Clare and her colleagues make to adapt to local customs and have a good experience in Egypt?
- How did the initiative shown by Clare and her colleagues assist them in navigating in unfamiliar surroundings?
- Where in your life do you act on assumptions that get in the way of being open to new information?
- How have you increased your awareness about *not* acting on assumptions?
- How can our mental models shape our experience?
- Where in your organization have you noticed assumptions operating that get in the way of working effectively?

Key Point Options

1. Americans come up against many assumptions when traveling or working in other countries. If Clare had relied on her American-based expectations, she might not have found any of the restaurants.
2. We make assumptions such as "there *ought* to be signage" and then make judgments according to those assumptions, no matter if the assumptions are correct or not.
3. A mental model is a picture or view of how we think things *should be.* It reflects our training and past experiences and helps us make sense of the world so we

can navigate through daily life. However, these mental models also carry our biases, filters, expectations, and judgments, which can get in the way of accepting differences and being open to new experiences.

Follow-up Activity

Step 1—Small-Group Discussion: Tell your own stories about adaptations you have needed to make while traveling.

Step 2—Large-Group Discussion: With the entire group, discuss the following questions:

- When have you had to change a mental model in order to be successful or effective?
- Where have you taken initiative to adapt to the unexpected?

CATCHING AN UNCONSCIOUS BIAS (4)

Contributor

Julie O'Mara, president, O'Mara and Associates

Type and Purpose(s)

Imbroglio; evaluate

Background

Before Julie tells this story she has typically done some training on diversity issues with the group so that they know that it is not appropriate to show biases, or to make comments or have thoughts that promote stereotypes about women.

Presentation Tips

When telling this story, start with a sleepy tone of voice; then demonstrate being wide-awake and alert when Julie catches herself making an assumption.

Set-up

Option 1—Although we try as hard as we can to change, we've been programmed to think and behave in certain ways.

Option 2—When we least expect it, our biases can appear at center stage.

Catching an Unconscious Bias

It was one of those days—there were twelve things I had to get done on my "to do" list. Grocery shopping didn't rise to the top until 11:00 o'clock that evening. There I was, in the store wearing sweats, no make-up on, pushing a cart loaded with groceries. Being an early morning person, I was really tired and feeling kind of spacey.

One by one, I put the groceries onto the check-out conveyor belt: orange juice, milk, eggs, bread, soup. As I watched the groceries being scanned, I looked up toward the bank storefront that is near the entrance to the store. The bank was closed even though the grocery store was open twenty-four hours that day. I happened to notice a woman standing at the bank counter. She was wearing a business suit and was searching through a tool box. Given what I could see, it looked like she was trying to fix a piece of broken equipment. I said to myself, "What is she doing? How would she know how to fix that piece of equipment?"

I suddenly caught myself and froze in my tracks. How could this be happening? I'm Julie O'Mara—a very knowledgeable diversity trainer, who has been working hard for years and years on this topic, both personally and professionally. Here I am, making an assumption that a woman would not be able to repair a piece of equipment.

In hindsight I'm glad I recognized that I was stereotyping and labeling this woman. I'm also glad that I "caught myself in the act" of making an assumption. This experience taught me a valuable lesson: Within each of us are years and years of programming around certain stereotypes. No matter how much work you and I may have done in the area of diversity, when we get tired or stressed, these stereotypes can suddenly appear. I caught myself in the act. What will you do to catch yourself?

Debrief Questions

- Why do you think this stereotype came up for Julie, who is so committed to gender equality?
- What do you think causes bias and stereotyping?
- In general, why is it important to catch ourselves in our biases and stereotypes?
- Has anything similar happened to you? Have you ever caught yourself stereotyping someone in your mind? Describe the situations.
- What stereotypes operate in the world that create assumptions about people's abilities?

Key Point Options

1. Even though we may intellectually know how race and gender stereotypes hurt our society and that women can do "men's jobs" and men can do "women's jobs," we may still find ourselves thinking and acting in ways that show bias and prejudice.
2. We all have prejudices and biases. We all stereotype to some degree. The key issue is to acknowledge this and strive to not make decisions based on any stereotyping. That is what is meant by "awareness." It is noticing your behavior but stopping at the point of making a decision based on stereotypes.
3. Stereotypes and biases are *learned* behaviors and thought patterns. They can also be unlearned. This is difficult to change because we live in a society that still has systems that reflect these biases, so we are immersed in them and the learning continues. Not acting on these built-in biases takes a commitment to act consciously and equitably in society.

Follow-up Activity

Step 1—Paired Discussion: Ask participants to find a partner and share with them a time when they have done some stereotyping. What was the stereotype? What did they think? Did they act on their stereotype or just think about it?

Step 2—Large-Group Discussion: What can we do to reduce the likelihood of acting on built-in biases and stereotypes? How can we amend the situation if we do act on them unthinkingly?

I NEVER NOTICED YOU WERE BLACK (5)

Contributor

LG Shanklin-Flowers, president, InReach

Type and Purpose(s)

Imbroglio; evaluate and evoke

Background

LG has more than twenty-five years' experience in organizational development consulting, specializing in creating inclusive cultures and dismantling racism.

Presentation Tips

You can substitute "he said, she said" as well as LG's internal dialogue with three different body positions (for example, turning a different direction) as you relay the internal and external dialogue of the two characters. LG's thinking voice is loud and brassy.

Set-up

Option 1—Uncovering our biases is like peeling an onion.

Option 2—Our unconscious judgments can block our appreciation of others.

I Never Noticed You Were Black

The opening workshop of a weeklong training program on diversity had been a success. Participants were approaching my colleague and me to talk about what they had enjoyed.

A gentleman—he was a district attorney—came up to me. He was a handsome, forty-something, white male in absolutely great physical condition—a runner—proud of his physique and his commitment to being healthy. He wanted to talk about his experience of me as a trainer and what he appreciated about me in that role. His first words—they still ring in my ears—were, "I never even noticed you were black." Now, for me as a black person that is *always* a red flag—when a white person says that they don't notice. I mean . . . how could you *not* notice my color? I don't live a moment of my life not noticing. I would *love* to *not* notice but as a consequence of racism, I notice it every minute of every day. So, when someone says to me, "I never noticed you were black," it says that person doesn't notice *me.*

To say the least, at this point I was a little offended. But, as a trainer, I needed to be pleasant and listen to what he had to say next. And out of his mouth came the words, "Because what I noticed *more* about you was your size." Now, this was supposed to be a compliment, you understand. You see, at this point in my life I was fat. But I never had anybody tell me that to my face. I mean . . . people have told me things about being fat. But it was never set up as a compliment. So now I'm really suspicious and wondering how this man could possibly get himself out of this hole he had dug. I ran through his words one more time. "He doesn't notice me because I'm black but he does notice me because I'm fat."

I decide to continue listening to him. And he says, "I really want to appreciate you. I will never be able to look at a fat person in the same way again. Before this workshop, I made all sorts of assumptions about fat people—they're not disciplined, they're not smart, and they certainly don't have anything to teach me. You, on the other hand, have done all of that and more. Clearly you live an incredibly disciplined life. You are so intelligent. I have learned so much from you. Now I have to take what I thought was true about a group of people and look at that."

Unbelievable. He had saved himself. He dug himself out of his hole and taught me a lesson as well. At one level, it was wonderful to able to move this man and his understandings about human beings—the particular stereotypes that he was operating from. At the same time, it reinforces a point that I am very conscious of: that there might be people who object to what I have to say based on my body size.

What haven't you noticed in your life? "Colors, shapes, and sizes."

Debrief Questions

- What were some of the stereotypes that this man held?
- How did he communicate these stereotypes to LG?
- How do stereotypes interfere with appreciating the true value of others?
- How do stereotypes interfere with our own learning?
- How can we interrupt stereotypes that we notice others engaging in? How can we give them a more accurate picture of the world?

Key Point Options

1. We all carry assumptions about others. Our early training and experiences have led us to create these assumptions.
2. Often the assumptions we have about others are wrong, or at a minimum, not useful. To the extent that we can notice our own assumptions and stereotypes and question the truth of them, we can appreciate differences.
3. Truly appreciating each other's unique gifts is the basis for equity and opportunity in our organizations and our lives.

Follow-up Activity

Step 1—Large-Group Activity: Post a large sheet of banner paper (or several easel pad pages) on a wall. Provide a number of colored markers. Ask participants to write stereotypes or phrases that they have heard or that have been said to them on the banner paper.

Step 2—Large-Group Discussion: Read and have participants discuss their reactions to the phrases. Ask participants what responses they can make when hearing these types of phrases. Have a discussion on how stereotyping groups of people hurts everyone.

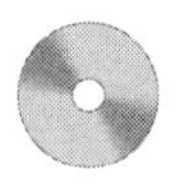

THE SCRATCH-AND-SNIFF TEST (6)

Contributor

Bob Shaver, director of the Basic Management Certificate Series, University of Wisconsin-Madison, School of Business, Fluno Center for Executive Education

Type and Purpose(s)

Imbroglio; evaluate and engage

Background

This situation occurred sometime around 1997. This was not Bob's first time at an outward-bound program.

Presentation Tips

This story is best told by portraying Bob and the other attendees as superior to Steve.

Set-up

Option 1—Seemingly insignificant things can have a significant impact on events.

Option 2—What role do "first impressions" play in life?

Option 3—The image we project can take on a life of its own.

Option 4—Our assumptions about others can impact our ability to achieve our goals.

The Scratch-and-Sniff Test

I had signed up for an outward-bound program specifically designed for older adults—no one was under the age of thirty and the average age was about forty. The first evening there were fifteen of us doing the typical scratch-and-sniff test that goes on whenever a new group gets together. You know the drill—who you are, where you've been, where you're going, and why you're there. After thirty minutes, almost everyone had mentioned that they had come to this rock-climbing program because of a fear of heights.

Right then, in walked a very good-looking young man—wearing cargo shorts and a tight shirt—who couldn't have been a day over twenty years old. We couldn't help but notice that he was sporting a large earring. Because of his dress and his walk, which I considered to be more like the strut of a cocky little rooster, the conversation immediately shifted. There was no way he was one of "us"—he had to be one of the instructors.

Now, even though I teach problem-solving and consider myself to be a rational human being, I got sucked into the group's conversation about this young man named Steve. Soon after, he came over and joined us. That just reaffirmed the biases we'd been discussing about this arrogant little young punk who was going to help us face our fears by teaching us how to climb a wall. No one could believe it! How could we trust somebody who behaved the way he did?

The next morning . . . in complete and utter silence . . . we watched Steve go up and down the rock like a billy goat—with no fears and no ropes—only using his hands and shoes to do what none of us really believed was possible. We were dumbstruck. Here's the man who's going to convince us that by the end of the program we'll be able do the same thing. Because of our first impressions—his obvious lack of maturity and experience, his strut, and his earring—we weren't going to be easily persuaded or won over. He would have to prove us wrong.

Then, something magical started to happen. Little by little he began to prove to us that he had the ability, he had the motivation, and he could stick to rocks like a fly on the ceiling. And he was going to help us do the same to overcome our fears. What amazed me was the way the group came to believe that Steve could, in fact, help us. We had finally scratched below the surface and allowed ourselves to be guided to success. By the end of the program he found a way for each of us to successfully climb the rock—we all made it. I was even able to climb upside down and over the edge, like you see in movies. That became possible because Steve helped me conquer my fear of falling.

That first evening—truth be told—we were deeply immersed in our own fears. At some level, we clearly felt that Steve's arrogant walk, and all the rest that went with it—his clothes and his earring—were ways of overcompensating for his own inadequacies. But, you know . . . when it came right down to it, when we scratched and sniffed below the surface, we realized it was our own inadequacies that had clouded our view of him. So, when you find yourself making assumptions about others based on their appearance, I suggest you "scratch and sniff" a little deeper to discover the real person.

Debrief Questions

- What assumptions did the group make about Steve?
- How did participants' first impressions of Steve initially get in the way of meeting their goals?

- What allowed people to change their initial impressions to permit a successful outcome to occur?
- In your own life, when have first impressions led you to the wrong conclusion?
- What misinformed first impressions have others had about you?
- How can you suspend your first impressions in order to gain a fuller appreciation of a person or situation?

Key Point Options

1. Our image and behavior creates our credibility or lack thereof. It often takes a great deal of effort to change that initial impression.
2. First impressions can be deceiving. We need to be open to new information about a person and not judge others on the basis of minimal information.
3. Acting on first impressions is not always helpful in meeting our goals. It can cause us to close ourselves off from new opportunities.

Follow-up Activity

Step 1—Paired Discussion: Talk about a time when either you were judged unfairly by another or you jumped to an initial conclusion about a situation that turned out not to be accurate.

Step 2—Paired Discussion: Discuss the following questions: What did it feel like to be unfairly judged on such minimal information? What caused you to revise your own initial first impressions about the situation?

Communication and Feedback

chapter EIGHT

Communication and feedback go hand in hand as an essential part of every relationship. Important aspects of building bridges between individuals include: the ability to listen well, without pushing our own agenda; the ability to present feedback in a positive, non-critical way; the ability to communicate clearly so there is a shared understanding; and the ability to notice the assumptions and beliefs that interfere with effective communication. It both reduces conflict and increases trust. Effective communication is the element that unifies us in acting on our best instincts and creating shared meaning regardless of our differences.

Providing feedback requires the willingness to take a risk whether or not you know the other person involved in a situation. This is portrayed in Chris Clarke-Epstein's "If You're Not Asked, Keep Your Mouth Shut?" and "Are You Listening?" by Sharon Bowman. The first tale involves being willing to walk up to a total stranger and deliver some uncomfortable feedback. In Sharon's case, the feedback is delivered to someone she knows extremely well—her spouse. She takes a risk by standing up for the type of listening she needs. In Lunell Haught's "The House Guest," we see how her interpretation of events leads to some very different conclusions about her daughter's actions. Well-intentioned directions that lead to an unexpectedly long journey is the topic of "How Far is Far?" by Laura Page. In our last story, we have a humorous look at what happens when communication is carried out over the telephone. John Renesch's "A Fish Tale" demonstrates the power of our assumptions and how they can interfere with our communication. In these five stories, communicating with and giving feedback to others provides endless opportunities for laughter and learning.

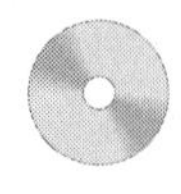

ARE YOU LISTENING? (7)

Contributor

Sharon L. Bowman, director, The Lake Tahoe Trainers Group

Type and Purpose(s)

Vignette; evaluate

Background

Good communication means understanding that people talk and listen in different ways. Sometimes, to make communication work, you have to ask for what you need, especially when the other person has a different way of talking or listening.

Presentation Tips

Use body movement and different voices to depict Jim and Sharon. Consider using the "stepping in" technique (explained in Chapter Five) when Sharon is sharing her inner dialogue.

Set-up

Option 1—People talk, and *listen*, in different ways.

Option 2—When you are conversing with others—at work and at home—how do you show that you're listening?

Are You Listening?

There was a time when I used to get home from work later than my husband. I'd walk into the living room and usually find Jim relaxing in his favorite easy chair watching CNN on television.

After I flopped down on the sofa beside his chair, he'd ask, "How was your day?" What followed was a scene that repeated itself numerous times: I'd start telling him about my day as he kept his eyes focused on the TV. At some point in the conversation, I'd *stop* talking. When he asked why, I'd say, "You aren't listening to me."

"Of course I am," he'd answer. And then he'd repeat everything I had said up to that point.

I would sit in silence and fume. What was wrong? Obviously he'd heard me. So why did I feel slighted?

Then, one day it dawned on me. I didn't *feel* listened to! To me, listening meant *looking* at the other person, making eye contact, nodding your head, and showing through body language that you really understood what was said. To Jim, it simply meant paying attention to the words. Two completely different ways of listening!

The next day I got up the courage to ask for what I needed: "When you watch TV while I'm talking, I don't feel listened to. It would be very helpful if you faced me and looked at me while I tell you about my day." Of course, Jim exaggerated the motions at first—dramatically swinging his legs over the side of the chair, resting his chin on his fist, staring into my eyes, and announcing, "Okay, I'm listening." I let the sarcasm go, told him about my day, and asked him about his. We repeated this scenario off and on for about a month.

One day, a few weeks later, I got home before Jim. I sat in his easy chair, and flipped on the TV. When he arrived home a bit later, he sat on the sofa and I asked him how his day went. As he began talking, I watched the news. Suddenly I noticed a silence. I turned and asked him what was wrong.

"You're not listening to me," he blurted. "Yes, I am," I replied. "No you're not. You're not looking at me while I'm talking," he protested.

Talk about a moment of enlightenment for both of us! Together we realized that he had learned a new way to listen and had gotten used to the face-to-face interaction that I had asked for. Now, a month later, he wanted the same attention—we both had learned to ask for what we needed. In fact, it was something we learned when we were small—"stop, look, and listen."

Debrief Questions

- What did Sharon and Jim learn from this experience?
- What listening barriers were getting in the way of their communication until they made a conscious decision to change?
- Who are people you know who are good listeners? What do they do?
- How do you know when you are listening well to someone else?
- How can being a good listener benefit you in your work and in your life?

Key Point Options

1. Listening is critical to building relationships. Without listening, there is no possibility of understanding.
2. We listen at a rate that is three to four times faster than we speak. This can cause us to lose focus of what someone is saying. While we may be able to repeat the words, we may not have actually paid attention to the person.
3. We often listen with filters that prevent us from understanding the actual intent and meaning of the speaker. Our filters are based on past experiences, current stresses, and habit. Examples of listening filters include your expectations of a

situation, your relationship with the speaker, your current personal situation, and your emotions in the moment.

4. Listening actively is not just about hearing the words. It includes paying attention to the meaning of the words, the speaker's feelings, and the person's non-verbal cues, such as body language.

Follow-up Activity

Step 1—Small-Group Activity: Divide participants into two groups. Assign each group the task of identifying (and posting on an easel page) barriers that get in the way of listening effectively. One group is to identify all the *internal* barriers to listening (for example, personal problems, judgments about the speaker, and so on). The second group is to identify all the *external* barriers to listening (such as interruptions, speaker mannerisms, and so on).

Step 2—Large-Group Activity: Have the groups post their barriers and read them to the whole group.

Step 3—Small-Group Activity: Now have each group identify possible solutions for the *other* group's list of barriers.

Step 4—Large-Group Activity: Have the groups post their solutions and read them to the whole group.

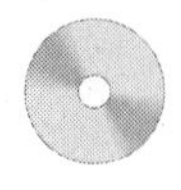

IF YOU'RE NOT ASKED, KEEP YOUR MOUTH SHUT? (8)

Contributor

Chris Clarke-Epstein, CSP, owner, SPEAKING!

Type and Purpose(s)

Vignette; evaluate and encourage

Background

Chris is a consummate observer of human behavior. Her stories have been published in several books about leadership and communication.

Presentation Tips

Consider using the "stepping in" technique (explained in Chapter Five) when sharing Chris's internal dialogue.

Set-up

Option 1—What makes it difficult for us to give feedback in certain situations?

Option 2—There are some life situations when you just don't know if you should give feedback.

If You're Not Asked, Keep Your Mouth Shut?

I was waiting at the front desk of the Phoenix Hilton to pick up a fax. The woman standing next to me was obviously dressed for a special occasion. I saw the rip in the side seam of her dress as I glanced over to check the time. "Now what?" I thought. After a few minutes of internal dialogue that consisted of thoughts like, "It's none of your business," "Someone else will say something," and "Just keep your mouth shut," I leaned over and said, "Excuse me, I'm sure you don't want to hear this, but you have a rip in your dress." A brief look of embarrassment was quickly replaced with a look of gratitude that matched her words, "Thank you so much, I would have been mortified if I had walked into the reception looking like this."

It has happened to all of us. You see yourself in a mirror and realize that you have some of your lunch stuck between your teeth. "Why didn't someone tell me?" you think. It's worse when you've been with friends. "They're supposed to care," you wail. "Why didn't they say something?" And yet when the shoe's on the other foot, when we sense someone's about to put a foot in her mouth or see him march out of the bathroom trailing toilet paper, we usually say nothing. [So my question to you is, "Do you care enough to say something?"]

Clarke-Epstein, C. (1996). "Lie #3: If you're not asked, keep your mouth shut?" *Silence isn't golden: How to unleash the real power of feedback.* Wausau, Wis.: Another Pair of Shoes Press, p. 15. Used with permission. This story may not be reprinted without permission of the original copyright holder.

Debrief Questions

- What risk did Chris take in telling the woman about her torn dress?
- How might the woman have reacted?

- If you were the woman with the torn dress, would you rather be told or not told about the tear? Why?
- What are the elements of good feedback? What needs to be present for it to work?
- When you give feedback, what if the person cannot change the situation? What might make it possible for the person to view things differently and be open to change?
- When is it critical to provide feedback to others in your organization? In your life?

Key Point Options

1. When you do not deliver critical feedback you declare your indifference. If you really do not care, this is no problem. But if your feedback concerns how your organization works, how your customers are treated, or what you are doing right—you need to care. You need to say something.
2. Consider whether you are not saying anything because it would embarrass you to say it or because it would embarrass the other person to hear it. Figure out how to overcome this embarrassment so that others can benefit from your feedback.
3. A useful model for deciding about giving feedback is to ask yourself three questions: Is it true? Is it necessary? Is it kind? If the answer is "yes" to the first two questions, then go ahead and deliver the feedback, as kindly as possible.

Follow-up Activity

Step 1—Large-Group Discussion: Brainstorm situations in which it might be hard to give feedback. List them on an easel or overhead. Then brainstorm elements of effective feedback and list them.

Step 2—Role-play: In groups of three, practice giving feedback. Rotate the roles of Giver, Receiver, and Observer. The Giver selects a situation and plans how to provide feedback. The Receiver reacts to the feedback. The Observer notices how the feedback was given and received and leads a follow-up discussion on what went well, what might have been handled differently, and how it felt to both give and receive this feedback.

THE HOUSE GUEST (9)

Contributor

Lunell Haught, Ph.D., owner, Haught Strategies

Type and Purpose(s)

Imbroglio; evaluate and explore

Background

It is not unusual for Lunell to be ready to go somewhere ahead of time. She was a trainer in county government at the time this situation occurred.

Presentation Tips

As you go through the dialogue about what Lunell is telling herself, you need to work yourself up into a frenzied state until you get to the part where she finds her daughter. Then, slow down the pace and remove all the stress from your voice.

Set-up

Option 1—Sometimes, situations are not what they seem to be.

Option 2—Anxiety and stress left unchecked can put us in surprising situations.

The House Guest

I invited a woman with a great reputation to conduct training with county government leadership staff. She was important to me personally, and was someone who I had tremendous respect for. I can't tell you how thrilled I was to have her join us. Because I wanted my five-year-old daughter, Jenaline, to meet strong, knowledgeable, professional women, I also invited her to stay in my home.

I changed my schedule so Jenaline could meet her plane with me. Being a very punctual person, I was anxious to be on time. I wanted to appear just as competent as my guest and not have any mess-ups on my part. When the time came for us to leave for the airport, I called out to Jenaline. She replied from down the hall that she wasn't ready to leave.

With each passing second, I got more and more anxious. What am I doing waiting for my daughter? She must not care about being on time. How dare she be so rude and lazy! She just can't seem to get it together, which must make me a bad mother. Why doesn't she care about the things I care about? This is going to be awful! My guest is going to arrive at the airport and I'm not going to be there. In my mind, I just went on and on and on about what a bad person I was and what a bad person Jenaline was and how incompetent we were.

Finally, I went down the hall to get her. I'm thinking, "All right, *this is it.* We are going whether you're ready or not." To my complete amazement, I found my daughter in the guest room making a lovely poster to welcome our house guest. There she was with her crayons, creating a wonderful drawing.

Watching her changed my whole perspective. The stress I felt completely disappeared. She *was* doing her part to welcome a guest into our home. She had *indeed* understood how important this person was and was doing *all* the things that I had taught her. In the blink of an eye I went from feeling negative, incompetent, and frustrated to realizing what a special daughter I have. And as I glanced at the clock, I realized we would also be on time.

Then it suddenly dawned on me. I needed to "seek out the truth." While I was busy telling myself one story that *wasn't* true, I was missing out on that one that *was*!

I suspect you've all experienced a situation similar to mine. And no doubt, it'll happen to you and me again in the future! When it does, remember to "seek out the truth."

Debrief Questions

- Why did Lunell become so frustrated? What feelings was she having?
- What was getting in the way of clear communication between Lunell and her daughter?
- When have you been upset or frustrated with yourself or others, only to find that your initial belief was not what was really going on?
- How does acting on such beliefs impact your communication with others?
- How can you prevent yourself from traveling up the Ladder of Inference (see key point option two) in your work and your life?

Key Point Options

1. Often, in our attempts to make sense of the world, we create a set of assumptions in the form of a story to explain what is happening. This directly impacts our communication with others.
2. Author and professor of organization behavior, Chris Argyris has created a model to help us understand our thinking called the Ladder of Inference. An event can be interpreted many different ways by traveling through four levels of reaction.

Level One is the observable data—what happened. Level Two is the meaning or inference you attach to this event. Level Three is the conclusion you reach about the other person's intentions and actions, and Level Four is the underlying assumption or belief that you adopt in order to support your conclusion (Argyris, 1990, pp. 88–89). In this instance, Level One was Lunell's daughter not being ready on time. Level Two was the panic this created for Lunell who was trying to demonstrate her capability to a colleague. Level Three was the conclusion she drew that her daughter was thoughtless, lazy, and careless. Level Four was the underlying question about her own capability as a parent and colleague. This model explains how two people can start with the exact same Level One data and reach entirely different conclusions about what happened and what it meant. Given a new set of data (that is, the welcome poster), Lunell was able to reach an entirely different conclusion about her daughter and herself.

Follow-up Activity

Step 1—Small-Group Activity: Post the four levels of Argyris's Ladder of Inference and have the group develop an example that illustrates each level. Have each small group report on its Ladder of Inference example to the large group.

Step 2—Individual Activity: Outline a Ladder of Inference example for yourself using a real situation that happened to you.

HOW FAR IS FAR? (10)

Contributor

Laura V. Page, managing principal, Page Consulting

Type and Purpose(s)

Vignette; educate

Background

Laura is well-known for her ability to teach interpersonal and organizational communication skills.

Presentation Tips

Exaggerate your vocal inflections and use gestures to demonstrate driving "up the mountain" and "down the mountain."

Setup

Option 1—In everyday conversation, *you* know what you mean. But how do you know that *I* know?

Option 2—In the English language there are multiple definitions for a single word. When talking with others, how do you know which one applies?

How Far Is Far?

I was moving my mother from Illinois to a new home in Florida after the death of my father. I decided to drive Mom down and take a small load of her personal things in a trailer attached to my car. Professional movers had sent the rest of her belongings earlier.

Along the way, Mom and I decided to visit some of my cousins who live in Boone, North Carolina. As we drove through the state, we thought we were getting close. However, we weren't sure *exactly* where Boone was located. So we decided to pull over to a gas station and find out.

I walked in and asked, "Where is Boone?" The young woman pointed out the window to the highway. It was the same highway we had just come off of! She said, "It's not very far." I assumed I knew what she meant, wouldn't you? So I got back in the car with mom and continued to drive. And drive. And drive. We went up a mountain and we went down a mountain. We went through a valley. We went up half of *another* mountain. We went way beyond "not very far." After several hours of driving, we *finally* reached my cousin's house in Boone.

During the time we'd been driving, it had gotten very dark, we'd almost ran out of gas, and my mother had started crying. And you know how I felt? I felt like going back and having a little talk with that young woman! "I heard what you said, but I sure didn't catch what you meant." In our conversations with others, how often can we say we "catch the meaning"?

Debrief Questions

- What do you think went through Laura's mind during the drive to Boone?
- What was the problem? What caused it?
- What might Laura have done differently when she stopped at the gas station?
- When have you experienced a similar miscommunication? What did you do to clear it up?
- How can you make sure your communication is clear and clearly understood by others?

Key Point Options

1. In the casual nature of our communication we tend not to be specific or ask specific questions. This can cause problems in understanding others and in achieving our goals.
2. Communication has not occurred unless there is a "meeting of meaning." Words can be exchanged but they might not lead to a collective understanding.
3. It is helpful to listen for *understanding* rather than *agreement* and to paraphrase what we hear in order to reduce the possibility of missing the meaning of a communication.

Follow-up Activity

Step 1—Individual Activity: Give each person in the group a worksheet with several phrases on it (for example, I'll be there in a little while; don't spend too much time on that; it cost too much; a small wedding; and so on). For each phrase, ask each person to determine a high and a low number that defines for him or her the "value" associated with the statement. For example, "How many minutes—high and low—is *a little while*?"

Step 2—Large-Group Discussion: After each person has completed the worksheet, have individuals share their high and low numbers with you; record them on an overhead or easel. Determine the "range" for each of the statements and discuss the implications.

A FISH TALE (11)

Contributor

John Renesch, business futurist, www.renesch.com

Type and Purpose(s)

Vignette; entertain and explore

Background

This situation occurred several years ago. The interview eventually was completed.

Presentation Tips

Use different voices for the narrator (John) and the executive. There is a pattern to the story (that is, first time, second time, third time) that you may want to emphasize with your voice.

Set-up

Option 1—Sometimes situations are not what they seem to be.

Option 2—Our assumptions can influence our communications with others.

A Fish Tale

As the publisher of the New Leaders Press newsletter, one of my responsibilities was to interview executives for feature articles. On the scheduled day at the scheduled time I phoned a CEO whom I greatly admired. I asked him questions about his company's use of "open book management," and about having an employee-owned organization. The company was a real pioneer and great role model for how well a company can do if you trust people and nurture human creativity. About halfway through the interview he stopped and excused himself for a minute. I heard some muffled noise and figured someone had entered his office for a signature or something similar. When he came back, he apologized. So, I started asking questions again. Besides making enough to payoff an LBO loan, I wanted to explore the hows and whys of his company's spin-off of dozens of other ventures in which they held an interest.

Soon afterwards he excused himself a second time. Once more I heard muffled noise in the background. I found myself getting slightly irritated even though I understood the life of a busy executive. When he came back, he apologized again and we continued the interview.

Then it happened a third time! This time when he returned, he said, "Excuse me, John, but I got a really good fish on the line here." Suddenly it dawned on me. How was I to know he was sitting in the middle of a lake in a rowboat with a fishing line in the water while he was talking to me on his cell phone?

In your communications, you need to "find the fish"—the fish that reflect your assumptions about what's happening on the other end of the phone line—and the fish that distract you from listening. The next time you're on a phone call, count the fish that you catch!

Debrief Questions

- What assumptions did John have about the conversation with the executive?
- How did these assumptions influence his reactions to the interruptions?
- When have you been in a situation where someone else was distracted? What was that like for you?
- What communication assumptions exist in your organization?

Key Point Options

1. Our assumptions are not always accurate; however, they do influence our behavior and responses to others.
2. When we act on our assumptions, we often hinder good communication.
3. Communication is composed of the words we speak, the tone of voice we use, and the non-verbal behaviors we engage in. Over the telephone, we miss a significant portion of what is being communicated. The less actual data we have during communication, the more likely we are to create a potentially false view of what is occurring.
4. Distractions (both face-to-face and over the telephone) also interfere with effective communication. This is a continuing challenge for virtual teams.

Follow-up Activity

Step 1—Small-Group Discussion: Discuss what sort of "fish" (that is, distractions) get in the way of your communication with others.

Step 2—Large-Group Discussion: Have each group share their distractions. Have people talk about how these "fish" interfere with work and what can be done to reduce their impact.

chapter
NINE

Customer Service

As you know, companies do not define service—customers do. Stories about good and bad service are often repeated and always remembered. At the heart of every customer service experience are the values of the customer. Upholding these values is the challenge of every individual and organization that provides service to others. These seven stories explore when a customer's values are beautifully served and the times when they are not. These service stories will elicit your own examples and remind you of the importance of putting the needs of your customers first.

Our first story takes us back to the fundamental beginnings of our values around service—the value of a smile as portrayed in Joe Barnes's "It's the Little Things That Count." "You Don't Qualify for the Senior Discount" by Laura Page, Robert McIlree's "The Customer Strikes Back," and Marcy Fisher's "I Was Aching for a Fight" all depict strong reactions by customers to how they were treated. Laura's reaction to an employee who followed a policy too literally was to leave the garden center without her prospective purchases and never to do business with the store again. Robert and his friends' responses were meant to retaliate light-heartedly on the unhelpful and unsuspecting store clerk. In Marcy's situation, she expected to be be poorly served and was both mollified and gratified by encountering a skilled and helpful customer representative. Each of these stories shows the power of one individual in shaping another's perceptions of customer service.

Two of the stories demonstrate the influence of organizational culture on shaping the delivery of service. "Sorry, We Can't Do It" describes the frustrating internal service barriers Shelley Robbins encountered when trying to get assistance from another department. In contrast, "Ladies and Gentlemen Serving Ladies and Gentlemen" by Chip Bell is a stellar example of an employee clearly knowing and articulating his organization's vision for customer service. Our final story is a beautiful example of exceptional service. In "The Taxi Driver," Sivasailam "Thiagi" Thiagarajan and his family receive an unexpectedly welcoming taxi ride even though warned repeatedly to take other transportation. Meeting customers' expectations for service means paying attention to the values of our customers and establishing systems around the business of serving those values.

IT'S THE LITTLE THINGS THAT COUNT (12)

Contributor

Joe Barnes, managing partner, Communications Success

Type and Purpose(s)

Vignette; evaluate

Background

On a business trip to Phoenix to do some training, Joe experiences the power of something as simple as a smile.

Presentation Tips

Consider telling this story in the first person (that is, as "Joe") and using the "stepping in" technique described in Chapter Five.

Set-up

Option 1—It is the little things in life that we often miss the most.

Option 2—When we write a letter, we sign it. The same is true in customer service—it also has a signature.

It's the Little Things That Count

After twelve hours of air travel, I had finally arrived and checked into my hotel in Arizona. Hearing my stomach growl, I hurried across the street to a convenience store to get some pretzels and a soda. While there, I noticed two store clerks smiling and joking around with each other. As I strolled back to the hotel, I had a revelation as I thought about my day.

It had started before the crack of dawn at a hotel in Pullman, Washington. I remember the front desk clerk being helpful. So was the van driver who took me to the airport as well as the airport personnel who assisted me through security. Yet, something was missing.

The flight attendant who served me on my flight at 6:00 A.M.—she seemed very nice. And, throughout two flights—the agents at the counter, even the attendants at the gate—they had all been very helpful. Yet, something was missing.

It wasn't until I boarded the shuttle van early that afternoon that I remembered seeing my first smile of the day. It was on the face of the van driver who took me from the airport to my hotel. The second one I received was from an elderly woman passenger who disembarked at a Christian residence center. She left all of us with a very warm smile as she departed the van.

Seeing these smiles made me wonder. . . . What's happened to the little things in life? Those that are the most worthwhile? A warm look, a kind word . . . a smile. At the end of the day, when all is said and done, "service is a smile." How many smiles have you received—or given out—today?

Debrief Questions

- What made an impression on Joe during his day?
- How did seeing a smile change Joe's day?
- In customer service, what does a smile convey? Why do customers notice when it is absent—especially if they are receiving good service in its absence?
- What is the difference between "service with a smile" and "service is a smile?"
- How do you react to seeing a smile when you are the customer? What difference does it make to you?
- How does a smile add to what you do? Where in your job is it especially important to have one?

Key Point Options

1. Businesses that want to succeed place a premium on a *smile* as part of their service philosophy. This true story illustrates the importance to a customer of both seeing a smile and not seeing a smile.
2. In this era where customers have numerous options and vote with their feet, a smile can make all the difference. Statistics from the Technical Assistance Research Programs (TARP) in Washington, D.C., state that only one out of twenty-seven dissatisfied customers will actually complain. Fully 65 to 90 percent of your non-complaining—but dissatisfied—customers will not use your service again (1980).

Follow-up Activity

Step 1—Small-Group Discussion: How can organizations convey the importance of a smile to their frontline service personnel? What does your organization do to ensure good "service with a smile"?

Step 2—Large-Group Discussion: Lead a discussion on strategies for reinforcing a service philosophy throughout an organization.

LADIES AND GENTLEMEN SERVING LADIES AND GENTLEMEN (13)

Contributor

Chip Bell, senior partner, Performance Research Associates, Inc.

Type and Purpose(s)

Credibility; explore

Background

One of the companies with whom Chip has consulted is The Ritz-Carlton Hotel Company headquartered in Atlanta, Georgia. Ritz-Carlton is an organization with a compelling sense of vision, a common sense of direction, and a shared picture of who they are and what they are about. Such organizations are able to communicate this picture in a way that everyone in the organization understands, believes, and takes inspiration. Such a vision creates aligned energy that gives guests consistency and trust.

Presentation Tips

Use different voices and body movement to depict the two characters, rather than saying "he said, she said."

Set-up

Option 1—How well does your organization operationally define its expectations for staff?

Option 2—When it comes to customer service behaviors, what sorts of compelling pictures does your organization paint for its employees?

Ladies and Gentlemen Serving Ladies and Gentlemen

The Ritz-Carlton Hotel Company headquartered in Atlanta has won the Malcolm Baldrige National Quality Award twice—once in 1992 and again in 1999. They won it not because they have great quality, but because they have *consistently* great quality, no matter which of their hotel properties you visit. No matter which of their employees you deal with, you can count on a consistent, predictable Ritz-Carlton "feel." I remember asking the CEO, "How are you able to achieve such incredible consistency?" He responded, "We make sure that the promise we make to our guests is a picture all of our associates can relate to."

One day I'm thinking, "You know, I should really check this out." I had just come from a stay at the Ritz-Carlton in Washington, D.C., and was on my way to the airport. The young man driving the hotel town car also happened to work the bell stand.

As we're riding along, I ask, "Tell me what it's like working at the Ritz-Carlton." "Oh," he said, "we are ladies and gentlemen serving ladies and gentlemen." I reply, "I beg your pardon?" He repeats himself, "We are ladies and gentlemen serving ladies and gentlemen."

I ask, "What does that mean?" He then begins to paint the picture for me. "It means that how I look is important—that my uniform is pressed and my shoes are shined. If I'm a gentleman serving ladies and gentlemen it means that when I'm doing something nice for a guest and they say 'thank you,' I would never say 'no problem.' Have you ever thought about that phrase? It's going be a 'serious problem' . . . but for you, 'no problem.' Why would we talk to someone in the negative? At the Ritz-Carlton, we respond with 'certainly' or 'my pleasure.' It also means that when a guest asks for directions that I would never point. Instead, I would say, 'It would be my pleasure to escort you there.' And, when a guest brings me a problem, I own that problem until the problem is resolved."

In just a few moments, the hotel bellman had painted a very clear picture of what it means for ladies and gentlemen to serve ladies and gentlemen. How could I *not* be impressed? How about you? How can you "paint a picture" of great service in your organization?

Debrief Questions

- What was the *consistently great service* referred to in the story?
- What stood out in this employee's description of his job?
- What does this story mean to you?
- How do you define the mission of your job?
- What are your organization's vision and values around customer service?
- How can your organization communicate its vision and values regarding customer service in a way that is compelling and consistently shared among all employees?

Key Point Options

1. Painting a picture—accessing visual images versus just words—is a powerful way to communicate core values in an organization. When we share a common picture that we can relate to personally, we can also act collectively.
2. It is the role of leadership in every organization to communicate a powerful and compelling picture of customer service. The Ritz-Carlton Hotel has translated a key phrase—"ladies and gentlemen serving ladies and gentlemen"—into specific behaviors that all associates understand and carry out.
3. When employees know and understand their organization's customer service vision and values, they are free to act with more initiative and confidence on behalf of the organization.

Follow-up Activity

Step 1—Small-Group Discussion: Have each person identify a situation in which he or she experienced exceptional service. Then answer: What occurred? What made it exceptional? Have the small group select one of the examples to report to the entire group.

Step 2—Large-Group Discussion: Have each group share its example and the answers to the questions for this situation. As a large group, list the characteristics that made the service examples exceptional on an easel or overhead. After compiling the list, discuss how these characteristics might be demonstrated by the organization that employs them.

I WAS ACHING FOR A FIGHT (14)

Contributor

Marcy Fisher, former vice president, Organization Development and Human Resources, Shell Technology Ventures, Inc.

Type and Purpose(s)

Imbroglio; evaluate and explore

Background

Prior to this incident, Marcy had had several negative customer service experiences with this department store, as outlined here. It was these experiences that led to her response.

Presentation Tips

Portray Marcy as angry and ready for a fight and the story clerk as cool, calm, and collected.

Set-up

Option 1—How do you prepare for the possibility of confrontation?

Option 2—Catching someone off balance can impact the outcome of an interaction.

I Was Aching for a Fight

One day while fixing the garbage disposal, I broke the allen wrench that I had just purchased at a major department store. Given the hassles I'd experienced in the past with this store, I got myself really angry and really pumped up. Not more than two months earlier, it took five phone calls to get a repairman out to the house to do warranty work on my new garage door opener. First, he missed two appointments. And then when he finally did show up, he said, "I'm not leaving until you pay me!" The nerve of that guy! I had to place a call to the store manager to get him to leave my house.

And then there was the incident with my new refrigerator. I carefully measured the size of the opening for it—even checked it twice! Three weeks after I ordered it, it came alright—only it was two sizes wider than what I'd ordered. The delivery guys wouldn't even help me put my old refrigerator back in place. When I called about the mishap, customer service said they sent the larger model because the one I wanted was on back order. Finally, four weeks after the wrong model was sent, I got the refrigerator I wanted.

When I got in the car, I knew I was in for a fight. Defiantly, I walked into the store and over to the hardware department and boldly set the tool on the counter. Ready for an argument, I gave the clerk my story. "My new garbage disposal seized up on me. So I got the booklet that came with it and found the instructions on how to fix the damn thing. I put this wrench exactly where it tells you to and pushed hard—just like it said to do. Look at this thing—it snapped in two, right in my hand. See the bruise I got? My hand flew back and hit the back of the cupboard." In a very pleasant manner, she said,

"Oh, I'm so sorry. I'd be happy to replace the wrench for you." Her response took all the air out of me. I was so surprised that I didn't quite know how to respond. In fact, I actually tried to start an argument with this woman about giving me a new allen wrench. I was convinced that returning the tool would be a difficult situation. She just kept saying, "No, ma'am. Really. I *want* to replace it." And she did. How could I have known that I would leave with *two* gifts: the new allen wrench and the experience of being treated well despite my best efforts to pick a fight?

When faced with angry customers, "go for the gift." Search for the opportunity to extend a higher level of service. While it may be a challenge—in the moment—to treat customers better than they're treating you, it is truly a gift you can—and need to—give them in order to recover the situation. Try it the next time you have an angry customer.

Debrief Questions

- How did Marcy's expectations influence her actions during this encounter?
- What did Marcy learn from this experience? How did her expectations change?
- What did the service provider do to defuse a potentially difficult situation?
- When have you had to go beyond the basic customer service response to provide a more advanced level of service? How did you handle that situation?
- What might customers be feeling if they were not able to have the fight they prepared for?
- How can you ensure that your customers are satisfied?

Key Point Options

1. As customers, we have to be careful how we prepare ourselves for potential conflict because we may not be paying attention to what is going on in the moment. Thus, we may miss the opportunity to resolve a conflict before it escalates.
2. As service providers we need to realize that even when a customer problem is handled skillfully, customers may or may not be able to let go of the anger they are feeling. Customers may need to *tell their story* and *get angry.* At that point, our job is to listen fully and let them vent. Before customers can be moved to a problem-solving mode, they may need to get angry, verbalize their feelings, and believe that they carried out what they had planned. The subtlety of providing this type of support is really an advanced level of customer service skill.
3. Customer follow-up can help ensure that a customer truly is satisfied with the outcome of a complaint. Do not be afraid to *ask* customers what they want, what would make the situation better, and what they expect of you and others.

Follow-up Activity

Step 1—Role-play: In groups of three, practice defusing difficult customer situations. Rotate the roles of Customer, Service Provider, and Observer. The Customer should select a situation that has happened frequently or is difficult to handle, introduce the problem, and play the role. The Service Provider should handle the Customer's problem as skillfully as he or she can, with a goal of providing exceptional service and defusing the Customer's anger. The Observer should notice the skills the Service Provider uses and the impact on the Customer.

Step 2—Small-Group Discussion: After each role-play, discuss what the Service Provider did well and might do differently. How did the Customer feel at the end of the role-play?

THE CUSTOMER STRIKES BACK (15)

Contributor

Robert McIlree

Type and Purpose(s)

Vignette; entertain and evaluate

Background

Bob and his friends were out of town on business during this incident, and had never been to this particular store before. It is a part of a nationwide chain that is open twenty-four hours a day.

Presentation Tips

Use different voices for all five characters. Portray the clerk as preoccupied and snotty.

Set-up

Option 1—As a customer, how do you get someone's attention when you need help?

Option 2—Never doubt the creativity and perseverance of well-intentioned customers.

The Customer Strikes Back

I was with several colleagues in Dallas, doing a computer upgrade project over a long holiday weekend. Because of some problems at the client site, we hadn't really slept in twenty-four hours. On Saturday evening, Paul, Jim, and I left around nine o'clock to get some dinner. On the way, Paul asked us to stop at a local drugstore.

He approached a clerk who appeared to be wasting time behind a counter and spoke up, "Excuse me. I need some help." She ignored Paul and continued what she was doing. He said again, a little louder this time, "Excuse me. I really need some help." Sighing deeply, she turned around and barked, "Can't you see I'm busy?" You could hear her gum cracking as she chewed. Trying one more time, Paul said, "Where can I find dermatological soaps?" As though Paul were completely clueless, she dismissed him with, "I have no idea. You'll need to look around yourself."

Well, you can imagine our collective fury. How *dare* she respond so rudely to a simple request for help? She obviously placed no value on Paul's needs. At that moment, Jim's face lit up. "Hey, I know how to get us some help. I used to work for a chain of stores just like this years ago. See those house phones? I think I remember how to gain access to the PA system. Go stand by a phone. I'll use this one. I'm going to dial 1, 2, 3. If you hear my voice, follow my lead."

Not more than thirty seconds later, over the loudspeakers throughout the store came Jim's words, "Customer in aisle four needs help with douche bags." Following close behind was Paul's voice. "Customer in aisle six needs help with incontinence products." By this time, you could hear the store manager running up and down the aisles, screaming, "Who's doing this? What's going on?" My voice came last. "Customer in aisle three needs help with condoms." The store manager went wild.

Then it hit us. The store's security cameras might have caught us on tape! We could get thrown out just for being vocal customers who couldn't get any help. We quickly flew out the door to continue our quest for soap and a good meal. Score one for the customer, zero for the store. We had struck back.

In my world, the hallmark of good service is to "value the voice" of the customer. Is it yours?

Debrief Questions

- What did you think of Bob, Jim, and Paul's responses in this situation? Why did they take such pleasure in what they did?
- How might the store clerk have handled the situation more effectively?
- What does this story tell us about customers and customer service?
- When have you been poorly served? What did you do about it?
- How can you handle a customer that is doing something inappropriate because he feels he hasn't been well-served?
- How can your organization ensure that its customers are well-treated?

Key Point Options

1. When you fail to provide good service, you never know how a customer might respond. Some will walk away without saying anything and never come back. Others will complain to the service person, to management, or to the head of the organization. Still others will use their ingenuity to strike back, sometimes at the expense of the company.
2. Customers define the experience of being well-served or not. To truly know how your service measures up, you need to ask your customers for feedback.

3. Do not assume that an isolated incident of poor service does not matter. Credibility and a reputation for excellence are precious assets that can easily dissipate due to the actions of only a few employees.

Follow-up Activity

Step 1—Large-Group Discussion: Brainstorm customer requests, attitudes, and behaviors that are difficult to handle. Post them on an easel page or overhead.

Step 2—Role-play: In groups of three, practice handling these types of customers. Rotate the roles of Customer, Service Provider, and Observer. The Customer should select a situation that has happened frequently or is difficult to handle, introduce the problem, and play the role. The Service Provider should handle the Customer's problem as skillfully as he or she can, with the goal of providing exceptional service and defusing the Customer's anger. The Observer should notice the skills the Service Provider uses and the impact on the Customer.

Step 3—Small-Group Discussion: After each role-play, debrief by discussing what the Service Provider did well and what he or she might do differently. Ask the Customer how he or she felt about the interaction.

YOU DON'T QUALIFY FOR THE SENIOR DISCOUNT (16)

Contributor

Laura V. Page, managing principal, Page Consulting

Type and Purpose(s)

Vignette; explore and evaluate

Background

This story can be used to illustrate concepts related to customer service strategy, trust, and perception.

Presentation Tips

Present the clerk as highly suspicious in her tone of voice and mannerisms. Laura's voice starts out calm and escalates to anger.

Set-up

Option 1—How do you know if you can trust a customer?

Option 2—It only takes one incident to change a customer's future buying habits forever.

Option 3—What impact can internal policies and procedures have on customer service?

You Don't Qualify for the Senior Discount

After retiring to Florida for a few years, my mom moved to a large, assisted-living home that was not far from a really nice garden center in the same town where I lived. Periodically, I would stop in to buy flowers and gifts. The Tuesday before Easter, I gathered several hundred dollars' worth of bulbs, planters, and potting soil for Mom and the other the residents.

When I got to the check-out counter I noticed a sign that said: "Tuesdays—10% off for seniors." I asked the clerk, "Could I please have the 10 percent discount for seniors? I'm buying all this stuff to donate to the senior center across the street where my mom lives. I would be happy to get the receipt signed by the activity director so you have a record of my donation."

She stared at me like I was a criminal and said, "No, we can't do that." "Why not?" I asked. She retorted in a suspicious manner, "You're not a senior, so you don't qualify. How do we know that this is just for seniors?" I was shocked. I couldn't believe her actions. I protested, "Well, I'm not buying it all for myself or to be reimbursed! This is a charitable gift for them."

"Well, how do I know that you're telling the truth?" she continued, in a dismissive tone of voice. "Well, that's why I'll go get a signature from the activities director," I explained, getting angrier by the minute. "How do I know you're not making that up?" she continued in the same vein. At that point, in sheer disgust at the clerk's harshness towards me, I walked out leaving the merchandise on the counter.

Besides not making the purchase, I've never gone back to this garden center. And I've told tons of people this story. Her actions told me that the clerk clearly didn't trust me, even though I was trying to be charitable. I wonder if the owner of the garden center knows what happened or would have granted the discount. In fact, I wonder if he knows that when it comes to customer service, "every action counts."

Debrief Questions

- Poll the participants: How many think that the clerk should have given Laura the discount? Why or why not?
- What was the store's intention for having a senior discount on Tuesdays?
- What were the beliefs and values from which the garden center was operating? Answer: It does not want to be cheated.
- If the clerk felt that she had to say "no," what could she have done to keep Laura as a customer?
- What kind of training might the clerk have needed in order to handle the situation more effectively?
- How many customers do you think actually take unfair advantage of this garden center?
- What would you have done if you had been the customer in this situation?
- What happens when organizations set up their customer service systems based on a lack of trust in their customers?
- What service policies in your organization cause customers to question your company's commitment to service?
- How important is each individual service person in creating the reputation of a company?

Key Point Options

1. The way Laura reacted was very typical of customers. The research shows that people tend to tell negative stories about service nine to twenty times (TARP, 1980). They tell negative service stories far more often than they tell stories about good service.
2. The garden center lost Laura's business for the future because of one bad experience. Each interaction with a customer creates a continuing perception that impacts all future actions of that customer. An organization's business is dependent upon each and every interaction.
3. How an organization views its customers forms the basis for setting up customer policies. When policies are too inflexible, the benefit they are trying to ensure becomes a liability. When an organization makes a policy based on the 2 or 3 percent of the customers who will cheat it, the organization ends up treating 100 percent of its customers like criminals. As a business, it hurts to be cheated, but the number of people who actually engage in this behavior is small. When people are given the benefit of the doubt, they appreciate it.

Follow-up Activity

Step 1—Large-Group Discussion: Identify specific responses the clerk might have used to communicate the store's policy without alienating the customer.

Step 2—Small-Group Discussion: Ask participants to tell similar stories that have happened to them. Then have the small groups answer the following questions: What were the results of these incidents? Have they continued to use these service providers? In hindsight, how could the service provider have handled the situation more effectively?

SORRY, WE CAN'T DO IT (17)

Contributor

Shelley R. Robbins, Ph.D.

Type and Purpose(s)

Vignette; explore and evoke

Background

This incident illustrates the frustration of dealing with an attitude of "we follow our policies" versus "we serve the customer."

Presentation Tips

Shelley's tone of voice is one of complete surprise and frustration. The voice of the marketing department is very matter-of-fact. Consider also using body movement to depict the characters.

Set-up

Option 1—People's choices and responses regarding customer service are often deeply embedded in an organization's culture.

Option 2—On a scale of one (excellent) to five (poor), how would you rate this response to a request for assistance?

Sorry, We Can't Do It

My role at the university was to develop continuing education programs. I was responsible for coming up with the programs, finding and hiring instructors, and scheduling course offerings on the calendar.

When it came time to create the brochures to advertise the first program, I sought out the assistance of the marketing department. I met with the marketing staff and said, "I'm new here and I really need your help. Our first program, Leadership in Action, is in three months and I need to get this brochure out in thirty days." The response I received was, "I'm sorry, we can't do it." I was completely dumbfounded. I thought to myself, "Isn't this their job? I thought I was the customer." I decided to take a stand.

So I replied, "Well, why can't you do it?" To which I heard, "We don't have time to do it; we have other projects on the calendar."

Selecting my words carefully, I said, "Well, in order to hold this program, the brochure has to be done. If I don't get the publicity out, I'll have to cancel the program. So I need to go out and hire someone to do this brochure for me." The reply came quickly. "Nope. Can't do that either. We control the budget for outside services. We also control the approval for these services, so . . . no, *we* can't do it and . . . we can't get you help to do it either."

I was left speechless. What was I to do? I cancelled the first program because we couldn't get the brochure out on time. But it suddenly dawned on me. I wasn't only the customer; I was also the supplier—of information. At any given moment, it's important to "know where you stand."

Debrief Questions

- What does this story tell us about the service culture of this university?
- How does this story illustrate internal customer service practices?
- What might you have done if you had been in this situation?
- How do you think *internal* customer service practices impact *external* service?
- What policies does your organization have that might get in the way of meeting customer needs?

Key Point Options

1. People and departments can get so concerned about their policies and procedures that they forget about the needs of their customers.
2. Internal service practices have a direct impact on external service. Often these internal practices are detrimental to an organization and its reputation for service.
3. Despite an individual's best leadership skills, persuading people to get on board may be difficult due to deeply embedded values in the culture of the organization. When an organization acts in ways that prevent innovation and prevent anyone from doing anything differently it can have the unintended result of preventing that organization from being successful.

Follow-up Activity

Step 1—Large-Group Discussion: Which departments in your organization provide exceptional internal service? What do they do to demonstrate that service? How does that make serving your external customers easier?

Step 2—Individual Activity: Reflect and write about what your department can do to provide both exceptional internal and external service.

THE TAXI DRIVER (18)

Contributor

Sivasailam "Thiagi" Thiagarajan, resident mad scientist, QB International

Type and Purpose(s)

Vignette; encourage

Background

Thiagi immigrated to the United States in 1967. This was his first experience with New York City cab drivers.

Presentation Tips

To enhance the storytelling, we encourage you to develop a distinct and different voice for each of the characters. This story is best told using third-person voice.

Set-up

Option 1—With the best of intentions, others may warn us of danger based on commonly held stereotypes.

Option 2—Opening our eyes to the possibilities of the unknown requires great courage.

Option 3—Others' fears and anxieties do not create our own reality.

The Taxi Driver

When I bought airline tickets for my family's trip from India to the U.S., the travel agent told me with a serious look on his face, "In New York, you'll have to transfer from JFK to La Guardia to catch your next flight to Indianapolis. Whatever you do, don't take a cab from JFK."

My wife, my baby son, and I left Bombay on a SwissAir flight that had a full evening layover in Zurich. The next day, a Swiss taxi driver gave us the same warning when he took us from the hotel back the airport: "Don't take a cab from JFK to La Guardia."

During our flight, a nice flight attendant stopped to admire my son. When she found out that we were transferring to La Guardia, she too warned us against taking a cab.

When we landed at JFK, my wife carried our sleeping baby and I dragged a couple of heavy suitcases outside to find a bus. As we stepped out onto the sidewalk, a yellow cab stopped in front of us. The driver immediately jumped out, opened the trunk, grabbed the suitcases, and started loading. I protested weakly and said, "We want to take a bus to JFK." He looked at me sternly and said, with an Irish brogue, "With the baby and all, you don't want the bus. So jump in." Being meek and subservient, I followed his orders. My wife, who was panic stricken, also got in. When he started driving away, I asked the taxi driver, "Shouldn't you start the meter?" He simply said, "Don't worry!" "Don't worry! What does he mean, don't worry? How will I pay the charge?" I wondered.

The taxi driver asked us about where we came from. He wanted to know if we were interested in having him drive us around to see some famous landmarks. Figuring that this was a plot to fleece us, I lied that we had a very tight connection. The taxi driver then insisted that we stop by his apartment because his wife loves saris. So we went. He stopped at a high-rise building, got out of his car, walked over to a wall, pressed a button, and said something. A few minutes later, a cheerful woman rushed out. She admired my wife's sari and wanted to know why I was not wearing a turban. I explained that I was not a Sikh. She invited us in for a drink but I told her about the tight connection.

When we finally arrived in front of the TWA terminal at La Guardia, the taxi driver unloaded our luggage. With a trembling voice, I asked, "How much is the taxi fare?" He winked at me and said, "No charge. Welcome to the USA and enjoy yourself!" Can you believe he said, "No charge"? He taught me the power of a simple act of service—going above and beyond. He added "value at no charge."

Debrief Questions

- What assumptions did Thiagi and his family have about New York City based on all the warnings they had received?
- How were their assumptions turned around by the service they received?
- How do we balance the value of receiving advice based on others' experiences and yet not fall into the trap of assuming our own experience will be identical?
- How does trust relate to customer service?
- What does this story tell you about the relationship between assumptions and customer satisfaction?

Key Point Options

1. Often people form stereotypes of an entire group based on one or two individual experiences. These experiences take on the aura of *truth* and subsequently become very hard to dislodge.

2. It is usually our *first* experiences that form the assumptions that then are applied to all subsequent experiences. These are especially true in customer service situations. Those who provide exceptional service manage the customers' initial interactions with the company.
3. We are each individuals, able to acquire new information and engage in new behaviors. It is important to stay open to the possibility of reframing our original viewpoint.

Follow-up Activity

Step 1—Small-Group Discussion: Think about your own assumptions about service—both those that have proven reliable and those that have not been. When was a time that you needed to change an initial assumption about a service provider? What led to your change in perspective?

Step 2—Large-Group Discussion: Have one or two groups share their examples. How have assumptions helped or hindered you in your life in general? How can you minimize the impact of these assumptions? Do you believe they can ever be completely eliminated?

chapter
TEN

Influence and Motivation

Influence and motivation work hand in hand. Both are about change. Motivation stems from within and impacts how we approach our lives, our work, and the choices we make. When we are internally motivated, the seeds are sown for us to influence others. Influence, typically, is directed toward others, encouraging some type of change in attitude or behavior. Both have a profound effect on people's actions and their reasons for taking them. In these six stories we see a leader's support of employees, the underpinnings of an organization's values and how those values influence others, what drives us to make decisions that others may question, and the willingness of some to change the status quo.

The importance of *awareness* in creating the ability to influence others is highlighted in Jon Preston's "Missing a Golden Opportunity." In real-time, Jon brings awareness of the importance of handling objections to his new sales rep. In his next story, "Upstaged by a Rookie," Jon is faced with a challenge—how to influence a more seasoned salesperson's closing techniques without detracting from his desire to help and to grow their relationship. Both sales representatives were highly motivated to succeed and they did. Joan Gillman tells another story of internal motivation resulting in profound life influence when she accepts "The Volunteer Job." Her experiences lead her to a richly rewarding expanded career.

Three of our stories deal with the difficulties of shifting organization culture. Geoff Bellman writes a well-intentioned memo—titled "The Cobbler's

Children"—on his observations about the human resources department's need to develop its own staff. What transpires becomes company legend. Our next inclusion tells the story of a company "bells and whistles" presentation designed to raise morale and increase customer satisfaction. Referring to earlier times when staff was proud to wear company logo hats, Chris Clarke-Epstein overhears one of the employees comment, "I Haven't Worn My Hat in a Long Time." In our last story, "Who Called This Meeting?" Shelley Robbins makes an ill-fated attempt to address an organization-wide need through the collaborative efforts of several key departments.

While the elements of each can be subtle, both influence and motivation are vehicles through which people relate to each other in the workplace and in their lives. Influence and motivation underscore the need for organizations and individuals to take risks, act with integrity, and take an honest look within.

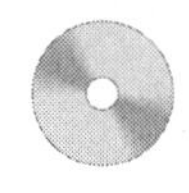

THE COBBLER'S CHILDREN (19)

Contributor

Geoff Bellman, consultant and author of *The Consultant's Calling,* 2nd ed. (2002)

Type and Purpose(s)

Imbroglio; evaluate and evoke

Background

In this experience that he had when he was an internal consultant, Geoff gained valuable insight into how influence and power work in organizations. He has also published *Getting Things Done When You Are Not in Charge* (Berrett-Koehler, 2001).

Presentation Tips

Give different voices to all the characters. Note that each of them displays a different set of emotions and reactions that need to be brought out.

Set-up

Option 1—Sometimes we try so hard to make an impact within an organization that we are blind to the implications of our efforts.

Option 2—How important are influence and motivation in creating change?

The Cobbler's Children

I was invited, as an internal consultant, to an off-site meeting of human resources executives. For some reason I couldn't attend. So, I decided to send a one-page memo, titled "The Cobbler's Children," to about half the people who were invited. The memo was about how "we"—human resources—support the development of people across the company but we don't do that for our *own* people. After I sent it, I went home. Over the weekend, I had chest pains. I couldn't sleep. I questioned what I had done. I worried about the impact on me, and how I would be seen in the organization. I felt as though I were in the right, but had done wrong.

Early Monday morning, my feelings were confirmed. I discovered a note on my desk from the vice president of human resources, asking me to come to his office immediately. As soon as I entered he barked, "What in the hell do you think you're doing to me?" I replied "Doing what to you? I'm not doing anything to you." He continued, "What did you mean by writing that memo and distributing it to people at the meeting?" So I responded, "I'm really concerned that within the department we're not developing ourselves while we're responsible for developing this organization."

He asked, "Why didn't you send a copy of that memo to me?" Being forthright I said, "I only sent the memo to people that I thought would read it and appreciate it and I didn't think that you would." He retorted, "I could have your ass out on the street in five minutes." I said, "I know you could, but you won't." He was taken aback by my comment and asked, "Why not?" I said, "Because I'm too good a performer and you're too good a businessman. *That* would be a foolish action for you to take." He paused and then said,

"Damn it, you're right, but don't ever do that to me again." I said, "I won't," and promptly left. I was shaking but felt we'd had an honest encounter. I was proud of both of us.

Word of my memo spread like wildfire, especially around the thirty-sixth floor, where human resources was housed. A week later I was at the elevator bank talking to a colleague who strongly supported my ideals and was on my side. Just then, the VP of HR came around the corner. When my colleague saw this VP, he stopped talking and moved one elevator away from me. He *physically* moved so that he would not be seen with me. That was *really* hard for me. I felt wounded by one of my own.

A couple weeks later, my immediate supervisor was assigned to work on employee development within the HR function—kind of a secret assignment. He took me aside and said, "I got this assignment from the VP. I wish you hadn't sent that memo, but I want to hear more about it and I want you to help me but you can't tell anyone that you are talking to me about this." So I helped him some and then he gradually kind of buried it.

Ten years after leaving this organization I still received occasional calls from people asking for copies of "The Cobbler's Children" memo. I've even had people say to me, "Remember when you got fired because of The Cobbler's Children?" I wasn't fired but isn't it interesting that story was created? In hindsight, how was I to know that taking thirty minutes to write a memo would make this much difference? Would I do it again today? Yes, but differently. I was politically naïve and should have been more sensitive to the powers surrounding me. As it turned out, the benefits did outweigh the risks I took.

So what about you? As you move forward in your life, when you want to have influence, be willing to "assess the risk."

Debrief Questions

- What was Geoff's intention in writing the memo? What motivated him?
- What are the unintended consequences of his memo?
- What made Geoff's friend move away from him when he saw the vice president at the elevator?
- What did you notice about the impact of influence and power in this organization? What was the impact on employee communications?
- How well do you think Geoff influenced his boss? His organization?
- When has it been risky for you to speak up about your beliefs? What did you decide to do in that situation? How has it impacted your relationships with others?
- In what workplace situations do you think it is important to *speak up,* even if your opinions disagree with senior leadership?
- When might it be better to *withhold* a viewpoint that disagrees with the organization's thinking?

Key Point Options

1. In some organizations, when an employee is considered difficult or out of favor with senior management, others can perceive it as a liability to associate with him or her. In this story, when Geoff's friend moved away from him, Geoff started to better appreciate the dynamics within the company.
2. If you are going to take a risk, make sure you are an exceptional employee that the organization truly needs. Geoff says, "If I had been an average performer my ass would have been out on the street in five minutes. But I was a very good performer and highly respected by my clients. I wasn't a very good department member in human resources, however."
3. Individuals in organizations need to decide when it is important to take a stand on something they strongly believe in. Standing up for what you believe can build a stronger relationship. Geoff felt proud of standing up to the vice president, as well as the VP standing up to him. He says, "We did that pretty well together. That was a foolish thing for me to do, to write that memo. But I was really proud of that encounter with him and I hope he was too."

4. Creating organizational change is a complex process. Numerous stakeholders each have an agenda they are committed to and each have the ability to influence others. Bridging the gap between all these viewpoints takes both vision and skill. In hindsight, Geoff believes, "I wrote [the memo] because my intent was to help the organization basically change. I probably had some ego in there too and was looking for a little recognition for my revolutionary nature. . . . But, I was most interested in helping that organization change. If I were to approach that subject again I would not do that in the way that I did it. I was naïve. I was not respectful enough of the politics and power or the dynamics of the organization. . . . Eventually that was a really important learning for me. It was probably the start of my beginning to appreciate power and politics in an organization. . . . I didn't play very well in recognizing how politics are important in getting things done."

Follow-up Activity

Step 1—Small-Group Discussion: Talk about ways an organization's leadership can promote open communication between employees and management. How can enterprises reduce the negative impact of politics and power and create a culture of positive influence and motivation? How can organizations encourage all employees to contribute their ideas and opinions?

Step 2—Large-Group Discussion: Ask groups to report on their conversations. Lead a general discussion on creating a culture that values honest and open communication.

I HAVEN'T WORN MY HAT IN A LONG TIME (20)

Contributor

Chris Clarke-Epstein, CSP, owner, SPEAKING!

Type and Purpose(s)

Vignette; evaluate

Background

Chris had been asked to consult to this organization and was in the audience during the company's presentation.

Presentation Tips

This story can be told as though it is a mystery that is unfolding. Chris often tells the story, allows for silence at the end, gives participants a break, and tells them that they will discuss the story when they return. The participants will then have had some time to think about the impact of it.

Set-up

Option 1—Leaders will search far and wide for solutions when faced with diminishing results on key organizational measures.

Option 2—Sometimes leaders think they know best!

I Haven't Worn My Hat in a Long Time

The company knew they had to do something. Customer satisfaction ratings were dropping, employee turnover was rising, and nobody wanted to talk about morale. Serious competition was looming. A group of leaders were appointed to do something about the situation and to do it fast. Meeting after meeting produced idea after idea. Consultants were hired and a final decision was reached. We'll create a video that tells everyone why they should be happy that they work here, they decided. We'll prove that the future's bright by showing our grandly produced video to everyone. Spare no expense, they said. Just get it done.

So, the script was written, the actors were hired, and the locations scouted. Production began and money was spent. The final version was shown to the executive team and they beamed at each other. This would do it; things would change now. After all, they had spared no expense.

Employees were ushered into the meeting room and given plastic cups filled with sparkling grape juice. The lights dimmed and the video began. The music was powerful and the videography impressive. The leaders sitting in the front of the room led the applause and everyone raised their glasses in a toast to the renewed commitment they were certain everyone in attendance felt. People filed out of the room talked about their weekend plans. That's when I heard him say, "I can't believe they're trying to get us to put our hats back on with that crap!"

No one else seemed to hear his comment. Curious, I followed him out of the building and asked, "What hat?"

"Oh," he replied offhandedly, "When I first started, fifteen years ago, we all had hats with the company's name and logo. I was like most guys; we wore them all the time. We wanted everyone to know where we worked. We were proud to work here. I haven't worn my hat for a long time." [What would make you "wear your hat"?]

Debrief Questions

- What do you think were the assumptions these leaders made about how to improve their business situation? About how to motivate their employees?
- What is preventing the employees in this situation from speaking up about how they really feel? What are the organizational dynamics operating in this situation that impact the company's ability to influence its employees?
- Based on this story, what do you think the prevailing organizational values are in this company?
- What motivates you in your work?
- Who is responsible for morale and motivation in an organization?
- What makes you proud of working for your organization?

Key Point Options

1. Just as customers define whether or not they have been served, employees define motivation and morale. A company that *tells* its employees why the organization is a good place to work is never as powerful as one that *asks* employees what they appreciate about the company and then follows through.
2. The fear of repercussion often keeps employees from speaking up about what they are observing in the organization and how they are feeling. An organization's efforts to influence employees are often derailed by this fear.

3. Often frontline employees are the first to be aware of problems affecting an organization. When organizations cut themselves off from direct employee feedback, they run the risk of operating with less-than-current information. This places the organization at a distinct competitive disadvantage.

Follow-up Activity

Step 1—Large-Group Discussion: Ask participants to create a list of all the benefits, programs, and services that a company provides to motivate, reward, and recognize its employees and create positive morale (such as a pension plan, profit sharing, company picnics, holiday parties, free parking, choice in health insurance carriers, bonus time off, and so on.)

Step 2—Small-Group Discussion: Have participants review the list and state which items are particularly motivating for them and which are not. Ask them to notice what they have in common with each other and what is unique to one or two members. Key point: Employees differ in what they consider motivating in the workplace.

Step 3—Large-Group Discussion: Discuss ideas for what your company can do to build morale among employees.

THE VOLUNTEER JOB (21)

Contributor

Joan Gillman, director, Special Industry Programs, University of Wisconsin-Madison, School of Business

Type and Purpose(s)

Vignette; engage and encourage

Background

Joan was promoted to director of the Small Business Development Center after two years as a program director so she needed to develop many new skills in addition to learning her new job responsibilities. The changes described in this story have taken place over a ten-year period of time.

Presentation Tips

Incorporate drama into telling this story. Express the emotions that are implied—trepidation at the beginning, and enthusiasm and appreciation at the end.

Set-up

Option 1—What can happen when we open ourselves up to opportunity?

Option 2—A single decision can significantly change the course of one's life.

The Volunteer Job

What was I doing? At age forty I had gone back to school to get my master's degree in health services administration—a complete change from being a full-time art teacher, researcher, and mom. Now, two years later, I was starting a new job as the director of the Small Business Development Center at UW-Madison, which I knew was really going to stretch me professionally. On top of this I had just agreed to volunteer five to ten hours a week as secretary for a national organization of people teaching entrepreneurship—and whose executive director had just quit.

I think it was the travel. When Alan, the association's president, mentioned that the organization would be meeting in Vienna in three years and that it would pay for one national and one international conference a year, I was thrilled. My new job only offered travel in the state of Wisconsin. And so I decided to take a chance, even though my friends and colleagues all thought I was nuts to take on this volunteer role in addition to my new full-time work.

Five to ten hours a week working as a volunteer was an understatement. There was *so much work* to be done in the association. My assistant and I needed to expand membership *and* clean up data *and* set up a record-keeping system. Then we were pushed to start running national meetings and expanding grants from zero to over half a million dollars.

I could have walked away from this volunteer work early on. That's what I suspect most people would have done. But some interesting things started to happen that I had absolutely no idea would occur.

I found I was learning and growing tremendously. Within two years, I was named the executive director of the association. Several years later, it became a paid position. From here, my network rapidly expanded. This opened up amazing opportunities for new friendships, new colleagues, and new opportunities—both nationally and internationally—like teaching in Hungary, consulting in Eastern Europe, and speaking in Saudi Arabia and the United Arab Emirates.

The travel? It's been beyond my wildest expectations. Little did I know all the places I would visit besides Vienna—places like Strasburg, Stockholm, Singapore, Sidney, and Taiwan. On one trip, I even got to attend a private concert given by the musical artist I most adore—Tony Bennett.

In hindsight, would I take a chance like this again? Absolutely. Choosing to volunteer as the secretary of the association was the one decision that has been the most beneficial to my career. It's really changed my life.

Every request for help and every opportunity in life—no matter how much work it might entail—often has a gift hidden inside. You just need to be willing to "take a chance." How willing are you?

Debrief Questions

- What do you think about Joan's initial decision to take on the executive director role at the association? What influenced her decision?
- What does this story tell us about the nature of opportunity?
- What does this story mean to you?
- What decision would you have made if you were Joan?
- What can we do to become more open in our lives to the opportunities that present themselves to us? What can we do to allow them to influence us?

Key Point Options

1. Opportunities are choices presented to us on an almost daily basis. Allowing these opportunities to influence us can open new vistas. Knowing what motivates us enables us to recognize a choice for the opportunity it truly is.
2. Opportunity often comes packaged with a lot of work. It takes motivation to seize such an opportunity and make the most of it. Only by acting on opportunities can we realize their benefits.
3. In this story, Joan experienced a series of events that some would call "synchronicity"—meaningful accidental coincidences. She experienced them because she was receptive to these events and made room in her life for opportunity to take her in different directions. When they occurred, Joan was also willing to search out their meaning and follow through on the possibilities they brought to her. She allowed this opportunity to influence her life. The power of synchronicity lies in being open to possibilities and following through on opportunities.

Follow-up Activity

Step 1—Small-Group Discussion: When have you made a choice or decision that has had an unexpected positive impact on your life? What motivated you to avail yourself of the opportunity?

Step 2—Large-Group Discussion: Ask each small group to tell one of the stories it discussed to the entire group. Ask the following questions: How do you know when to say yes to an opportunity? How can you allow more room in your life for opportunity and yet not get overloaded or neglect other commitments? How can opportunity influence your life?

MISSING A GOLDEN OPPORTUNITY (22)

Contributor

Jonathan M. Preston, senior manager of a major pharmaceutical firm

Type and Purpose(s)

Vignette; educate and evaluate

Background

This situation happened about twenty years ago. Since then, whenever Jon sees a missed opportunity to handle an objection, he tells this story.

Presentation Tips

There are three characters in this story: Jon, Diane, and the physician. The physician shows two different types of reactions—your voice and body language need to change to reflect them. Also reflect with your voice that Jon's coaching is done in a caring manner.

Set-up

Option 1—What is the real purpose of a sales representative in the field?

Option 2—The adage "Silence is golden" is not always the best approach to take when a problem arises.

Missing a Golden Opportunity

As a new sales operations manager, I was given the task of working in the field with Diane, a new sales rep. Together we called on a doctor who was known to be a little abrasive.

Diane did a great presentation on drug A—an antibiotic. He was agreeing with her, and nodding and saying, "I love this drug. I use it all the time. In fact, I wouldn't be here right now if I weren't using it myself." Then she went to drug B—a new class of anti-hypertensives. Right away the physician interrupted her and said, "Excuse me. I will *not* use drug B because it causes orthostatic hypertension and dizziness. I would *never* give it to my patients." On and on and on he went. She paused for a moment, looked at him, and then said, as she turned to her next visual, "Well, how about this next drug?" And on she went to her third product. His response was, "Now there's a drug I use."

Afterwards we went outside and Diane asked how she did. I said, "I guarantee you that that gentlemen will never, under any circumstance, use drug B. He will never use it because you missed a golden opportunity to handle his objections. Think of all the patients who could have used drug B who won't get it because you inadvertently confirmed all of his thoughts by saying nothing." Since Diane was eager to learn, we role-played how she could have better handled the situation. For example: She could have asked the doctor a few probing questions to determine whether his objections were based on his clinical experience—which was highly unlikely since it was a new drug—or on side effects that the competition had told him about. When we were finished, Diane said, "I can't wait to get in to see this doctor again and try out what I've learned."

From that day forward Diane never forgot that "objections offer opportunity"—the opportunity to explore an issue in more depth, to learn a new approach, and to build stronger relationships. In the future, whenever you hear an objection, stop and consider the opportunities it's bringing your way.

Debrief Questions

- What does this story tell us about motivation and influence?
- What did Jon do to influence Diane to learn a new way of looking at objections in the field?
- What is at stake if Diane does not learn to address client objections?
- What motivational issues do sales organizations have? How might these issues differ from those in your workplace?
- How do you go about influencing someone else's behavior or performance?
- In this story, Jon was able to coach Diane, in part because she was motivated. How can organizations coach their employees to become better able to influence others?
- What can organizations do to create a culture of motivated employees?

Key Point Options

1. Good questions can be more valuable than good answers, especially when influencing others. In a sales culture where handling objections is a part of daily work, learning what questions to ask, and then not being afraid to go ahead and ask them, is critical to success.
2. Objections typically fall into two categories: those that are grounded in personal experience and those that are hearsay—that reflect the opinions of others. Opinion-based objections can be handled with facts. Objections based on negative personal experience are more difficult and need to be handled in greater depth. For example, if a physician had a negative patient experience with one of the company's drug products, Jon would probe for more specific information.

He would inquire about the patient—was the person on any other drugs that could have had a negative effect? What were the circumstances, dosages, and so on? It is critical to be willing to explore an objection and handle it, despite the fact that it seems insurmountable. This is at the heart of sales influencing skills.

3. Coaching sales personnel is a judgment call. Jon was told to never jump into a sales representative's presentation. He was coached to talk to the representative after the sales call—and not to steal the presentation or make the representative look bad in front of the client. Jon not only coached Diane but he *role-played* the process to show her how a difficult objection could be handled, which Diane found highly motivating.

Follow-up Activity

Step 1—Individual Activity: Write down as many questions as you can identify that would be helpful in eliciting a client's objections to or dissatisfaction with a product or service.

Step 2—Large-Group Discussion: Based on individual comments, create a list of useful questions that uncover a client's objections to or dissatisfaction with a product or service. For example: What is your main concern about this product? Who else shares this concern? What makes you feel this way? List the questions so all can see them.

Step 3—Large-Group Discussion: Ask the group to identify different types of objections and the kinds of responses a sales or service person could make to effectively handle them. For example, provide documented information, empathize with the client's feelings, and so on. List these items so all can see them. Identify how these responses might influence a client to purchase the product or service.

UPSTAGED BY A ROOKIE (23)

Contributor

Jonathan M. Preston, senior manager of a major pharmaceutical firm

Type and Purpose(s)

Imbroglio; educate and explore

Background

This situation happened to Jon about twenty years ago when he was a new district manager. He and "Bud" are still great colleagues today.

Presentation Tips

All three of the characters in this situation need to be portrayed in a colorful manner through mannerisms, tone of voice, pacing, and so on.

Set-up

Option 1—How do you give feedback to a more senior and seasoned colleague?

Option 2—Are the number of years of work experience a good gauge of someone's skills?

Option 3—It can be challenging to maintain a relationship *and* to let someone know what you think.

Upstaged by a Rookie

Bud had been with the company about twenty-one years when I met him. He's known as one of the legends in our sales force.

In my new role as district manager, I noticed that he had great conversations and great access to his physician clients but when it came to closing the sale, he wasn't ever asking them to *use* the products. I brought it up to him a couple of times and he responded, "They *know* why I'm there. I don't *have* to ask them." So, not wanting to rile him too much, I said, "Okay." And then I thought, "Maybe if I could get an opportunity to show him." And that pretty much was the end of it.

One day we went to see Dr. P. who's one of the most trusted and respected physicians in the area, and someone Bud has great rapport with. Now, it just so happens that some bad press from the competition and outside sources had recently hit the newspapers about one of our new arthritis products. Even though the drug was really a great product, a lot of patients were calling their doctors and asking to be taken off the drug—or, when the doctor tried to put them on it, they refused.

After Bud's presentation, this product came up in conversation. Bud said his usual, "Can we leave you some starters of this arthritis product?" Dr. P. said, "Sure, Bud, you can leave them here." The discussion then turned more social. After they chatted about their kids, there was this pregnant pause. And I said, "Dr. P., can I ask you a question? And he said, "Sure." And I said, "Are you using the new arthritis drug with *all* of your patients that have osteo- or rheumatoid arthritis?" And he said, "Oh, hell no. I don't use this drug in anybody over the age of fifty-five because of the terrible bleeds it causes and all the deaths I've heard about." By the way, the over-fifty-five age group just happened to be the market for this product.

At this point Bud comes unglued. Good thing he had a trusting relationship with this physician because he stands up and says, "What are you doing with all of those starters I've given you?" Dr. P. says, "I'm only using those for people under the age of fifty!" You could hear Dr. P. starting to get very defensive. And then Bud, as only Bud can do, went through the entire litany of all the facts and data about the drug—including all the sources of the negative information. Then Bud asks, "Have I given you enough information now so that you'll commit to using this arthritis drug with people over the age of fifty?" "Of course," Dr. P. says. "Why didn't you tell me all this before, Bud? You have been coming in here for months representing this drug. I believe you, Bud, and I have great rapport and trust in you. I'll go back to using this drug with everybody that comes in with osteo- or rheumatoid arthritis. Thank you for telling me."

When we were done, Bud and I go outside and walk over to the trunk of Bud's car. As Bud reaches into his trunk to get some starters, he looks up at me and says, "Don't you say a thing." From that day forward Bud was one of the best closers I've ever seen. He truly understands that "trust kindles commitment." Only when trust is present in a relationship can either person's behavior be influenced. So, the next time you attempt to influence someone to engage in a particular behavior, remember trust kindles commitment.

Debrief Questions

- Jon wanted to positively influence Bud's selling skills. As the new district manager, what risk did Jon take jumping into Bud's sales call?
- Why did Jon take *this* approach with his salesperson?
- We know how Bud and Dr. P. reacted. However, what *possible* reactions might Bud have had? What *possible* reactions might Dr. P have had?
- How did Jon's coaching affect Bud's motivation to sell?
- How did you feel as you listened to this story?
- When have you wanted to give feedback that you thought might not be appreciated? How have you gone about giving it? How did that work for you?
- Consider how influence and motivation work in organizations, especially in a sales culture. Jon was the new district manager and Bud was an experienced, high-profile salesperson. What organizational politics issues might be present in such a situation? What implications did Jon's actions have for their future working relationship?
- What organizational influence and politics issues exist in your workplace? How do they show up?
- How do you know if someone's actions are for the benefit of the organization or for the benefit of him- or herself? Are these two goals mutually exclusive? Why or why not?

Key Point Options

1. When a new leader comes on board in an organization, the existing dynamics change. Each new manager brings different ideas, skills, and expectations. This always causes a shift—sometimes subtle, sometimes dynamic—in the existing culture. This manager influences the organization in new ways.
2. Everyone uses influence everyday. We can use it for the good of the organization and our customers and to help others and ourselves do their jobs well. Or we can use it to undermine others' success and the success of the organization. Personal integrity is at the core of determining the difference between these differing motivations.

3. Influencing strategies can include the following approaches: *reciprocity*—you get something from someone and so feel obligated; *commitment* and *consistency*—you take a stand on something so you need to act consistent with it; *social proof (comparison)*—we want to be like others who are doing it; *liking*—I know and like you; *authority*—you are a recognized authority and so have credibility; and *scarcity*—it is rare, so it is valuable (Cialdini, 2001).
4. Influence investigates the causes of human change—whether that change is a behavior, an attitude, or a belief (Rhoads, 2002).

Follow-up Activity

Step 1—Small-Group Discussion: Talk about the six types of influencing strategies (stated in the third key point): reciprocity, commitment and consistency, social proof (comparison), liking, authority, and scarcity. What are the pros and cons of each type? Give a situation that illustrates each type of influencing strategy. Why would this strategy work in this situation? Post your responses so everyone can see them. Note: The facilitator might want to have six groups with each group reporting on one style.

Step 2—Large-Group Discussion: Have the small groups report on their discussions. Ask the entire group: What influencing strategies do you see most often used in your organization? What influencing strategy or strategies do you use most often?

WHO CALLED THIS MEETING? (24)

Contributor

Shelley R. Robbins, Ph.D.

Type and Purpose(s)

Vignette; explore and evoke

Background

When Shelley worked as a director of training and human resources development, she often ran into situations when she needed the cooperation and collaboration of people in other departments and areas. What surprised her was that when she tried to get cooperation, other people were not interested even though she thought it was for the good of the company and that everyone shared the same goals.

Presentation Tips

Portray the individuals from the information and technology and sales departments as matter-of-fact and polite, even though they do not express cooperation with their words. Depict Shelley as completely surprised and a bit confused by what she learns.

Set-up

Option 1—What are the dilemmas of being an early adopter of cross-functional teams?

Option 2—It is one thing to believe all employees are working toward the good of the organization; it's another to experience people's true motivations.

Who Called This Meeting?

The results of the company-wide needs assessment were very clear: People were asking for training in how to use word processing, spreadsheets, and other basic computer software. As director of training and human resources development, I knew the organization didn't have a lot of money to buy such training. So, I decided to see what I could organize internally by bringing together the people who had the expertise and the resources.

I invited people in the information and technology department—they had the knowledge. I invited people in the sales training area—they had the facilities and the resources. I also invited people from my department—we were responsible for training.

When I started the meeting, the first thing somebody said was, "Who authorized this meeting?" I was completely stunned. I had no idea this would be questioned. So, I quickly made up a response and said, "My boss, John, authorized this meeting." He was the vice president of human resources so I figured this was a pretty safe reply. In the meantime, I'm thinking to myself, "Here I am. I've discovered this company-wide need and am trying to address the situation. I didn't think I needed a higher authority."

Continuing on, I laid out the results of the needs assessment. "Employees have indicated a need for computer training. Here in this room are all the people in the company who I believe have the knowledge and the resources to help them. I was wondering if we could provide them with training. I'm willing to organize everything if those of you in IT are willing to instruct and those of you from sales training are willing to free up your training room."

I turned to the head of sales training and asked, "Would you be willing to help?" She looked at me and simply said, "No." I inquired, "What do you mean by 'no'?" She replied, very matter-of-factly, "I'm sorry. We aren't going to let you use those training rooms." Then I turned to the people in IT and asked if they could help. They replied, "We would really like to help but we're too busy. And, we have a lot more important things to do. We're sorry, but we won't be able to do this."

They talked a bit longer during which time I tried my best to persuade them. Then it hit me. Neither group was going to change its mind. I walked away and dropped the project. I didn't have a budget to go outside and hire a person or buy the software to do the training. I learned that for projects to have a chance of succeeding, I would need to understand how power and authority play out in organizations. Reflect for yourself. Notice how "power plays" in your organization.

Debrief Questions

- What does this story say about interdepartmental alignment?
- How does this story relate to meeting requests that are to benefit the entire company?
- What else might Shelley have done to influence the group to be more willing to meet these requests? Given the culture, what could she have done prior to the meeting to influence a positive outcome?
- What might you have done in Shelley's situation?
- What do you think are the issues with being an early adopter of cross-functional teamwork?
- How can you motivate and influence others to take an action for the good of the organization when it may personally mean more work?

What are examples of situations in your department in which you have needed to collaborate with other departments to meet internal needs? How have you made that work?

Key Point Options

1. Not seeing the merits of cross-functional teamwork can lead to departments focusing so exclusively on their own goals that they miss meeting organization-wide goals. This tunnel vision is created by the motivations of those involved, and has significant impact on overall success. This is an issue of organizational alignment and clarity of its mission, vision, and values.
2. Sometimes bureaucratic organizations find it is almost impossible to get things done when they need assistance from others. The accepted organizational norms are politically based instead of being based on internal and external customer needs. Influencing these groups to focus on the customer can be exceedingly difficult.
3. "Optimizing the system" in an organization means that each area takes ownership of supporting the needs of the whole organization versus optimizing individual business entities. A key way to optimize any system is through collaboration and feedback.

Follow-up Activity

Step 1—Individual Activity or Groups from the Same Department: On a sheet of paper (or on a prepared worksheet), write down three lists:

- What work is your department responsible for? What motivates you to accomplish this work?
- What departments or groups is your department dependent on to accomplish its work? How can you influence these departments or groups to get what you need?
- What departments or groups depend on your department to accomplish their work? What motivates you to provide good service to them?

Step 2—Large-Group Discussion: What happens when one part of the system breaks down or one part of the system refuses to collaborate?

chapter **ELEVEN**

Leadership

The concept of leadership has an almost limitless number of aspects. From supporting deeply held organizational values, believing in the capability of others, and profoundly influencing those around you, the many faces of leadership shine forth in these five stories. These leaders help create a shared vision of the future with those around them. Take your training participants on a journey of discovery and use these stories to hold out the possibility of further developing their own leadership capabilities.

Bedrock organizational beliefs are at the center of "A Culture Rooted in Gunpowder," by Merrill Anderson, and Katherine Hudson's "The Bamboo Years." Merrill learns how the inception of safety as a fundamental value over a century ago still continues to influence his client's company. In "The Bamboo Years," Kathy is touched by a Japanese customer's commitment to invest in his company's continued growth, even during difficult economic times.

The story contributed by Paula Bartholome illustrates the pitfalls of overlooking the leadership abilities of another. In her story, "Expecting Too Little," the entire board had discounted the possibility of a contribution from a fellow board director. Two of our stories illustrate the impact one individual can have on another in shaping that person's future. They show how mentoring and developing are leadership actions. Kathy Nielsen shares the story of Harry Hopkins's role as key economic advisor to Franklin Delano Roosevelt in "The Worth of a Contribution." In "Fostering Full Potential," LG Shanklin-Flowers shares her experiences in managing a resentful employee and developing her skills to achieve a successful outcome.

Whether individually or organizationally, each of us has experienced the power of leadership in our lives. That power gives us the ability to influence others in profound ways, as well as the ability to realize our true potential.

A CULTURE ROOTED IN GUNPOWDER (25)

Contributor

Merrill Anderson, Ph.D., CEO, MetrixGlobal, LLC

Type and Purpose(s)

Credibility; educate

Background

This situation occurred while Merrill was a consultant working for a professional services firm. Merrill often digs into a company's history to understand present behaviors and decisions.

Set-up

Option 1—Where does an organization's culture come from?

Option 2—How deeply rooted are the various aspects of culture in an organization?

Option 3—Digging deep into an organization's past can uncover surprising revelations about its current practices.

Presentation Tips

Use gestures to depict the gunpowder plant design and how the houses were situated on and around the property.

A Culture Rooted in Gunpowder

Almost immediately after my colleagues and I were contracted to work for a textile manufacturer, the client wrote up two consultants on my team for safety violations. Now, this is fairly serious in this company. Employees who had three safety violations—three write-ups—were terminated. Even if you had *one*, it wasn't considered to be a good thing.

In the eyes of Jim and David—who were the consultants—this was warfare! As far as they were concerned, these two safety violations were trivial. One occurred when Jim was facilitating a client meeting in a conference room with David. David needed a marker to write on an easel. So, Joe threw the marker to him. An employee who attended the session noted this as a violation of safety and security rules and so Joe was written up.

Soon after that it was David's turn. He had just returned from the manufacturing facility and was running down the stairs to get to a meeting. An employee who was in the stairwell noticed this, got his name, and wrote him up. Since these are activities that consultants routinely engage in, Jim and David did not view them as bad. They thought the write-ups were petty—just the client's way of making their jobs more difficult.

I decided to do some digging. This manufacturer had a long, long history dating back to the 1850s—before the Civil War. I visited some of their early facilities, which were part of a state park. Long ago, these facilities were used to manufacture gunpowder. The individual mixing areas had seven-foot-thick walls around them. Behind these walls there was another seven-foot-high wall that an observer could look over. It was obvious that the company wanted to minimize risk to any individual worker and went to a lot of expense to guard their safety.

Past the gunpowder plant, the next building in the complex was, in fact, the plant manager's residence. He and his family lived closest to the mixing mills. And, his managers lived on the hillside, behind his residence. If you continued going up the hill, past a wooded area, you found the spot where the rest of the workers lived. What struck me was that those most responsible for the safety of others were the most vulnerable to the consequences of safety violations.

I came back and shared my findings with my colleagues. There was no doubt in my mind that the emphasis on safety and security was a cherished and time-honored tradition. Safety and security were deeply rooted in "guarding the gunpowder." Jim and David quickly came to understand that what people were really doing—*guarding them from unsafe conditions*—was a lifelong value of the organization.

Your organization has deeply held values, too—that it protects to this day—much like this organization's value on safety. Think about it. What values does your organization guard like gunpowder?

Debrief Questions

- What was your initial reaction to the safety infractions that caused Jim and David to be written up? How might you have responded in the same situation?
- What was this company's value regarding safety?
- How did your opinion of the company's safety culture change once you understood its history?

- What values guide your life? How do these values show in your actions and decisions?
- What does this story tell us about the role of leadership in communicating organizational values?
- How can an organization ensure that its values are clearly understood by its employees?

Key Point Options

1. This example illustrates how having clear, deeply held values in an organization assists in the ongoing implementation of a shared culture of accountability over a 150-year period of time. Employees throughout the organization acted collectively on behalf of these values.
2. Each employee is a leader in carrying out the values of his or her organization.
3. For individuals, core values can form the foundation of a personal mission, helping to guide actions and decisions throughout one's life. For organizations, core values are at the heart of their mission and vision, and directly influence carrying out their purpose.
4. Often our values and the values held by organizations are a function of history. We are all shaped by what we have experienced in our lives.

Follow-up Activity

Step 1—Large-Group Discussion: What deeply imbedded values is your organization committed to? How do these values show in its employee expectations, customer practices, and leadership actions? Post the list of values on one sheet of paper. On a second sheet of paper, post how each value is visibly demonstrated in the organization.

Step 2—Large-Group Discussion: How can an organization's leadership effectively instill shared values with its employees, contractors, and business partners?

Step 3—Individual Activity: Reflect and write on the following questions: What does this mean to my role in demonstrating values and helping to instill them in others?

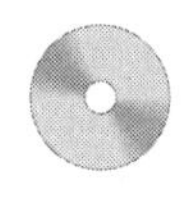

EXPECTING TOO LITTLE (26)

Contributor

Paula Bartholome, principal and corporate jester, Parallax

Type and Purpose(s)

Vignette; encourage

Background

Even though this situation happened a number of years ago its message is timeless.

Presentation Tips

The voice of the volunteer needs to be soft but strong.

Set-up

Option 1—We sometimes don't realize the power of our expectations.

Option 2—Adages in life, such as "If you never ask, you'll never get!" exist for a reason.

Expecting Too Little

I was growing increasingly concerned. I was the board president of a not-for-profit organization that had been around for a long, long time. The vast majority of the organization's funding came from the public sector. This was a problem for two reasons—public monies were coming under pressure and the restrictions on its use were increasing. The only way around this was to engage the board in fundraising—both giving and getting monies—if we were to be credible when asking others for support.

Over numerous objections and amidst a great deal of doubt, the board agreed to host a major fundraiser—a first! Each board member was responsible for buying or selling at least one table's worth of tickets for the event. This amounted to raising $350. Many told me how much of a hardship this was going to be on several of the board members. One person, in particular, was mentioned regularly—a sweet woman who supported herself in a modest job and often baked cookies for the board. It wasn't fair, I was told, to expect her to have the same level of participation as other board members.

Not long after we started working on the plans for the event, I was in the organization's offices. There was a lot to get done and I wanted to be sure that I did my part. I was running from one meeting to another when, on the stairs, I ran into the woman who everyone was so worried about. Her face and her eyes were beaming! I asked where she was going and she drew herself up to her full height and said, "I'm going to the development office to drop off a check!" "Great!" I said, "How many tickets did you sell?" She looked me squarely in the eye and said, with great pride, "Sell? I *bought* my entire table myself!"

You know what? She was the first board member to step up and participate in our major fundraiser. And, nearly ten years later, she's *still* participating in it.

Whether working with volunteers or paid employees, the issue is still the same. To get participation, you need to invite it. In your own work, where might you "invite participation"?

Debrief Questions

- What leadership action did the board president take that so surprised the other board members?
- What meaning does this story hold for you?
- Think of a project you are involved in and/or oversee. In the project, who is like the woman who bought her table?
- Who are the people in your organization who may never have been asked to help with a project? What leadership action on your part might shift that level of participation?
- What do you need to make clear to others so that they can *choose* whether or not to engage?
- What specific words or phrases are helpful in inviting participation from others?

Key Point Options

1. Do not assume people will not be able to participate or volunteer because of their life or work circumstances. Expect others to take initiative and demonstrate leadership and often they will.
2. We sometimes use others' circumstances as a reason not to notice our *own* reluctance to do something.
3. Clearly asking for and inviting participation is an act of leadership.

Follow-up Activity

Step 1—Individual Activity: Think of a project or work that you are involved in where you need to invite participation. Record what you would say to the other person(s).

Step 2—Role-play: In groups of two or three, practice the statements that each of you wrote down. Also assess with your partner(s) what might be preventing you from asking for help from this individual(s) and what you can do to overcome this.

THE BAMBOO YEARS (27)

Contributor

Katherine M. Hudson, president and CEO, Brady Corporation

Type and Purpose(s)

Credibility; educate and encourage

Background

Kathy has a strong belief in the power of stories to build organization cohesiveness and to enhance personal learning. She incorporates stories in all aspects of her work.

Presentation Tips

You may want to use a bamboo plant as a prop.

Set-up

Option 1—When is the best time to invest in an organization's future growth?

Option 2—Bamboo plants can teach us about when to invest in organizations and in ourselves.

Option 3—Let's talk about "the bamboo years."

The Bamboo Years

Earlier in my career [at Eastman Kodak], I had occasion to visit an important customer in Kyoto at the beginning of the Japanese economic crisis. This customer's father had worked very hard to build a successful family business from scratch. Over the years, they developed a strong and loyal relationship with the company I was working for at the time.

At this particular meeting, I was surprised when the customer handed me an order for an extremely expensive piece of equipment. "Given the difficult economic conditions in your country, are you sure you want to make this investment now?" I asked.

He pointed to a large bamboo plant in his office and explained, "[See how it grows? It has long spurts of growth and then it stops for several years.] It's during the times of slower growth that the bamboo plant builds the strong rings that serve as the foundation for its next growth spurt. During that pause, it is wise to make whatever investments you need to make and ready your organization for the future."

I have never forgotten that meeting, and often think of it in executive planning sessions. It seems particularly appropriate in these times of economic uncertainty. [At Brady Corporation, we now refer to these times as "the bamboo years." What are "the bamboo years" in your organization?]

Hudson, K. M. (2001). "Let me tell you a story." *Brady Corporation 2001 Annual Report.* Milwaukee, Wis.: Brady Corporation, p. 3. Adaptations based on presentation given by Katherine M. Hudson, "Fireside Chat," Future Milwaukee, March 20, 2002. Used with permission.

Debrief Questions

- What did the bamboo plant signify to the customer in Kyoto?
- What organizational lesson did the customer derive from the plant?
- How did Kathy transfer that concept to her current company?
- Where in your life have you chosen to focus on the positive future rather than on the current obstacle?
- How were you able to make that shift in perspective?
- What are the bamboo years in your organization?
- What has your organization done to invest in continued growth and development?

Key Point Options

1. By taking a lesson from the bamboo plant, enterprises need to invest during times of slower growth so that they may be better prepared for their next growth spurt and a likely economic slow down and recovery in the future.
2. It is the willingness to take risks, albeit calculated ones, during slow times that leads to future growth.
3. Each person goes through "the bamboo years" in his or her own life. Seeing this as a period of preparation for future growth is the key to moving forward and achieving success instead of stagnating and focusing on failure.

Follow-up Activity

Step 1—Individual Activity: Take ten minutes to think about and write on the following questions: To date, what have been the bamboo years in your life? What have you done to invest in yourself to prepare yourself for future growth? What has been the impact of this investment thus far?

Step 2—Paired Discussion: With a partner, take ten minutes to discuss your responses to the questions from Step 1.

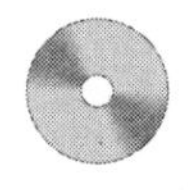

THE WORTH OF A CONTRIBUTION (28)

Contributor

Kathy A. Nielsen, president, Nielsen Associates, Inc.

Type and Purpose(s)

Credibility; encourage

Background

This story addresses people who question what their true priorities are on a day-to-day basis. This is especially significant for those who work in a culture where everything is considered to be of the highest priority.

Presentation Tips

Consider using a gravelly voice to depict President Roosevelt and seating yourself during his dialogue.

Set-up

Option 1—How do you value the worth of a contribution at work, no matter what its size?

Option 2—What factors help to determine a person's top work priority?

Option 3—Time is not a key determinant of the worth of a piece of work or its priority.

The Worth of a Contribution

When Franklin Delano Roosevelt was president, Harry Hopkins was his key economic advisor. Harry, who had a brilliant financial mind, displayed a hard-driving enthusiasm for the New Deal. He also had a "piercing understanding" of war problems. In 1933, as head of the Federal Emergency Relief Administration, he readily tackled the problem of providing immediate relief for the homeless and the hungry. Later that year he put 4,000,000 men to work in less than one month. Yet, Harry was also a severe diabetic. Unfortunately, towards the end of Roosevelt's administration, five years after he had been appointed the president's personal representative and advisor and had traveled overseas on numerous diplomatic missions, Harry's diabetes went out of control.

One day Harry marched into FDR's office and said, "Mr. President, because of my illness I can only come in one or two hours a day. I believe this isn't adequate to serve you and my country. As a result, I feel I should resign my position and let someone else take my place." Upon hearing that, FDR turned to him and said, "Harry, if all you can do each day in an hour or two is come in and advise me, you will have served your country and me extremely well. *That* is your number-one priority." And with that, Harry continued to advise President Roosevelt until the president's death in 1945.

Roosevelt understood the "worth of a contribution," even one as seemingly small as one or two hours a day. As I review my priorities, I now consider the worth of my contribution. How about you?

Debrief Questions

- According to FDR, what was Harry's number-one priority?
- What does this story represent for you?
- Suppose you could only come in to work one or two hours each day. What could you do that would give the organization the best use of your time and talent? What item would be your number-one priority? What would be your most valuable contribution?

Key Point Options

1. Often individuals are not clear on what their organization or their leaders expect from them. Without knowing these expectations, it becomes impossible to prioritize one's work to make a meaningful contribution.
2. Making a contribution is based on alignment between individual goals and organizational goals. Only when these goals support each other can both the individual and the organization succeed and grow.
3. Effective performance is a combination of knowing your key priorities, giving them your complete concentration, and making time for them.

Follow-up Activity

Step 1—Individual Activity: Divide a sheet of paper into three horizontal sections and label the three sections: Organization Goals, Department Key Priorities, and My Key Priorities. Now fill in each section, giving special attention to your priorities that support department priorities and organization goals. What are the links between your key priorities, your department's priorities, and your organization's goals?

Step 2—Individual Activity with Supervisor: Meet with your supervisor to discuss the worksheet. Make changes to the goals and priorities based on your supervisor's input. Meet at least annually to review your key priorities.

FOSTERING FULL POTENTIAL (29)

Contributor

LG Shanklin-Flowers, president, InReach

Type and Purpose(s)

Instructional; educate and encourage

Background

LG has worked with numerous organizations, both internally and externally, and strongly values developing others to reach their highest potential.

Presentation Tips

This story is primarily one of narration. To add variety, alter your voice based on the emotions that are implied in the script. Also note the patterning language in the middle of the story ("all").

Set-up

Option 1—What's the role of a leader when someone's been earmarked for dismissal?

Option 2—As a leader, how do you turn around a difficult employee situation?

Fostering Full Potential

I inherited Veronica. She was a receptionist who I was point-blank told to fire. But, in all fairness, as director of personnel, I couldn't make that decision without directly experiencing her abilities. Before my arrival, Veronica had, in fact, been acting as the interim personnel director. She was the person who coordinated information, knew all the systems, handled all the insurance, and tracked peoples' vacation and sick days. Everyone in the agency depended on her.

It became very clear, very quickly, that Veronica was tremendously resentful towards me. She felt she should have gotten the director job. And now, she had to train me! While there were many, many things that she understood about the logistics of running a personnel department, there were also lots of things that she didn't get about personnel management.

Over many months, we had a series of conversations and meetings during which I worked on developing a relationship with Veronica. I discovered she was correct in being upset with the organization for not developing and promoting her. No one had recognized her potential, yet I knew that I had to address her resentment. Over time, she began to talk truthfully about how she felt mistreated and used.

Now, although her title was that of a receptionist, she had demonstrated far more potential. So, I negotiated an expansion of responsibilities and committed to upgrading her salary. In very little time, Veronica built and followed up on *all* the systems; and she communicated with *all* the insurance companies. *All* while she continued to carry out to her receptionist duties.

I also got her some help. One of her challenges was that she couldn't spell. This became a point of contention for my supervisor.

"How can someone take messages if she can't spell?" A staff person who was also an English teacher worked with her. Veronica didn't stop there—she also worked on developing her other areas of deficiency.

Ultimately, Veronica left for a key administrative position in another organization. It was then that I realized how much she and I had both grown. What started out as a serious challenge for both of us turned into a win-win situation. I had "fostered her potential," and she had fostered mine.

Debrief Questions

- Why was Veronica resentful of LG as the new director of personnel?
- How did LG go about developing a relationship with Veronica? What did LG do to foster her full potential?
- What leadership characteristics did LG exhibit to make a decision not to fire Veronica?
- How would you have responded to being told to fire a staff person you had never worked with? What does this say about the organization's employee relations practices?
- Who (a mentor or a manager) has supported your development? What did this person do? What impact did his or her behavior have on you and your work?

Key Point Options

1. Integrity in employee relations is critical to staff motivation, productivity, and satisfaction on the job. Without clear expectations and honest feedback, employees cannot succeed or make a meaningful contribution to the organization.
2. Each leader can make a significant difference in employees' work lives. One person's thoughtful, caring leadership benefits both the employee and the organization.

3. Employees typically want to do their best and want to develop in their work. Often performance problems are the result of poor communication, lack of support, and unclear goals.

Follow-up Activity

Step 1—Small-Group Discussion: When have you been in a position to mentor or develop another person? What did you do to encourage that person? What impact did that have on you and the other person?

Step 2—Individual Activity: Reflect and write on the following questions: Who could use your mentoring or development today? How could you begin to demonstrate this behavior towards him or her?

chapter
TWELVE

Living Our Values

Our values compose the fundamental core of who we are as human beings. Instilled through our early experiences, they help formulate our attitudes, beliefs, choices, and behaviors. Both personally and professionally, values help direct our lives. Identifying our values is the first step to knowing who we are—doing this enables us to notice who we are becoming. Values provide a benchmark against which we measure our own growth. These stories show the importance of our personal journeys as well as the ways in which values influence our society. They are both inspirational and thought-provoking.

Two of the stories highlight what it means to be conscious of our values and how they influence our choices. Geoff Bellman's desire to live with integrity teaches him that "Time Brings Perspective" when he reflects upon a "failed" project and takes ownership of the results. And Kate Lutz reaches deep inside to write "In Search of Cappuccino . . . With a Little Chocolate on the Side" about her daughter's choice to live courageously and rebelliously with cancer.

The next two stories focus on the influence of our earliest experiences in shaping our lifelong values. Ed Scannell gives us a humorous look at the early messages that play out in adulthood when he experiences a traffic accident in "Values Aren't Accidental." In "A Legacy of Generosity," Chip Bell's early experiences with his grandmother's value of generosity help shape his future relationships. Finally,

"A Nation's Values Connect Us" takes a retrospective look at the impact of the September 11, 2001, terrorist attacks. After the event, futurist David Zach began to notice and track our nation's response, compiling a list of trends that became newsworthy.

These five stories offer a look at our deepest values and most fundamental human responses. They are an opportunity to learn about who we are.

A LEGACY OF GENEROSITY (30)

Contributor

Chip Bell, senior partner, Performance Research Associates, Inc.

Type and Purpose(s)

Vignette; encourage

Background

Chip's father was a big storyteller. Many of his stories come from his early years growing up in South Georgia.

Presentation Tips

This story is best told in a relaxed tone, preferably with a southern drawl.

Set-up

Option 1—Our early life experiences help shape our values around giving.

Option 2—One truly memorable experience can shape our relationships with others forever.

Option 3—What happens when we approach the world from an attitude of abundance rather than scarcity?

A Legacy of Generosity

I grew up in a small country town in South Georgia. Like most folks in my era, I didn't get an allowance. I made all my spending money mowing lawns. I got one dollar for a regular size yard and two dollars for a big yard. My grandmother . . . now, she had a two-dollar yard! I loved mowing it 'cause there weren't a lot of two-dollar yards in the town where I grew up.

In the summer of 1954, there was a major drought in South Georgia. I was ten years old and yards hardly didn't grow at all that summer. I was looking at a pretty bleak year in terms of spending money. Towards the end of that summer, my grandmother called me up and said, "Chip, I want you to come and mow my yard." I was so excited I went right over and mowed her yard. When I showed up at the back door to get my two dollars, she met me there and handed me a five-dollar bill . . . and said the most wonderful words that I've ever heard: "Keep the change." And it did *change* my relationship with my grandmother, a relationship I kept until she died in her eighties.

When you feel generosity it literally changes your relationships—it definitely did between my grandmother and me. Her spirit continues to guide the choices I make about my own legacy of generosity. Who has influenced you with their generosity of spirit and what is the "legacy you wish to leave"?

Debrief Questions

- What did it mean for Chip to have this experience with his grandmother?
- What did Chip's grandmother teach him about the value of generosity?

- What experiences of generosity have you had in your life?
- How have your early experiences helped shape your values?
- What does the spirit of generosity—an attitude of abundance—mean in your work?
- What are some ways you could demonstrate generosity at work? At home? How can you develop a "giver" mentality?

Key Point Options

1. Relationships are the foundation of our lives. It is important to manage them with a sense of generosity—a sense of abundance. Generosity is a core value of building relationships.
2. People tend to associate with organizations that they feel have their best interests at heart. Organizations that communicate that generosity of spirit engender customer and employee loyalty.

Follow-up Activity

Step 1—Paired Discussion: With your partner, share a time in your life when someone has shown generosity to you. What did it feel like? What impact did it have on your relationship with this person? On your life? On your values?

Step 2—Large-Group Discussion: Have people share their insights from the paired discussion. Then explore the following questions as an entire group: How have you shown generosity to others? What impact has this had on your relationships with these individuals or organizations?

TIME BRINGS PERSPECTIVE (31)

Contributor

Geoff Bellman, consultant and author of *The Consultant's Calling,* 2nd ed. (2002)

Type and Purpose(s)

Imbroglio; engage and explore

Background

Geoff is a highly respected international consultant and author of five books. He has made significant contributions to the organization development field over the last twenty-five years. Even the most skilled professional, like Geoff, can experience a blind spot that upon reflection provides a rich opportunity for expanding his leadership awareness.

Presentation Tips

The narrator's vocal inflections move from frustration to deep self-reflection as the story progresses. You may want to sit on a stool when you get to the self-reflection part of the story.

Set-up

Option 1—As leaders, we all have "stuff" that gets in the way of our work.

Option 2—With the passing of time, we, as leaders, might have a different perspective about a situation.

Time Brings Perspective

A long-term client asked me to lead its executives through a three-day meeting. My contact person at the client organization was a younger, less experienced woman. I offered ideas for the meeting, but she rejected them as not being what the executives wanted to do. Although I had a gut feeling about what was needed, she chose a plan that reflected her boss's recommendations. With great hesitation, I agreed to facilitate the plan that she proposed. I didn't take the time to fully explain my perspective to her.

Finally, the meeting date arrived. By lunchtime on the second day, it became clear that what had been planned wasn't working. I spoke to the most senior executive about this and he agreed that we needed to end the meeting. Everyone was immediately sent home. As you can well imagine, I was upset with my contact and called her right away to talk. I was clear about what I observed but critical of her and her lack of judgment.

Some time later, I received a box of materials I had left at the organization. I put it aside, planning to open it later. Weeks later, I moved it. Months later, I still hadn't opened it. Almost a year later I thought, "Why haven't I opened that box? I cannot open that box. Why?" It was only when I recognized my own failure and let go of the blame I'd placed on my client contact that I was able to open it. I called her and wrote several letters of apology, acknowledging what I'd done to cause the meeting to fail. While I never heard back, I also never forgot the lesson it taught me.

What had I recognized about myself? I recognized how protective I am of my reputation and image. Look at the extremes I took to protect myself—blaming someone else instead of looking at my own part in it. I now more clearly know my vulnerabilities and what gets in the way of my work. ["Time truly brings perspective."]

Quade, K. & Brown, R. M. (2002). *The conscious consultant.* San Francisco: Jossey-Bass/Pfeiffer, pp. 57–58. Used with permission. Adaptations based on interview with Geoff Bellman, April 5, 2002. This story may not be reprinted without permission of the original copyright holder.

Debrief Questions

- What might you have done if you were the consultant who did not agree with the client's plan?
- Why was it important for Geoff to contact the client liaison after his reassessment of the failed client meeting?
- What meaning does this story hold for you?
- What does this story tell us about leadership values?
- How do you know when it is right to stand up for something you believe in?
- Think of times when an organization has taken ownership for a mistake or error in judgment. What was the result? What impact did it have on company credibility and the perception of leadership?

Key Point Options

1. At times, we can get in the way of our own best work by not acting on what we know to be true. Leadership means paying attention to our instincts and standing up for what we believe.
2. It is only after acknowledging the places we get stuck in our lives that we are truly able to move on. Recognition and self-forgiveness are key to growth, and they reflect our values.

3. Our society has a business culture that continually reinforces that it is not acceptable to fail. This leads to blame, turf issues, protecting the status quo, and numerous other business practices that derail an organization's success. Geoff believes that by acknowledging and *accepting* where we have failed, we become more fully human and therefore better able to connect with others. To acknowledge where we have failed is to live in integrity with our values.

Follow-up Activity

Step 1—Paired Discussion: Select a partner. Each person takes five minutes to discuss the following questions: When have you needed to acknowledge that you made a poor decision? What was that like for you? What did you do to correct the situation? Then take an additional five minutes each to discuss these questions: When have you taken a stand for what you believed to be right even though it disagreed with others? What was that like for you? How did the situation turn out?

Step 2—Large-Group Discussion: Ask several of the pairs to discuss their situations with the large group. Recap the discussion highlighting how we know when we are acting with integrity.

IN SEARCH OF CAPPUCCINO . . . WITH A LITTLE CHOCOLATE ON THE SIDE (32)

Contributor

Kate Lutz, professional storyteller

Type and Purpose(s)

Crucible; encourage and evoke

Background

Kate chose a career as a professional storyteller in part due to the tragic death of her daughter. She has a compelling story to tell and a message of hope for others.

Presentation Tips

Tell this story in a serious tone of voice but end on a note of hope and triumph over adversity.

Set-up

Option 1—Being a rebel and being a victim may be flip sides of the same coin. What is it that makes them similar, yet different?

Option 2—What are the antidotes to preventing "victim" behavior?

In Search of Cappuccino . . . With a Little Chocolate on the Side

I had just gotten home from a great vacation, feeling relaxed. I was in one of those "the world is a wonderful place! I could do anything!" sort of moods. Wanting to share my excitement, I called my daughter, Karen, in New York City, who was finishing her third year of law school. I said, "Hi, I had a wonderful—" when she broke in. "Mom, right after you left I found a lump in my neck and the doctor did a biopsy right away but they have to do it again because they can't tell if it's malignant." I tensed up. My whole body curled around the word "malignant." I wanted to scream, "Not *my* daughter. She just *ran* the New York City marathon! She loves broccoli. And has a heart full of dreams. It can't be!"

Scheduling and biopsies take time; we waited, she in New York and me in Denver. The doctor called me after the second biopsy—Hodgkin's, a lymphoma cancer. He didn't want to tell her when she was alone. I called her that evening, a friend holding me, and my daughter tight in her boyfriend's arms. A telephone line connected us like a thin, fragile umbilical cord from mother to child. The word "cancer" hung in the air between us.

Every six weeks my internal "mother's clock" went off and I boarded a plane to New York. During phone calls Karen reassured me that everything was fine, but I needed to see and hug her. Words weren't enough. Chemo wasn't going well; the cancer was resistant to many drugs. Many months, and many drugs later, her hair fell out leaving a shiny, bald head—one that was hard to resist patting and kissing. She hated that, sputtering, "I'm not a baby, leave my head alone!"

One crisp, windy, autumn day, we raced to the subway for her chemo appointment. On the subway car, her shiny, bald head stood out proudly among the crowded commuters. We had our routine down pat: while Karen checked in for her treatment, I began browsing through the *New York City Guide to Coffee.* We were on a mission to find New York's best cup of cappuccino . . . with a little chocolate on the side. Cappuccino and chocolate became the antidote for chemotherapy.

After the chemo we headed for a coffee shop. As usual, I trailed behind. Karen was easy to follow, a shiny bald head rolling with the determination of a bowling ball amid the heads on a New York City street. I followed the shiny baldness until I saw a man stop abruptly and stare at my daughter. With indignation, he looked straight at her and snarled, "Skinhead!"

My she-bear right arm began winding up. I was set for a knock 'em down sidewalk brawl right there on the street. "How dare he . . . " I would have happily slugged him several times except my daughter took my hand and pulled me forward. "Mom, it's just a name. I'd rather be a *rebel* than a *victim*!"

Karen refused to be a *victim* of cancer. [She chose to "search for the cappuccino and chocolate"—the antidote to being a victim.] With her rebel spirit she lived with cancer for eighteen months, graduating from law school, buying a house with her significant other, and starting a job. She even grew a little hair!

[We can all choose to be rebels instead of victims. What is the cappuccino and chocolate in your life?]

Lutz, K. (Nov. 29, 2000). "Cappuccino, Chocolate, Chemotherapy," unpublished story, Denver, CO. Adapted and used with permission. This story may not be reprinted without permission of the original copyright holder.

Debrief Questions

- What did Karen do to cope with her illness? To not become a victim? What did she do to live life fully despite cancer?
- What lessons does Karen's story have for us?
- Where have you shown a rebel spirit in your own life? Where have you chosen *not* to become a victim in a difficult situation?
- How might you apply the value of being a rebel instead of a victim to your work environment?

Key Point Options

1. No matter what life hands us, we can choose our response. Choosing to be a rebel instead of a victim allows us to take ownership of our lives and live fully.
2. Stephen Covey, author of *The 7 Habits of Highly Effective People,* believes that in our lives, there are some things that we can do something about—our areas of *influence.* And there are also some things over which we have no real control—our areas of *concern.* "Proactive people focus their efforts in the Circle of Influence.... Reactive people focus their efforts in the Circle of Concern. They focus on weaknesses of others, problems and circumstances over which they have no control" (1989, p. 83). People who are most satisfied and most effective focus on their areas of *influence.*

Follow-up Activity

Step 1—Large-Group Discussion: Draw two separate circles on easel paper. Label one "Circle of Influence" and label the second "Circle of Concern." Ask participants to identify elements of their industry that are of concern and beyond immediate control; consider legal, societal, and global areas. Write these comments in the Circle of Concern. Then ask participants to identify ways to respond to these concerns and write them in the Circle of Influence. Lead a discussion about taking ownership in areas that can be influenced versus spending time complaining about things over which we have no real control.

Step 2—Individual Activity: Repeat the activity using a personal example. Also have each person people answer: How can you increase the amount of time and attention you place on your Circle of Influence versus your Circle of Concern?

VALUES AREN'T ACCIDENTAL (33)

Contributor

Edward E. Scannell, CMP, CSP, director, Center for Professional Development & Training

Type and Purpose(s)

Vignette; explore

Background

Ed tells this story to illustrate the values and early messages to which different age groups have been exposed. He often tells his audiences that the story is a little embarrassing but that he believes most adults can relate to it.

Presentation Tips

The story can be told seriously but should end on a humorous note since Ed finds his own reaction amusing.

Set-up

Option 1—There are messages that are burned into our brain at an early age.

Option 2—According to values educator Dr. Morris Massey, most of our values are locked in at an early age.

Values Aren't Accidental

Phoenix, Arizona. Four o'clock in the afternoon. Rush hour traffic was very busy. I could hear the sirens in the distance! Moments earlier I'd been hit by an approaching car.

I'd wanted to make a left-hand turn across three lanes of traffic. The drivers in two lanes of oncoming vehicles had graciously motioned me to turn in front of them. As I crossed in front of a large pick-up camper, which was in the middle lane, a third car came up on its right-hand side traveling the forty-five mile-per-hour speed limit. Neither of us saw each other as he plowed into me.

Four cars were involved in the accident; two of them were totaled and two were towed away. I was tossed around a bit—having my seat belt on obviously made all the difference in the world. Thankfully, no one was sent to the hospital.

But, I must confess. As I lay there waiting for the paramedics to arrive, I smiled to myself as my mother's warnings from childhood raced through my mind. "Eddie, make sure you don't have any holes in your socks and have on clean underwear. What if you got into an accident?"

For all of us, "values aren't accidental." They were instilled in our early years. Think about it for yourself. What accidents of life bring you face-to-face with your values?

Debrief Questions

- What early values were taught to Ed by his family?
- How many of you have had the same thoughts about being in an accident? For those of you that didn't share Ed's thoughts, what reaction did you have? Why might some of you have had a different reaction?

- What early scripts are etched into your brain that affect how you react in situations?
- How many of our reactions to crises are dictated by early influences in our lives? How do these reactions help or hinder us in our lives? In our work?

Key Point Options

1. According to Ed Scannell, national speaker Frank Bucaro says, "Values are caught, not taught," and values are instilled early in our lives.
2. The early messages we receive influence our behavior and reactions for the rest of our lives.
3. People raised in similar eras often share common early messages and values.
4. Early messages or values can empower us or limit us.

Follow-up Activity

Step 1—Individual Activity: Write down five early messages you learned while you were growing up. Consider messages about getting along with others, family values, religious values, values you learned in school, and so on.

Step 2—Large-Group Discussion: What messages did you identify? How do these messages influence your behavior and reactions today? Which messages have been particularly helpful to you in your life? Which, in hindsight, are funny or no longer useful?

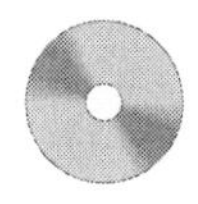

A NATION'S VALUES CONNECT US (34)

Contributor

David Zach, futurist

Type and Purpose(s)

Credibility; educate and explore

Background

As a futurist, David is constantly scanning the environment, looking for interesting anecdotes.

Presentation Tips

Consider various ways of physically indicating the highs and lows as you describe the trends in this story.

Set-up

Option 1—How do people respond during times of crisis?

Option 2—Tremendous change can occur as a result of crisis. Some of these changes lead to temporary fads and some become trends that are here to stay.

A Nation's Values Connect Us

Like everyone else in this country on September 11, I was stunned. Reality was sinking in. I knew that my business as a futurist, which involves extensive travel, had basically collapsed. That afternoon, as I walked my dog, two little kids suddenly came bounding out of one of the neighboring condos screaming, "Puppy!" They were thrilled and totally absorbed in my two month-old dog. Watching these children, I realized innocence still lived on, even in the face of something horrible. These children made a connection for me.

As the days progressed, I found myself noticing more and more anecdotes—on TV, the radio, and in newspapers—things that were odd, or funny, or interesting.

The first thing that caught my eye was that marriages and engagements were reported to be up, along with romantic gift purchases. From my office, which is above a restaurant, I learned that there were more requests for tables for two. Of course all this led me to expect a baby boom starting around May of 2002. After sharing these tidbits with some friends I found out that afternoon hotel reservations had gone up as well. Even membership on the Internet dating service match.com had increased 20 percent. So had puppy dog sales—they were up 30 percent the first months following 9/11. One way or another, people were making connections.

Curiously, divorces were both up and down—many who were planning on getting divorced looked at each other and said, "You know, honey, life is too short. Let's work it out." Other couples that weren't in the throes of divorce said, "You know, life is too short. I'm out of here."

There were also increases in the sales of Korans as well as attendance at religious gatherings. Although attendance has tapered off a bit, it has still been higher than it was prior to 9/11. Interest in other cultures went way up and there was a significant increase in enrollment in Arabic classes. I realized people were connecting to their foundational values.

Thinking about all of this, I sat with my computer and made a list of all my observations: marriages, engagements, babies, hotel reservations, religion. When I met with my friends over the next several weeks, I shared my list. I added the list to my presentations.

The *Milwaukee Journal Sentinel* heard about my list and that led to an article in that newspaper. Then I got a call from a booking agent and was featured on a CNN segment. From that came a half-hour interview on public talk radio. The more I spoke about these trends, the clearer I became on what was really going on. "Crisis creates connections." The trend or long-term issue is that humans really need to connect with other people.

Debrief Questions

- What was Dave's response to the crisis of September 11, 2001?
- Which of these trends had you been aware of?
- What reactions and responses did you notice after September 11?
- What changes have affected your life since that day?
- What do you do to live a full, connected life despite uncertainty about the future?
- What trends have you noticed in your industry since September 11? In your organization?
- What implications do these trends have for your organization's success?

Key Point Options

1. In crisis, a typical response is to find or create order once again in our lives. Trends define the collective "order" that we are seeking. They illustrate the values by which a society lives.
2. Crises can help us focus on *we* instead of *me.* We develop an awareness of what is truly important to us in our lives when we look to connect with others.
3. In times of crisis, we need to look beyond our petty differences and find the unity among all of us. At the same time, we need to appreciate the small joys of daily life such as playing with a puppy.
4. Noticing themes and trends is an important organization skill. It is the basis of strategic planning and positions companies for future success. It reflects an organization's beliefs and values.

Follow-up Activity

Step 1—Paired Discussion: Each partner takes five minutes to discuss the following questions: What personal values have you become aware of since 9/11? What are you doing to act on those values in your life?

Step 2—Large-Group Discussion: Have pairs report on their discussions. Help participants to identify common themes.

Performance and Coaching

chapter
THIRTEEN

Every successful person has received skillful coaching at some point in life. Coaching and performance feedback enable us to look at our strengths, assess our areas for improvement, and make conscious decisions about each. Too often, organizations provide poor coaching or none at all. These six stories highlight the importance of coaching in achieving our organizations' goals as well as our own. They give us a thoughtful and at times humorous and engaging look at the pitfalls of performance management as well as what it takes to be successful in this arena.

Sheriene Saadati's two stories depict the impact of lack of awareness on an organization's management practices. In "The Forest for the Trees," a committee over-designs the performance review feedback form to the point where no one wants to use it. "Is He Qualified?" shows us how timely coaching averts a poor hiring decision, causing a senior-level executive, who was coached, to become an ardent fan of behavioral event interviews.

Several stories portray the results "no coaching" has on well-intentioned employees. Their responses might reflect what you have observed in your own organization. Marcia Ruben, in "Thanks, I'll Do It Myself," recalls working with a manager who chose to rework projects herself after delegating them. With both audacity and creativity, Sandra Hoskins relies on "The Roll of the Dice" to develop her budget after the organization's comptroller ignores her requests for assistance.

When managers operate on their own assumptions about an employee's performance capability, the lack of coaching and performance feedback can result in legal action. In "The Case of the Magician's Assistant," a pregnant employee is terminated because her manager believes that she will no longer fit through the trapdoor in the magic act. Attorney Hortencia Delgadillo walks us through the legal ramifications of this manager's unfounded actions and the ensuing discrimination lawsuit.

Finally, one of our stories shows how timely and specific feedback coupled with a supportive coach can help cultivate improved performance and increase an individual's confidence in his or her own capabilities. Joan Lloyd outlines a specific performance management system used by athletic coaches, following the steps of "Isolate, Exaggerate, and Integrate." She shows how she benefits personally from using this technique, as well as how she employs it successfully in her company.

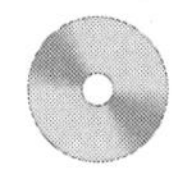

THE CASE OF THE MAGICIAN'S ASSISTANT (35)

Contributor

Hortencia Delgadillo, attorney-at-law

Type and Purpose(s)

Instructional; evaluate and evoke

Background

Hortencia is an attorney who has worked in employment discrimination for many years. In this case, the employer was asked to bring in a paper model of the magic act apparatus, complete with trapdoor so the investigators had a better idea of the actual situation.

Presentation Tips

This is a narrated story that needs to be told with some flair.

Set-up

Option 1—Think twice before taking action based on your assessment of an employee's ability to perform work.

Option 2—Your assumptions about someone's ability to perform work can get you in hot water.

The Case of the Magician's Assistant

Jennifer was delighted to be hired as the magician's assistant. Her role was to perform in one of the magician's special illusions. During each show, Jennifer disappeared on stage . . . and then reappeared "as if by magic." What Jennifer actually did was step behind a screen, crouch down, and slip through a trapdoor in the floor of the stage to the area below it. On cue, she reappeared by pulling herself up through the opening in the floor.

When Jennifer learned she was pregnant, she shared the good news with her co-workers and her supervisor. Imagine her surprise when she learned that her supervisor was *not* happy for her. Soon after, he told her, "You're being replaced because a pregnant woman cannot fit through the trapdoor. It's for your own good." Shocked, Jennifer realized she had just been removed from her role in the magic show. "How dare he fire me," She thought. "How can he be so sure I can't do the act? The fact is, who *knows* what size I'II be when I'm eight months pregnant?"

She immediately filed a pregnancy discrimination claim with the Equal Employment Opportunity Commission. Her employer only offered one argument in its defense. You see, Jennifer had been removed from her role in the magic act in *anticipation* of how difficult it would be for her to fit through the trapdoor toward the end of her pregnancy. Once she was too big for the trapdoor, she would be unable to perform the magic act and would be in breach of her contract. Even though Jennifer was a very petite woman, her supervisor explained that his decision was based on his experience with his own wife who had "ballooned up during her seventh month of pregnancy."

The unfounded assumption about Jennifer's limitations during pregnancy was enough to close the case against the employer. He didn't have any facts. However, the investigator was curious. He had to find out just how big the opening was to the trapdoor and allowed the employer to send in a drawing that folded out to its exact dimensions. Staring at the drawing, there was no doubt in the investigator's mind: Even pregnant, Jennifer had more than enough room to pass through the trapdoor. So, the next time you make a decision about performance, be sure to "get the facts."

Debrief Questions

- What were Jennifer's feelings about how she was being treated?
- What mental model (or mindset) was her boss holding?
- How was the boss's mental model created?
- How does his mindset interfere with his demonstration of good management practices?
- What type of leadership training would be helpful in this organization?
- What reactions do you have to this case and its outcome?
- When has a boss's mental model about your performance impacted you in your job?
- How might this ruling affect decisions in your workplace?
- What training does your workplace have regarding fair and legal employment practices?

Key Point Options

1. Individuals are responsible for assessing reasonable risk on the job. An employer cannot make this kind of decision for an employee.
2. Employers cannot deny employment opportunity based on concern for someone's welfare or based on the experiences of someone else in a similar situation.

3. Communication is essential. The company might have discussed its concerns about the magic act with Jennifer and considered possible solutions together.

Follow-up Activity

Step 1—Small-Group Discussion: Talk about the group's perceptions of what men and women are capable of on the job. Are there any jobs or job duties for which either women or men are better suited? Which ones might those be?

Step 2—Large-Group Discussion: Small groups report their conclusions. Discuss the following questions as an entire group: What are the legal and employment implications of making hiring decisions based on these views? How does gender stereotyping affect both women and men in the workplace? How can an employer determine if someone is the right fit for a "nontraditional" job?

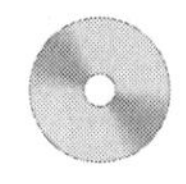

THE ROLL OF THE DICE (36)

Contributor

Sandra Hoskins, ISP, PMP, president, The Kellan Group

Type and Purpose(s)

Vignette; entertain and explore

Background

This was Sandra's first management job in information systems, in an insurance company. Previously she had been a senior analyst in an IT shop. Sandra reported to the president of the organization. Afterwards, he told her that her approach was an innovative way to approach budgeting.

Presentation Tips

The audience may be drawn to the entertaining aspects of the story. You may need to bring their focus back to the key points in order to successfully debrief the story. Portray Sandra as a new employee wanting to do her best and the comptroller as preoccupied, at first, and eventually very angry at her behavior.

Set-up

Option 1—When new managers are forced to figure out procedures on their own, the results can be quite unexpected.

Option 2—Resourcefulness is a key managerial skill.

The Roll of the Dice

One of my first responsibilities as the new manager of information systems was to complete the departmental budget. Twenty million dollars had been allotted by the organization for products, services, and projects for the coming year. Because the IS department was new, the company had virtually no history on which to base the budget.

I had no idea where to start. At the time, I had a computer science background with limited exposure to accounting. After a great deal of pondering, I swallowed my pride and approached the comptroller for help. Since he was immersed in year-end closing, he had very little time to help and told me to "try my best." After a great deal more thought, I walked to my dry erase board and listed all the things that I thought the department might need to spend money on: hardware, software, communications, travel, paper, insurance, training, and (last but not least) payroll. Staring at the board for what seemed like forever, I finally decided to take a lunch break. As I was standing in line at the deli waiting to pay, I noticed a cup and two dice on a display stand. As I stared at the cup and dice, the light went on in my head. I had found my budgeting tool!

Back in my office I put the dice in the cup and rolled them. The first die that came out became the first number for a specific expenditure; the number on the second die became the number of zeros that I added to the first number. I repeated the process for each item I had written on the dry erase board until all the numbers added up to $20 million. After printing and binding my budget, I submitted it on time. I was *extremely* proud of myself!

About six months later, the comptroller came to see me. He asked me where the assumptions were that should have accompanied the budget. Being somewhat surprised and curious, I explained that the only assumption I made was that I would be over on some numbers and under on others. His hands started to shake. And his face turned from ashen to pink to a deep shade of purple. I thought he was going to implode. After much stammering, he finally boomed, "What is it about you computer people? You never record assumptions for anything you do. If I prepared financial statements without assumptions, I would go to jail!"

I was stunned by his reaction. To date, my solution was working well. We were, in fact, over in some areas—most notably payroll—yet under in others, such as insurance. Overall, we were under budget. However, I did learn a very valuable lesson: If you don't get the answer you need "ask and ask again" until you do.

Debrief Questions

- What responsibility did the comptroller hold for the outcome of this situation?
- How did Sandra's approach meet and not meet the expectations of the budgeting process?
- What are your reactions to Sandra's creative budgeting process?
- How might you have gone about preparing a budget for which you had no training or information?
- What did you learn from this situation about managing performance and the importance of coaching in the workplace?

Key Point Options

1. When someone in a new position asks for help, chances are the person needs assistance. If the task is important, it is in the best interests of the organization to coach this person.

2. Key priorities in an organization need to be clearly defined so they can be thoroughly and consistently carried out. Not communicating expectations limits an employee's ability to meet goals and successfully perform.
3. Performance is a function of both the willingness and the ability to do a job. In the absence of ability, the organization needs to assist employees in developing the necessary skills to carry out the job.

Follow-up Activity

Step 1—Individual Activity: Think of a time when you did not know how to carry out a specific part of your job and received good coaching and feedback to assist you. Answer these questions about it: What did you do to get that assistance? What impact did that coaching have on your carrying out the job? What impact did it have on your level of motivation?

Step 2—Small-Group Discussion: Have participants share their situation and their answers to the questions with others in their group.

ISOLATE, EXAGGERATE, AND INTEGRATE (37)

Contributor

Joan Lloyd, Joan Lloyd & Associates, Inc.

Type and Purpose(s)

Instructional; educate and encourage

Background

Coaches, particularly athletic coaches, are in the business of helping people to improve performance. They have honed these techniques over time. Joan felt that if she could study what they do and apply it to the workforce, managers in particular could learn some valuable techniques and skills. She researched professional coaches, for example, Mike Holmgren when he was the Green Bay Packers' coach. She also studied people like Jerry Warren with the Professional Ski Instructors of America's Demo Team; these coaches teach all the ski instructors in the United States. Joan has also reviewed the work of Olympic coaches and golf pros.

Presentation Tips

Use body movements and different character voices to depict the dialogue of the various characters. Move to a different spot for each scenario: Joan and Jerry, and Joan and the consultant.

Set-up

Option 1—What exactly do athletic coaches do to improve someone's performance?

Option 2—If you want to improve someone's performance, especially that of *good* performers, follow the advice of athletic coaches.

Option 3—How many of you have hired someone to improve a skill like golf or tennis? Ever think about the technique the person used to help you improve?

Isolate, Exaggerate, and Integrate

Jerry Warren of the Professional Ski Instructor's Demo Team is considered one of the best ski instructors in America. I really love to downhill ski so I hired him to coach me for four days.

On the first day I said, "Jerry, you see that hill over there? It's deep and it's steep and it's full of mogels. I want to be able to ski that." He replied, "All right Joan, let me see you ski." So I showed him my stuff by skiing down a moderate hill. Jerry watched me a few times and offered some feedback. "If you are going to really ski that deep, steep stuff you need to improve your turns." I replied, "All right, tell me what to do." He instructed, "I'd like for you to ski down this hill on one foot." "You must be kidding me," I chuckled. He replied, "No, I want you to do that." So, I tried with my right foot. And I fell over and I did it and fell over again. Pretty soon I was successful. He asked me to try the same thing with my left foot. It took me some practice, but I was able to do it. I could carve turns separately on each foot!

When I had finally done what he wanted to his satisfaction, Jerry said, "Now I want you to put your feet together and integrate that back into your skiing style." Not only was I a lot better at doing turns, but I also improved a whole notch in my ability to ski deeper, steeper terrains.

At the end of the four days, I told Jerry that I had another motive in hiring him. I wanted to know how he coached people. He said, "There's a specific technique called isolate, exaggerate, and integrate. I watch your performance and isolate one little gap, one little thing that I think you could improve on. And then I pull that piece out and create a drill for it. In your case, the drill was skiing on one foot to improve your balance. Finally, after you have the drill perfected,

I reintegrate it back into your performance. Every coach uses this technique."

I decided to try this technique with a consultant who was working for me who was too eager to sell solutions and not patient enough to listen to her clients' needs. She would interrupt the customer and put forth her ideas. I observed this a couple of times and then isolated what the problem was. I said, "In order to really do some client solution selling, I would like you to practice this drill. The drill is to paraphrase and summarize what the client is saying at least twice before you talk solutions." It just about killed her, but she finally noticed how eager she had been to jump in and that she really had not been listening. It definitely improved her ability to sell and quote business.

Skiing with Jerry influenced my approach to coaching others—especially good performers who want to get better. It's really the way to achieve peak performance. All you have to remember is: "isolate, exaggerate, and integrate." Now where can *you* try it?

Debrief Questions

- What stood out for you in this story?
- How did Joan apply the coaching method in her own life and work?
- Why do you think the "isolate, exaggerate, and integrate" coaching method works so well?
- What are the benefits and barriers to using this method?
- Where might you use this coaching method to improve your own performance?
- Where might you use this method to coach another on his or her performance?
- How can organizations incorporate this method into their performance management philosophy?

Key Point Options

1. This coaching method can be used in a variety of ways in organizations. It works especially well with good performers who want to get better. We often spend so much time on poor performers that we do not take the time to help good performers excel.
2. Performance is judged by results. This three-step coaching method works well in part because it builds on the person's own motivation to improve and on his or her desire to excel in some way. Results are directly linked to the individual's level of participation and practice.
3. Research on habits shows that it takes adults about a month to change behavior. When using this method to change habit-based performance, it is important to isolate and practice the new behavior for enough time for true change to occur.

Follow-up Activity

Step 1—Paired Discussion: With your partner, pick an example of performance that would benefit from improvement (your own or someone else's). Using the "isolate, exaggerate, and integrate" model, break down the specific steps, identify the gap that you observe between current and desired performance, and create a drill for practicing the new behavior. Be sure you can monitor the drill over a period of time to create behavior change. Discuss how you will reintegrate the behavior back into performance.

Step 2—Large-Group Discussion: Ask one of the pairs to present its plan. With the entire group, talk about making the commitment to act on the plans they created.

THANKS, I'LL DO IT MYSELF (38)

Contributor

Marcia Ruben, principal, Ruben Consulting Group

Type and Purpose(s)

Vignette; evaluate

Background

This was a new job for Marcia; she reported to a manager in the sales department. It is a story that she uses both in teaching management and leadership, and in her one-on-one executive coaching sessions. One of the common issues she has noticed is an inability of people to delegate—not being willing to let go of control. Often these individuals think that other people cannot do it as well as they can themselves.

Presentation Tips

Alter your voice and behavior to match the changes that Marcia goes through over time. Consider "stepping out" of the action by turning away from your group when telling Marcia's inner thoughts.

Set-up

Option 1—What type of impact can a leader's behavior have on a new employee?

Option 2—As leaders, our blind spots can have a powerful effect on employee behavior.

Thanks, I'll Do It Myself

My colleagues and I in the sales department were responsible for producing materials and monthly audiocassette tapes for the sales force. I worked really diligently on every assignment—writing it, thinking about it, editing it, and reworking it. I always finished my work way before deadline so my manager could have ample time to review it. But, in every case, she wouldn't look at it until right before the deadline. Then she'd rewrite the whole thing! No matter what I did, she would totally rewrite and redo what I had done. She never took the time to tell me what she wanted. I started to doubt myself. Over and over again I would go through things in my head—I thought I had done a good job on this project and I spent a lot of time on it—it wasn't something I just dashed together—yet I was being told I had done it all wrong.

After this happened several times, I decided to change my behavior. My boss was training me all right—she was training me to no longer do a thorough job.

A couple months later I gave my manager and her boss, who was the director in the sales department, copy for an audiotape I'd been working on. Of course, my boss totally rewrote it, but the director responded in a different way—she took the time to sit down with me and help me rework what I had written. For the first time I started to learn the thinking process that I needed to go through in order for me to be more successful in the future.

Immediately afterwards I started to observe that it didn't matter who gave newly developed written materials to my manager—she always had the same reaction. She'd lock herself in her office and redo all the work, no matter how talented the staff. It *had* to be done *her* way—there wasn't a lot of room for anybody else's creative thinking.

I realized as long as I continued to work for her there wouldn't be an opportunity for me to grow. As a result, I made a commitment to myself that I would always take the time to coach people before they began an assignment so they could be successful. What about you? Do you "take the time"?

Debrief Questions

- What does this story tell us about delegation, performance, and coaching?
- What may have caused Marcia's manager to act the way she did?
- What impact did Marcia's manager's actions have on her motivation at work?
- What might Marcia have done to change the dynamic between herself and her manager?
- What were your reactions to Marcia's dilemma with her manager?
- When have you been delegated to in a way that *was not* effective? What did the delegator do or not do to create that experience?
- When have you been delegated to in a way that *was* effective? How did that influence your performance and your interest in your work?

Key Point Options

1. Delegation is a skill leaders often handle poorly because they have fears about employees not following through or not producing acceptable work. Perfectionist leaders, in particular, struggle with delegating, coaching, and developing others.
2. How positively you feel about a particular assignment often has to do with the way in which that assignment was communicated to you. This directly affects your motivation for the specific assignment, as well as for the job overall.
3. As an employee, taking initiative to complete work assignments, asking for feedback on them, and being accountable are ways to ensure your work is making an effective contribution, regardless of your leader's style.

4. Delegating assignments can be a wonderful opportunity to grow and develop your employees' skills, provided you are willing to coach employees and provide feedback.

Follow-up Activity

Step 1—Small-Group Discussion: Define the steps to effective delegation and explain why each step is necessary. Write the steps on an easel page and post to create your own delegation model.

Step 2—Large-Group Discussion: Have each group present their delegation model to the rest of the participants. Ask the entire group to identify barriers to delegating. Why do managers not delegate well? Lead a general discussion on delegation and the link to employee motivation and development.

Step 3—Paired Discussion: Have each person spend a few minutes sharing a recent situation when he or she delegated work. Use one of the delegation models to critique the experience. Identify what the person did well and what he or she might do differently the next time a delegation needs to occur.

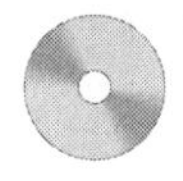

THE FOREST FOR THE TREES (39)

Contributor

Sheriene Saadati, organization consultant

Type and Purpose(s)

Vignette; evaluate

Background

Sheriene was an internal consultant in this situation and brought experience in setting up and implementing performance management systems.

Presentation Tips

Use your voice and body movements to depict total confidence up front and a humbler tone at the end. Also note the patterned language early on in the story.

Set-up

Option 1—Sometimes we get so caught up in the details that we lose sight of the big picture.

Option 2—Our performance is only as good as the systems in which we work.

The Forest for the Trees

The CEO was totally supportive of a company-wide performance management process. He totally believed that everybody should be educated in it. And, he totally believed that a written form should be completed and turned in to him. He even tied the task of completing the form to people's bonuses! For me, as an HR employee, this was a dream come true!

There came a point in time when management wanted to review the form again. Imagine a bunch of executives sitting in a room staring at a form. They made that form so detailed and so specific that it became eight pages long. They couldn't "see the forest for the trees." It covered the person's goals for the next year . . . it covered how the person was going to reach those goals . . . it covered long-term developmental goals . . . *and* it covered how the person was going to reach those long-term goals. On and on and on it went. To help people learn how to use the new form, it was released along with a bunch of training.

A year later my colleagues and I did a review of the performance management process. It was not unheard of for a boss, who was going to Indonesia, and a direct report who was going to Thailand, to meet in a centrally located airport, such as Hong Kong, and quickly fill out their forms and turn them in so they could get their bonuses. Because the form was now so cumbersome, people found ways to work around it.

When the executives who designed the performance management system lost sight of the "big" picture, those who were to follow the system could no longer "see the forest for the trees" either. So, I ask you, when you participate in designing systems in your organization, do you see the forest . . . or the trees?

Debrief Questions

- What were the intentions of the company regarding performance management?
- How did these intentions become derailed by the well-intended efforts of the executive group?
- What do you think the human resources department could do about the performance management system to recover the original intentions?
- When the form no longer worked well for people, what was their response? When have you seen this type of response in your own organizations?
- What type of performance management process does your organization use? How is the review process structured? What is your role as an employee (or leader) in this process?

Key Point Options

1. A performance feedback form is only a form. It is not the entire system. Forms and processes need to clearly translate the intent of an organization's philosophy without getting in the way of that philosophy.
2. When organizations become too cumbersome, energy, motivation, and willingness to follow policy all suffer. Employees become highly creative in meeting the *letter of the law,* so to speak, without actually carrying out the intent. In this story, managers completed their staff performance reviews but essentially ignored the framework on which it was built. By ignoring the framework due to ineffective systems, organizations lose the opportunity for employees to truly be engaged in and proud of their workplace. This sells both the employees and the organization short.

Follow-up Activity

Step 1—Small-Group Discussion: Ask the groups to discuss the intent of the performance management systems in their organizations. Ask them to identify the elements that make them both successful and user-friendly. Then, discuss areas in the performance management system that need improvement.

Step 2—Large-Group Discussion: Ask the small groups to report on their discussions and to post their responses so everyone can read them. Identify common themes from the responses. Ask participants to identify aspects of their performance review systems that could be improved based on the group's discussion. Close by reviewing the intention of a performance management system.

IS HE QUALIFIED? (40)

Contributor

Sheriene Saadati, organization consultant

Type and Purpose(s)

Instructional; educate and evaluate

Background

Sheriene was an internal consultant in this situation.

Presentation Tips

Portray David as wanting to learn but being a bit embarrassed at the moment he discovers his questions were inappropriate. Depict Sheriene as interested in being truly helpful in her coaching.

Set-up

Option 1—Formal training may not be sufficient to initiate a permanent change in behavior.

Option 2—What role can real-time coaching play in helping others to develop their skills?

Is He Qualified?

The corporation decided to completely change the direction of its business and go into an entirely new area. Consequently, a whole new set of skills was needed at very high levels in the organization.

To meet this need, several of us in human resources put together a new competency model along with a series of training sessions. My role was to teach executives how to interview people for these competencies using behavioral event interviewing techniques to gather the right data. These executives were directly responsible for hiring the individuals who reported to them. Since the new positions were so important, either another trainer or I sat in on the first few interviews that the president or VPs conducted with potential new hires.

One day I was with David, a high-level executive, interviewing a very competent candidate for a critical senior position. David started asking a series of questions. "How would you describe your personality? What interests do you have outside of work? How successful were you on your last big project?" To me, these questions clearly weren't behavioral event interview questions. Every once in awhile I'd pop in a few of my own to try and redirect the conversation.

After the interview was over and the candidate had left, I started to quiz David on his approach. "What did you think about this particular individual?" He began describing personality traits, such as "he's a very outgoing guy"—and personal interests and hobbies—"he belongs to some of the same clubs that I do." I continued, "What about his experience in closing deals? What about his international work experience?" David remained silent, reflecting on what I had just said. I went on: "What data do you have about similar work experiences? What sense do you have as to whether he's ever done this sort of work before today?" David simply responded, "I really don't know."

As we continued our debrief meeting, David completely changed his opinion of the candidate. One by one, we went through the specific characteristics and traits and experiences for which we were looking. He realized that he had not asked the right questions, didn't have the data to make an informed decision, and that his personal biases almost caused him to make the wrong hiring decision.

David was so moved by this experience that we received support throughout the company to continue training those in senior-level positions. He even told the story about his own learning to other colleagues and used himself as an example! David learned that "data drives decisions." Think about your situation. Do you have the right data?

Debrief Questions

- What was David's original interviewing style?
- What concerns did the consultant have about David's interviewing style? Why?
- What impact would there be on the organization if all the senior-level new hires were interviewed using David's original approach?
- What is your own interview style? Where have you learned your current interview techniques?
- What do you do in job interviews in your business to ensure that you have objective, specific, and comprehensive information on which to base your decisions?

Key Point Options

1. In hiring, when you do not have a clear profile for whom you are looking, you tend to look for someone like yourself rather then what the position actually

requires. It takes discipline and sometimes another person's viewpoint to help you to figure out if this is the right candidate or not.

2. Hiring people like yourself is one of the ways organizations undermine their commitment to fairness, equitable hiring practices, and appreciating diversity. This has led to numerous lawsuits over the years and more stringent legislation in these areas.
3. Behavioral event interviews focus on the use of targeted questions that allow candidates to respond using past experiences to demonstrate mastery of a skill required for the job, such as, "Tell me about a time when you successfully dealt with an irate customer. Describe the situation and your role in it."

Follow-up Activity

Step 1—Small-Group Discussion: Select a job and create a series of behavioral event interview questions (see above key point) for this position. Answer the following questions in the process: What specific skills are required for this job? What questions would elicit direct evidence of the candidate having these skills? Post your responses so that everyone can read them.

Step 2—Large-Group Discussion: Have the small groups present their interview formats. Identify the behavioral event questions. Talk about any required skills for which it was difficult for each group to find behavioral questions. Ask participants to discuss what makes their current interview practices successful and what could be improved.

chapter
FOURTEEN

Problem-Solving

There are a myriad of problem-solving techniques available for use. The possible solutions to problems life presents to us can be almost endless. These five stories focus on the enduring ability of individuals (or animals!) to tackle a problem head-on. They showcase a number of problem-solving approaches, attitudes, and creative solutions. In exploring the problems of others, we develop a broader and more resilient set of problem-solving tools to use in our own lives. These stories will make you think and make you laugh as we pay tribute to our perseverance in unraveling life's dilemmas.

The importance of *awareness* as an element in solving a problem is highlighted for Bob Shaver while on "The Road to Peoria," as well as in "The Disapproving Neighbor" by Kate Lutz. Bob learned that without awareness, you might just end up in another city. Kate's account is a humorous look at acting on our own misinformation and the lengths to which we can take that action. Another key element of the problem-solving process is the ability to identify the root cause of the problem. To this end, Suzann Gardner asks us to name the basic problem between "The Porcupine and the Snake" who share, for a brief time, the same home.

Our creativity in thinking "outside the box" is celebrated in Sandra Hoskins's "Viewing the Problem Through a Different Lens," as well as in "For Lack of a System" by Larry English. Sandra's colleague refused to give up on an expensive, technical problem and took a completely different approach to arrive at a value-added long-range solution. In Larry's situation, one part of his client's organization created a distinctive coding scheme to track their difficult customers.

Our perseverance, ability to think outside the box, and willingness to ask new questions are all part of our uniquely human spirit. These capabilities shine forth in the everyday problems we are asked to solve. The stories in this chapter honor this gift.

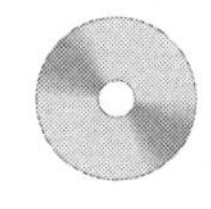

FOR LACK OF A SYSTEM (41)

Contributor

Larry P. English, president, INFORMATION IMPACT International, Inc.

Type and Purpose(s)

Vignette; entertain and explore

Background

When telling this story, do not give away the punch line through your own laughter or facial expressions. It is best to tell this story in a serious manner. This story is also mentioned briefly in Larry's book, *Improving Data Warehouse and Business Information Quality* (1999), in relation to information quality.

Presentation Tips

Larry was working on information quality initiatives within the insurance company when this situation became apparent.

Set-up

Option 1—When we go to solve a problem, we need to ask ourselves who else in the organization will be impacted by the solution.

Option 2—There can be unintended negative consequences to "the perfect solution."

For Lack of a System

The insurance company needed to understand its risks—exactly what it was paying for through its claims. Employees were downloading claims data so the information could be examined in this manner. As they started analyzing the medical diagnosis codes, they uncovered what appeared to be a problem. One region had a high incidence of hemorrhoid codes—so high that it was way outside the normal distribution. We wondered, "What's going on? What's causing this problem? Is there some sort of an epidemic we don't know about?"

Several of us got in touch with the regional claims supervisor. We explained that other departments were using the data, including the actuarial staff, and asked her what she knew about the situation. She exclaimed, "Oh. That's *our* data that we use to pay claims. I didn't know anybody else saw it. We use that particular code to identify claimants who are PITAs—you know—a 'pain in the ass.' How else are we to identify problem customers who we need to approach with special caution? If we have to get back in touch with them, this code helps us recognize that there was some sort of problem. This way we're better prepared to deal with the situation."

No matter what the problem may be, all "problems seek solutions." The challenge that comes with this is that the solution may have surprising consequences. So, whenever your problems go in search of a solution, consider whom else the solution may impact.

Debrief Questions

- What problem was the regional claims staff attempting to solve?
- What impact did the regional claims staff's solution have on others?

- What were the unintended consequences of the staff's creative solution?
- What other creative solutions have you come into contact with in your life?
- What was your reaction to these "thinking outside the box" ideas?
- How can an organization foster creative problem-solving with its employees and leadership?

Key Point Options

1. People often create or use information in ways that meet their internal needs without being aware that anyone else is affected. As a result, there may be negative unintended consequences to others who depend on that information.
2. When an organization fails to create a necessary system, good old ingenuity takes over and fills the gap. Human beings are highly creative when faced with a challenge that presents a problem to solve.
3. Organizations need to build systems that meet the needs of frontline employees. They also need to train these employees in the nuances and intricacies of the business so they can make the best use of available systems. This is key to employees being able to effectively do their work.

Follow-up Activity

Step 1—Small-Group Discussion: Have the group identify a time when one of the members created an unusual solution to a problem. What did that person do? What was the impact of the solution? Did it have any unintended consequences?

Step 2—Large-Group Discussion: Have small groups report on their examples. Are there any common themes identified about the methods, the impacts, or consequences of their solutions?

THE PORCUPINE AND THE SNAKE (42)

Contributor

Suzann Gardner, associate professor, Alverno College

Type and Purpose(s)

Minerva; explore

Background

This story is an old fable told for many years by one of Suzann's retired colleagues.

Presentation Tips

Have some fun with the animal characters in this story. Create a unique voice, facial expressions, and mannerisms for each.

Set-up

Option 1—Surface issues or symptoms can mask the real problem.

Option 2—How do we go beyond what we hear or see in a situation to address what is really going on?

The Porcupine and the Snake

There was a big flood in the valley where a porcupine lived and his home was flooded out. He moved about the countryside looking for a new dwelling but couldn't find one—everything was underwater. So he decided to seek higher ground.

The porcupine started up a hill and came upon a snake. He said to the snake, "Do you know of any place where I could live? I'm homeless." And the snake said, "My family would be happy if you came to live with us. We have more than enough room. Come and stay with us." "That would be great! Thank you so much," said the porcupine. And off he went with the snake.

The snake's home was near the top of the hill since snakes live in high ground. Once they arrived, the snake introduced the porcupine to the snake's family—they were all very welcoming. The home itself consisted of a series of tunnels right beneath the ground. At first the porcupine thought, "I'm never going to fit. These tunnels are so small and I'm not that small." But, when beckoned, he instead said, "Fine," and went down into the series of tunnels to settle in with the snakes.

It didn't take long before the snakes were not happy with the situation *and* the porcupine was not happy with the situation. Generally, everybody was pretty miserable. The porcupine and the snakes came to the agreement that the porcupine would have to move out. The situation was just not working. The porcupine couldn't figure out the cause. The truth is, the porcupine hadn't dealt with his core problem. "The core is the cause."

Debrief Questions

- What was the problem the story referred to? Why couldn't the porcupine and the snakes get along? Note: Give participants some time to answer this question. Responses might include: they are different species, the porcupine has quills and the snakes have skins and the porcupine quills would irritate the snakes, the porcupine didn't feel comfortable around a different species, they didn't map out their territory, lack of communication, and so on.
- Look at identifying the *core* problem. What is the *core* problem? Answer: The core problem is that the porcupine could not deal with the fact that he was homeless. The core is the cause of ensuing problems.
- What does this story teach us about searching for the root cause of a problem?
- When have you found that what you *thought* was the reason for a problem was not *actually* the underlying or real reason for the problem?
- Why is it important for organizations to develop methods for finding the root cause of a problem?

Key Point Options

1. This is a symbolic story. When there is a problem or a conflict, usually there are layers to the conflict. Often people don't look at what the real problem is. They just look at the *symptoms* of the problem. By trying to address the symptoms, they don't actually address the real issue.
2. The core is the cause. The porcupine was homeless and was taking advantage of a possible solution. However, he was not really solving his long-term problem. The porcupine was not doing anything to try to find a more compatible and permanent home.
3. Often in organizations, people believe that the real problem has to do with getting along or not getting along. Just as in this story about the porcupine and the snake, there is usually a deeper reason for the surface symptoms of conflict and a lack of unity.

Follow-up Activity

Step 1—Small-Group Discussion: Identify a problem that one of the group members is currently trying to resolve. What are the possible causes of this problem?

What is the root cause of the problem? Why do you believe this is the root cause? What assumptions are you making about the problem and the possible solution(s)? What constraints are contrived or real? What ideas does your group have for resolving this situation?

Step 2—Large-Group Discussion: Ask several of the small groups to present their problem analysis to the large group. What root causes did the small groups identify? How can we become more skilled at identifying root causes when working with future problems?

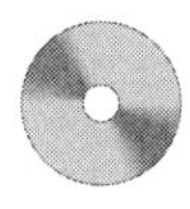

VIEWING THE PROBLEM THROUGH A DIFFERENT LENS (43)

Contributor

Sandra Hoskins, ISP, PMP, president, The Kellan Group

Type and Purpose(s)

Vignette; explore

Background

This situation happened to a colleague of Sandra's in 1986 yet the lesson it brings home to groups and organizations is enduring. At the time the problem occurred, the company had sixteen employees and approximately $2.5 million in revenue.

Presentation Tips

Sharon's actions, through the story narrative, need to be expressed in a persevering manner. She is not a person who gives up.

Set-up

Option 1—In a problem situation, sometimes the solution that is implemented differs radically from what we know really needs to be done.

Option 2—Lack of technology can be beneficial to solving a problem.

Viewing the Problem Through a Different Lens

Sharon was working with a small company that manufactured prosthetic limbs for children. These limbs were manufactured out of wood, leather harnesses, wires, and mechanical parts, with the average arm or leg weighing about twenty-seven pounds. Do you know what the average child under the age of five weighs? Less than twenty-seven pounds! Think about it—this meant that young children might have prosthetic arms or legs equal to or greater than their own body weight.

The company's long-term goal was to reduce the weight of the limbs by substituting nylon for wood. Knowing that their technology was outdated, they began to search for a computer program that did three-dimensional modeling in order to create molds for manufacturing lightweight nylon limbs.

It didn't take long for the company to discover that the type of computer program it wanted cost tens of millions of dollars. Only companies like Boeing, General Motors, and Ford could afford them. The company was ready to throw in the towel.

But, Sharon refused to give up—she decided to take a second look at the problem. She recommended that the company develop a computer program to track information that would help it predict future work and create a competitive edge in the marketplace. The organization began to collect data on children's growth statistics—such as the amount a femur or a forearm increases as a child grows and how frequently artificial limbs were being replaced. It also started to track the specific circumstances that caused these limbs to be replaced. In one instance, a student lost his artificial limb on a river boat cruise when, as a joke, his classmates rolled the arm out on to the dance floor and someone threw it overboard!

It took another ten years before affordable computer programs with three-dimensional modeling became available. Only then was the company able to realize its earlier goal and build lightweight nylon limbs. On the upside, over that ten-year period, data from the computer program that Sharon created allowed the organization to offer value-added services to its customers that they could not find anywhere else.

When a suitable technology solution isn't readily available, it isn't unusual for companies to deem the problem unsolvable. In reality, Sharon's willingness to "take a second look" provided the company with a strategic market advantage that they still leverage today.

Debrief Questions

- What did Sharon do to view the problem in a different way?
- What does this story tell us about problem-solving, even when there are no affordable solutions?
- How often do you run across problems where the obvious solution is not feasible? What can you do to reframe these problems?
- How can you manage uncertainty in problem-solving, especially when you don't know how the future will affect the situation?
- What seemingly insurmountable problems face your organization? Your industry? What is your organization doing to position itself for future success despite these barriers?

Key Point Options

1. Lack of a technology solution must never exclude other available options from being considered. Sometimes the solution to a problem is radically different

from what was anticipated. Breaking the problem down into smaller chunks can lead to a very different result than expected.

2. Creativity is a key ingredient to problem-solving. While others in her company gave up, Sharon insisted on finding a creative interim way of addressing the problem. She had both a long-term vision of future needs and the persistence to implement this short-term goal now.
3. Reframing a problem can help people generate unique solutions. Often a problem cannot be completely solved but can be positively impacted in some way. Only by viewing the problem through a different lens could Sharon identify such a creative alternative. Even though the best solution was not available for another ten years, her unique viewpoint allowed the company to position itself for future success.
4. Assumptions are at the heart of a lack of creative problem-solving. The enterprise initially dismissed all thoughts of any worthwhile solution on the assumption that cost was the only parameter that counted. When Sharon chose to look beyond that barrier, she was able to ask the right questions relevant to clients' future needs.
5. Uncertainty is not just about what you do not know, it is also about what you cannot know. There is always uncertainty attached to financial numbers (in this case, the cost of a new computer program), which is why knowing the assumptions behind these numbers is important.

Follow-up Activity

Step 1—Small-Group Discussion: Identify ways to increase both individual and group creativity when problem-solving. What specific questions or actions can bring out the creative side in each of us?

Step 2—Large-Group Discussion: Have groups report on their findings. As an entire group, brainstorm what organizations can do to build a culture of innovation and creativity.

Step 3—Individual Activity: Apply one of the creativity methods identified in the large-group discussion to a problem that you are currently working on solving. What method did you choose and why? How will you implement this method?

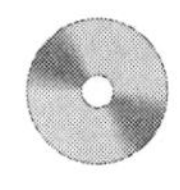

THE DISAPPROVING NEIGHBOR (44)

Contributor

Kate Lutz, professional storyteller

Type and Purpose(s)

Minerva and pattern; entertain and evaluate

Background

This story is based on a traditional East Indian tale that Kate learned from another storyteller, Bobby Avstreih, who first heard it in an ashram in India. Traditional tales frequently travel by word of mouth rather than the printed page, with each teller changing the story slightly to fit their style.

Presentation Tips

The voice of the old woman is shrill and scolding. The voice of the man is patient and soft. The rest of the dialogue is almost like the refrain to a song due to its pattern form.

Set-up

Option 1—How much does our own perspective color our understanding of a problem?

Option 2—How do *you* handle dissatisfaction with a person or situation?

The Disapproving Neighbor

The rooster crowed. The old woman got up, went downstairs, and made two cups of coffee and two bowls of cereal. Putting these on the table, she called her husband to breakfast. No sooner had he sat down than she looked out the window and began scolding, "Look at that woman's house! It's covered with spider webs and splattered with mud! How can she see out her windows? That woman! Why can't she keep her house as clean as I've kept mine?"

Her husband patiently listened.

The next morning, the rooster crowed. The old woman got up, went downstairs, and made two cups of coffee and two bowls of cereal. As her husband sat at the table looking out the window, she began again, "Look at that woman's laundry. It's gray and dingy! Who would want to wear clothes looking like that? Doesn't she know how to wash? Why can't she get her laundry as white as I get mine?"

Her husband's ears burned. Taking his coffee, he went outside. But, even on the porch he could hear her scolding voice.

On the third day, after the rooster crowed, the old woman made the usual two cups of coffee and two bowls of cereal. And, she called her husband. Oddly, he came to the table with a bandanna under his chin that was tied on the top of his head, like rabbit ears. Over both of his ears he had stuffed rolled up socks. But still he could hear her complaints as she looked out the window, "Look at her children; their hair is covered with spider webs. And, oh, I can't believe it, their cheeks—that must be bird poop! Oh, why can't she wash her children as I always washed mine?"

Every morning it was the same: The old woman scolded about her neighbor's dirty house, dirty laundry, and dirty children. Her husband . . . well, he ate less and less breakfast.

Each morning. Well, you know the routine: the crowing rooster, the old woman, two cups of coffee, and two bowls of cereal. Surprisingly, one morning her husband sat promptly at the table. The old woman began her usual scolding before she'd even sat down. "Look at that woman's house . . . why, it's a miracle! Her house is freshly painted! Her laundry shines like the sun. Her children—their faces are freshly scrubbed and smiling. Why she must have been up all night working! A miracle, my prayers have been answered. Everything she owns is clean!"

Her husband looked up from his coffee and softly said, "Old woman, last night, after you went to bed, I went outside and *washed our window!*" [So I ask you, in your life, where do you need to "wash your window"?]

Lutz, K. (Oct. 18, 2000). "A fable: The dirty window." Unpublished story, Denver CO. Adapted and used with permission.

Debrief Questions

- What was the source of the old woman's dissatisfaction?
- How did her husband's reactions influence the story and its outcome?
- How often do we look to others as the cause of our problems?
- Quote: "Truth is a river in which I stand, not a rock on which I sit" (source unknown). How does this story illustrate this quote?

- What impact does our own bias or lack of awareness have on our ability to solve a problem in our lives or in our work?
- What impact does it have on our ability to take ownership for solving the problem?

Key Point Options

1. Each of us has filters through which we view the world. These filters influence our perspective and may not give us accurate information. This can affect our ability to see a problem clearly.
2. Often those filters are less about the other person or situation and more about our own values, opinions, and "shoulds."
3. When we become aware of the filters we use to perceive the world, and how these filters influence our judgment, we can become open to new ways of looking at things and new solutions to the problems we encounter.

Follow-up Activity

Step 1—Pair Discussion: With a partner, take five minutes each to discuss the following: When was a time when you were very dissatisfied with a person or situation in your life? What problem did this create for you? How might you "wash *your* window" by reframing the situation to provide more options?

Step 2—Large-Group Discussion: Have one or two participants tell their stories to the entire group. In a group discussion, develop a list of steps for reducing dissatisfaction and increasing options.

THE ROAD TO PEORIA (45)

Contributor

Bob Shaver, director of the Basic Management Certificate Series, University of Wisconsin-Madison, School of Business, Fluno Center for Executive Education

Type and Purpose(s)

Imbroglio; explore

Background

This situation happened to Bob at a time when he was overloaded with work. He looks back on this situation with great humor.

Presentation Tips

Bob's anxiety level goes from low to high as this situation unfolds.

Set-up

Option 1—What are factors that impact how well a person can solve a problem?

Option 2—If you believe that people want to do their best to solve a problem, what can cause them not to find a solution?

The Road to Peoria

I received a request to teach a supervisory program for a company headquartered in Peoria, Illinois. The training director sent me a detailed, multicolored map of the city, showing the hotel and the training center, and another map that showed the route from Madison, Wisconsin, to Peoria. Now, Peoria is about a four-hour drive from where I live so it's not the sort of thing that I normally look forward to—driving down one day, teaching all day for the next two days, and then driving back again at the end of the second day. To entice me to come, the training director mentioned that we'd be able to gamble and check out the casinos while I was in town. This sounded great because other than driving, I had nothing scheduled the day before the training.

Two weeks before my trip I discovered a special tourism insert in the Sunday newspaper. The insert included several stories about the riverboat casinos, the John Deere Museum, and other places of interest. Thinking no more of it, I threw it in with my training materials. I didn't have time to examine it.

I left Madison very early in the day so I could enjoy some sightseeing along the way. When I arrived outside the city, I pulled over to the side of the road because I didn't know which way to go. From my bag in the back seat of the car, I got out the detailed city map and was having trouble following it. It just didn't make any sense. Then I heard, "Tap, tap, tap." My heart raced when I looked out the window and realized it was a state trooper. You see, I pay lots of road use taxes since I have a tendency to speed. The trooper wanted to make sure I was fine because there was quite a bit of road construction. "What are you trying to do?" he asked. I told him, "I'm trying to get down by the riverboat casinos." He replied, "I can't take you there but I can get you through the construction. I'm headed in that direction."

Finally, I got to the downtown area and found the road to the casinos. But the street names still didn't match up with the city map. So, I stopped at a restaurant to get a cup of coffee and asked the waitress, "What am I doing wrong?" She examined me like I was an alien from another planet and said, "Do you know where you are?" I said, "Yes, I'm in Peoria and I'm trying to get to the riverboat casinos." She laughed and said, "No, you're in Moline. Peoria's ninety miles from here!"

At that point the light bulb went on. I had followed the map in the tourism insert but I had never really examined it. As a result, I wound up at the riverboat casinos in *Moline*, not those in Peoria!

As you move forward in life, take time to "examine the map" you have. Or you may find yourself someplace you don't want to be!

Debrief Questions

- What led Bob to the problem he encountered—arriving at the wrong city?
- What problem-solving skills did he use along the way? How well did they work?
- What might Bob have done to circumvent the problem?
- When have you been faced with a seemingly insurmountable problem that just didn't make sense? What did you do to work it through?
- What approach do you take to solving problems? Do you use a specific method or set of steps? If so, what method?
- What does your organization tend to do when faced with difficult problems? What problem-solving methods does it use?

Key Point Options

1. Many of our problems do not start out as problems. Initially, Bob's task was *not* how to go from Madison to Peoria. That was just a four-hour road trip. It only became a problem once he found himself in a place where his map didn't match the roads. Then, his problem became getting to Peoria from Moline.
2. Solving problems, which is typically a performance expectation, can be affected by four factors: First, the *motivation* to solve the problem. Once he realized he was in the wrong place, Bob was clearly motivated to get to his destination. Second is the *ability,* your own ingenuity and creativity. Bob had the ability to read the map—in fact he had read a number of maps. He also had the ability to drive the car. Third, *support*: the client provided him with detailed maps of the area and the state trooper went out of way his way to be supportive. Bob also asked for help when the problem seemed insurmountable. The last, and in this case, the most critical factor is *awareness.* Bob was so focused on getting to the casino in the newspaper insert that he forgot about all the other essentials, like noticing what city he was in or what city was referenced. Without *awareness,* all the other factors still would not have led Bob to his correct destination.
3. Using the "right maps"—the right frame of reference or theory—can make or break the problem-solving process. Outdated or inaccurate information in this instant-access, global economy can undermine achieving a workable solution, either individually or in a group. It is important to explore how current your "maps" are and whether you are using the "right map" when you problem-solve.
4. Acting on our assumptions is another trap to creative problem-solving and reaching our goals. When we do not question our assumptions, we miss important information or interpret all incoming information according to those assumptions. It is a universal human trait and one we need to be conscious of so that it does not derail us.

Follow-up Activity

Step 1—Small-Group Discussion: Identify a problem needing to be solved by someone in your group. Take the four factors of problem-solving—motivation, ability, support, and awareness—and apply them to this problem. Write your responses so everyone can read them. What is the motivation of the problem solver? What abilities does he or she have to assist with solving this problem? What support systems are in place or can be put into place? Where does the problem solver need to focus his or her attention in order to arrive at a solution?

Step 2—Large-Group Discussion: Have each of the small groups present its problem and the four factors affecting it. Discuss how the model applies to organizational problem-solving.

Teamwork and Collaboration

chapter
FIFTEEN

The four stories featured in this chapter focus on the power of collaboration—teamwork, partnership, and cooperation in our lives and in our work. Organizations and communities take great pride in and expend immense effort on building a collaborative framework, which demonstrates a deeply held commitment to shared outcomes. The magic of working together and the synergistic impact of multiple ideas can outstrip the efforts of individuals in some highly unique ways. Building on a collective spirit to achieve their goals, the characters in these stories show us both the noble and the roguish aspects of seeing the opportunity in the moment.

"Doing the Packarena" will make you want to get up and dance as you appreciate Katherine Hudson's employees building team spirit. Their creativity resulted in news cameras filming hundreds of employees demonstrating the Packarena on the company's front lawn. The power of win-win outcomes is the topic of Sivasailam "Thiagi" Thiagarajan's tale, "The Contest." A wise contestant breaks through the competitive mindset to offer new possibilities. In "A Family United," Clare Novak shares a story from Aesop's Fables that was brought to her by one of her Egyptian students. It illustrates the strength of unity in numbers. Finally, you will appreciate the humor in Robert McIlree's "The Slingshot." It exposes the antics of college students on a team mission to preserve what little sleep they can.

Working together has unlimited potential and is fundamental to who we are as human beings. By working, laughing, and thinking together, we grow as individuals. These stories bring us a deeper appreciation of our connection to each other.

DOING THE PACKARENA (46)

Contributor

Katherine M. Hudson, president and CEO, Brady Corporation

Type and Purpose(s)

Credibility; entertain and evoke

Background

Brady Corporation is a Fortune 100 company transforming its culture.

Presentation Tips

Learn how to perform and teach the dance called the macarena. You may also want to contact the Brady Corporation for a copy of the Packarena Playbook so you can also perform the movements to this dance!

Set-up

Option 1—Remember the song and the dance called the macarena? (Show the movements.) Have you ever considered how an organization might use it to showcase its values?

Option 2—Communicating the importance of teamwork and collaboration goes beyond posters and presentations.

Doing the Packarena

In the summer of 1996, the Green Bay Packers were looking forward to a promising season. So for our annual Bradyfest picnic, an executive in our Signmark division decided to put together something that would appeal to Brady's ardent Packers fans. He settled on a routine set to the music of the macarena, the popular dance at the time, but with football movements: you take the snap, you step back, you pass, you receive the ball, you celebrate the touchdown.

A local television station came out and filmed a performance of the Packarena from our front yard here at corporate headquarters. About 300 people from all segments of the company showed up in Packers shirts to perform for the cameras. The Packers cheerleaders came down from Green Bay. Well, as soon as the Packarena aired, our switchboard was jammed: People wanted a copy of the "Packarena Playbook," the instructions to do the dance. Soon thereafter, we went to elementary schools to teach the dance to kids. The Green Bay cheerleaders learned it and did it during halftime at one of the Packers' home games.

It's probably the most publicity Brady has ever received. The Packarena was the talk of Milwaukee for weeks. More important, it was the talk of [the] Brady [Corporation].

Debrief Questions

- What intangible benefits did the Brady Corporation receive from the Packarena, both internally and externally?
- Why do you think creating the Packarena created such strong team spirit at Brady Corporation?
- When have you been part of a team that had fun as well as got the job done?
- What do you think creates this kind of team spirit?
- What is your organization doing to create spirit in the workplace?
- How can you use humor in your company to build morale and teamwork?
- What approaches can you take to encourage employees to collaborate?

Key Point Options

1. Humor enables people to connect and be more engaged in the workplace.
2. Engaged employees are more productive and share information more freely. For fifty years, the Gallup Organization has studied how employee attitudes relate to performance. In their latest findings, Gallup discovered that the workgroups that exhibited the highest levels of employee engagement were more likely to have above-average employee retention, customer loyalty, safety records, productivity, and profitability ("Employee Engagement," 2002).
3. Creating fun in the workplace creates a culture of acceptance, camaraderie, and collaboration. This leads to higher productivity, morale, and performance.

Follow-up Activities

Activity 1

Step 1—Small-Group Discussion: Have small groups discuss and then make a list of suggestions for creating teamwork and team spirit in the organization.

Step 2—Large-Group Discussion: Compile the small group suggestions and identify the most popular ones. Discuss what benefits these ideas might bring to the organization and its employees.

Activity 2

Step 1—Small-Group Discussion: Have small groups design a dance, based on some organizational value, for the enterprise.

Step 2—Large-Group Activity: Have each team demonstrate its dance for the entire group.

Step 3—Large-Group Discussion: What values did the dances portray? How did each dance depict its value? What was the experience like for your team to develop the dance?

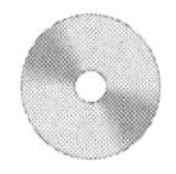

THE SLINGSHOT (47)

Contributor

Robert McIlree

Type and Purpose(s)

Imbroglio; entertain and explore

Background

This story is about an incident that occurred while Bob was in college in 1979. Looking back, it was a stroke of luck that he and his friends didn't injure someone. While it was construed back then as a college "prank," times have changed.

Presentation Tips

Uses pauses in key spots to allow for laughter from the audience.

Set-up

Option 1—Conflicting needs between teams can fuel outrageous responses.

Option 2—Have you ever thought about what can happen when two teams that impact each other hold opposite goals?

Option 3—Never underestimate the power of teamwork.

The Slingshot

I was a member of a fraternity during my undergraduate days in the late 1970s at UW-Madison. At that time, the university had nationally ranked rowing teams that would practice on the lake around five o'clock in the morning once the weather grew warmer. As I saw it, there was a problem with this. Their coach would follow them in a motorboat with a bullhorn, shouting instructions: "Pull-2-3-4, pull-2-3-4." Naturally, the sound of the coach exhorting his troops onward carried across the lake and into our living quarters—which regularly disturbed our sleep at that ungodly hour of the morning. As far as I was concerned, he wasn't being very considerate of our needs.

After a week or so of this abuse, I began searching for a way to take action. It was then that I decided to put my technical education to good use. First, I went to a lumberyard and purchased two four-foot wooden poles about three inches in diameter. Next, I had a frat brother, who worked at the university hospital, quietly appropriate about thirty-five feet of heavy gauge surgical tubing. Then, I drilled holes on both ends of the wooden poles and tied the surgical tubing to them.

Still not finished, I rummaged through closets for old blue jeans. I cut up two pairs of jeans, stitched the material together, and attached the tubing to the material with heavy thread and super glue. The result was a three-man slingshot—two guys held the poles up while one would pull back on the tubing and pouch and let it fly.

Our frat house was on Lake Mendota, with the property sloping down to the shoreline. The house was three stories high, with a basement, and a large deck off the top floor overlooking the lake. We tested the device off of the top deck using golf balls, tennis balls, oranges—anything small enough to fit inside the pouch. We found that items of this size could easily be propelled 150 to 300 yards into the water, depending on the angle and how far back the apparatus was pulled. Our testing greatly amused all who watched us—including the patrons on the pier at the restaurant next door.

After a week of bad weather during which the crew teams could not practice on the lake, they were back at it again early one morning with the bullhorn-wielding coach in full glory. Since we had been indulging in our usual late-night party activities, we were, to say the least, quite dismayed. I found my two cohorts and told them it was our day of reckoning. In no time, we retrieved the slingshot and headed upstairs to the deck.

Problem was, we had practiced so much that we had run out of "ammunition." So, I ran downstairs to the kitchen to see what I could rustle up as a substitute. "Tomatoes . . . no, sack of potatoes . . . yes! Soup, bread, eggs. Ah . . . melons. Unripened melons!"

I took my newfound ammunition up to the deck. We first tried firing the potatoes, but due to their odd shapes they weren't aerodynamic enough to reach the boats. We then tried a melon, which worked much better but didn't fly as far due to its weight. Frustrated, I took a second melon, pulled back on the slingshot as far as I could, and pretty much blindly fired it at the lake.

Unbeknownst to me, one of the boats had moved in closer to shore. My desperation shot landed squarely between two crewmembers and smashed a large hole in the boat, which quickly turned upright and capsized! While the crewmembers swam to shore, their coach cruised straight to our dock and ran into the yard, bullhorn in hand. While we watched and laughed from inside the house, he shouted words I hesitate to repeat for about five minutes before he went back to his boat and took off.

Everyone laughed hysterically about this all day and into the next week . . . until the frat house received a letter from the dean of students office informing us that if we didn't pay $1,400 to the athletic department to replace the crew boat, none of us would graduate, be able to register for future semesters, or get transcripts. This was a lot of money in the late 1970s. Imagine asking your parents for a semester's tuition to fulfill this debt. It was then that we realized that we neglected to "consider the consequences" of our actions. Even though we had hit our target, the outcome had an unintended negative consequence associated with it. So, what's my message to you? The next time you set a target and create a plan to accomplish it, consider the consequences.

Debrief Questions

- What does this story show us about teamwork?
- How effective was this team? Why or why not?
- What were the unintended consequences that this team experienced? Why did they occur? How might they have been avoided?
- When have you created a team in order to achieve a goal of yours?
- How successful were you in reaching your goal?
- How do employees in your area learn effective teamwork?
- How can you apply the lessons from this story to teams in your department or organization?

Key Point Options

1. Conflicting needs between teams with opposing goals whose work impacts each other can derail the success of a project or organization-wide effort. Team leaders need to pay attention not only to the needs and goals of their own team, but the needs and goals of other groups within the organization that impact their teams. Collaboration is more than working well within your team.
2. There are four elements of teamwork: (1) membership (that is, knowing who is on the team); (2) a reason for existence (that is, a team charter that includes goals and so on); (3) ground rules (or expectations); and (4) roles and responsibilities. A team can experience unintended consequences of its actions even if the four elements of teamwork are clearly defined and understood.
3. Team spirit can be difficult to define and create. It often depends on the commitment to or passion for the goal that is the reason for forming the team.

Follow-up Activity

Step 1—Small-Group Activity: Have each group take the slingshot story and identify the four elements of teamwork for this particular team. Ask each group to discuss the details of each of the four elements given what they know and can infer from the story.

Step 2—Small-Group Activity: Have each group take one example of a team from their respective organizations. Have the group describe the four elements of teamwork and how appropriate each of them is for this team. Have the groups answer: What would this team need to do to become (or continue as) a high performing team?

A FAMILY UNITED (48)

Contributor

Clare Novak, president, Novak and Associates

Type and Purpose(s)

Minerva; explore

Background

While training in Egypt, a student in one of Clare's workshops gave this story to her. It is based on one of Aesop's Fables.

Presentation Tips

Watch that you do not give away the key point of the story when you introduce it.

Set-up

Option 1—The wisdom of a parent can be far-reaching in its implications.

Option 2—Strength can be defined in many ways.

A Family United

A father had four sons. As he got older, he wanted to give his sons the wisdom of his experience.

He asked his sons to meet with him and showed them a bundle of sticks laid out on the ground. He picked up the first stick and asked his first son to break it. The oldest son easily broke the stick. Then the father picked up two sticks and asked his second son to break them. The son broke both of them, but with not as much ease as the first son. The father then bent over and picked up three sticks and asked his third son to break them. It took quite a bit of effort, but the son was finally able to break all three of the sticks. Then the father picked up four sticks and asked his fourth son to break them. The son tried with all his strength, but was unable to break the sticks.

After a few minutes, the father leaned back and said to his four sons, "You were able to break one stick, two sticks and three sticks, but you were not able to break four. What does this tell you about your relationship to each other? What does this tell you about where your strength lies? There is 'strength in numbers.'"

What about your relationships? Who are your allies? In whom does your strength lie?

Debrief Questions

- What lesson did his sons learn? How might they have answered their father?
- What does this story mean for you?
- How does this story relate to teamwork in your organization?
- Where can you create the power of unity in your life?

Key Point Options

1. There is power in unity and strength in collaboration. A united front can withstand more pressure than an individual acting alone and can achieve greater results.
2. Organizational change is dependent on groups of people acting in unity with a shared goal.

Follow-up Activity

Step 1—Small-Group Discussion: Think of a time when you were able to achieve more by working collaboratively. What were you able to accomplish? How did that feel?

Step 2—Large-Group Discussion: Decide how and where you can set up more collaborative efforts to achieve organizational goals.

THE CONTEST (49)

Contributor

Sivasailam "Thiagi" Thiagarajan, resident mad scientist, QB International

Type and Purpose(s)

Minerva; explore and evoke

Background

Thiagi created this story to as a way to illustrate values around competition and winning.

Presentation Tips

Use a mysterious tone of voice in appropriate parts of the story. You will also want to use different voices for each of the characters.

Set-up

Option 1—We learn about competition at an early age, just like the children in this village.

Option 2—What does winning mean to you?

The Contest

Every child in the village had heard about the exploits of past contest winners from their grandparents. Nobody knew when the contest tradition first began but everybody knew how it was conducted.

The contest was very simple. Two contestants stood facing each other. They spread their feet and assumed a stable posture. Then they placed their palms against those of the other person. The referee stood near them and started the contest by beginning to count. The rule for winning the contest was very simple. All children had memorized it: You win if you make the other person's feet move before the referee finished counting to twenty.

Everyone played the game in the village—men and women, boys and girls. From a very early age, children were taught competitive strategies. Among adults, there were secret meetings to share special techniques. In these meetings, the older and wiser people taught others how to strengthen leg and arm muscles, how to stand barefoot and dig your toes into the ground, and how to push suddenly to topple the other contestant. There were *other* secret gatherings where men and women learned how to cast spells to weaken the opponent, how to talk to the opponent to make him lose his confidence, and how to stare at the opponent's forehead to mesmerize him. Some people even bribed their opponents with money to get them to pretend to lose. However, this type of bribe was very expensive because of the public humiliation of losing.

On the seventh day of the first month on the lunar calendar, the village gathered on the banks of the river for the championship contest.

Over the last four years, the ceremony had been anticlimactic—nobody had challenged the champion. Rumor had it that there wouldn't be any challengers this year either and the champion would once again win by default. Despite this, all the villagers poured into the arena hoping for some surprise and excitement.

The champion came to the middle of the arena and yelled out the traditional challenge. The village elder, who served as the referee, stood by his side, ready to count to twenty. There was a hush in the crowd even though no one was expected to step forward.

But wait. There was movement in the back of the crowd—someone *was* stepping forward: a thin, old, holy man with a gray beard. Although he looked weak, he strode purposefully to face the champion. Without delay, he assumed the palm-to-palm starting position.

Some spectators started laughing. Others became apprehensive, thinking that the holy man had secret powers to hurt the champion. They held their collective breath. The village elder started the count. Before the count of three, the holy man moved his feet. The crowd began howling in disappointment. But the village elder kept counting because, after all, rules were rules. The holy man whispered something into the champion's ears. When the count reached seventeen, the champion moved his feet. The crowd was stunned and confused.

The village elder called for his advisors. They talked among themselves in subdued tones. Then the elder stepped into the middle of the arena and said: "I proclaim that both contestants won. The ancient rules say that a person wins if the other person's feet move before the count of twenty. Since both contestants' feet moved, both of them have won!"

Later, people asked the champion, "What did the holy man whisper to you?" According to the champion, this is what the holy man said: "You have already won. Would you like to achieve a greater victory? If you move your feet, I too can win. That way you can demonstrate how generosity makes everyone win."

That's the year the villagers learned that a person could win without requiring someone else to lose—that "generosity creates a collaborative spirit."

Debrief Questions

- What strategies had the villagers employed over the years in order to win the competition? Which were *positive* strategies and which were *negative* strategies?
- What did you think about the way the competition ended? How fair or unfair did you think it was? What did you think about the holy man's strategy?
- Where do we learn about competition, collaboration, and win-win outcomes?
- How does generosity come into play in this story? Where have you been generous in your own life to achieve a positive outcome?
- Where are there opportunities in your organization for increased collaboration between work teams, areas, or departments?

Key Point Options

1. As a society, we have powerful messages about competition and winning being positive. We also are taught that in order to win, someone has to lose.
2. When we take our focus away from doing our best and place it on undermining our opponent, competition can create negative consequences and hurt relationships.
3. The concept of win-win outcomes demonstrates a value that there can be more than one winner and that to win does not require someone to lose.

Follow-up Activity

Step 1—Paired Activity: Have participants partner with each other. Have each person draw six Tic Tac Toe grids on a piece of paper (or create a handout with the grids). Each pair will have a total of twelve grids to use during the game. Instructions: "You are going to play Tic Tac Toe for one minute with the following goal: Each of you is to try to win as many games as possible. For each game that you win, you receive five points." Play the game for sixty seconds.

Step 2—Individual Activity: Have each person total their winnings. As the trainer, post these winnings on a sheet of paper that everyone can read. For example, "How many of you won zero points? Five points? Ten points?" and so on.

Step 3—Paired Activity: Have the pairs draw twelve more grids (or pass out another handout to each person). Instructions: "Now I want you to work with your partner as a team and play Tic Tac Toe for one minute. This time, the goal is for your *team* to win as much as it can. I will give you two minutes to plan your collaborative strategy." Give the planning time and then time the game for sixty seconds.

Step 4—Paired Activity: Have each team total its winnings and post them on a sheet of paper that everyone can see.

Step 5—Large-Group Discussion:

- Which method resulted in winning more points? (*Answer:* The second method.) Why? Answers may include: the games could be played faster, you always had a winner (no draw games), you had time to work out a strategy, you were collaborating instead of competing, you had a common goal, and so on.
- Which strategy—competition or collaboration—would have better met the *first* goal, which was simply to win as many points as you could? Answer: the collaboration strategy. Note: Some participants may protest that this constitutes cheating. You may need to debrief the activity regarding this emotional reaction.
- How often do we wind up competing against other departments rather than collaborating?
- What is the impact on the organization's overall productivity and effectiveness?
- Where might we create more collaboration in the organization? What benefits would this bring?

Training Fundamentals

chapter
SIXTEEN

From life lessons to humorous episodes, the opportunity to learn is everywhere. What makes it possible for learning to take place? This question is at the root of each of these six stories, which cover learning a new skill, the training process, or classroom pitfalls. As managers, facilitators, and presenters, we notice how unique human qualities play out in the ways our participants learn and do not learn. If any part of your job requires you to teach or train others, these stories will enhance your understanding of the fundamentals of training and bring forth a few smiles as well.

Two of the stories contrast the differences in individual learning styles. In "How My Sons Learned to Dive," mom Suzann Gardner watches her two sons take very different approaches to their summer diving lessons. Paula Bartholome observes the different learning values of two of her students who are "In Pursuit of a Goal" while enrolled in her university course.

"I Didn't Ask to Be Here" recounts a trainer's nightmare—the reluctant participant required to come to training. It was a woman who had not received proper job coaching and was sent to trainer Jean Barbazette to be "fixed." In another classroom vignette, "Preparing Yourself for the Unexpected," Larry English shows his immediate response and how he coped in the moment with a group of seminar participants relying on him to take leadership after the September 11, 2001, terrorist attacks. How he arrived at his leadership response and what he chose to do speaks to his commitment to his group and his religious calling early in life.

In "The Jock and His Wife Go Water Skiing," John Renesch notes the *lack* of self-awareness that prevents the jock from successfully achieving his goal of learning how to water ski. In summary, "Teaching a Dog to Whistle" by Sharon Bowman takes us back to the fundamental question: "What is the difference between teaching and learning?" The answer to this question—and others trainers have been asking for decades—lies within these stories. They demonstrate that training is clearly not a spectator sport.

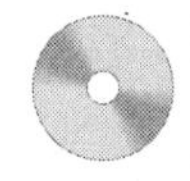

I DIDN'T ASK TO BE HERE (50)

Contributor

Jean Barbazette, president, The Training Clinic

Type and Purpose(s)

Instructional; educate and explore

Background

This story is about how to deal with a problem learner and what Jean learned from dealing with this situation firsthand.

Presentation Tips

Demonstrate the various emotions that Jean felt through vocal changes and gestures. Also depict the problem participant's frustrations in your tone of voice and actions.

Set-up

Option 1—How important is it to offer people choices, even in situations where there may not be many available?

Option 2—Our behavior is influenced by the choices we are allowed to make . . . or not make.

Option 3—Your reactions and behaviors can significantly influence the outcome of a problem situation for everyone who is involved.

I Didn't Ask to Be Here

Imagine being in Oahu teaching a customer-service workshop for a government agency. I was there for three days—teaching two day-and-a-half workshops, back to back, to a total of twenty-four employees.

The first day and a half with a group of twelve was marvelous. It was an absolutely wonderful group. They were the epitome of Hawaiian hospitality. They even took me to lunch at the end of the program.

At one o'clock in the afternoon on the second day, I was in the classroom to meet with the second group. Just then, a supervisor who said she had responsibility for training stopped and asked if she could observe. I said, "Sure, that's fine." One by one I greeted employees as they came through the door. I happened to notice one woman who didn't have much to say. She was sitting back from the table with her arms folded. Her body language said, "I don't want to be here."

To start the session, I asked people to introduce themselves to a partner so their partner could introduce them to the entire group. As they talked in pairs, I walked around the room. When I got to the second pair I noticed they weren't speaking to one another. I said, "Is there a problem?" The two women, one of whom I had noticed earlier, said they were going to introduce themselves. I said, "Okay."

Later that afternoon, as I was assigning people to case study discussion groups, this same woman—her name is Mary—slams her pencil down and says, "This is a [blank, blank] waste of the taxpayers' money and I am not doing this." I'm thinking, "Here I am in a wonderful mood and now it's being destroyed. I feel totally caught off guard by this person's behavior."

I told the discussion groups to go through the case study. Then, I said to myself, "Count to ten. Just wait her out. Here's an opportunity to practice what you teach other people all the time." As I counted to ten and gathered my wits about me, I dashed out into the hall to find someone to talk to. At the same time, the supervisor who was observing the workshop also dashed out. She approached me and said, "I knew this was going to happen." I said, "Really? How did you know that?" And she replied, "Oh, I'm Mary's supervisor." I retorted, "Why didn't you tell me that before? I'd like it if you'd let me go back in there alone and handle this myself. Why do you think that this is happening?" She said, "Well, she's the only one out of the twenty-four people who was *told* to come and we'd like you to fix her." I responded, "I'm not sure that can happen. I don't do lobotomies. If there's something I can help her with in terms of what she can learn and how she treats the public I'd be willing to help with that."

I went back in and declared an early break. You would've thought there was a fire. Eleven people were falling all over each other racing to get out. They couldn't stand to be near Mary who had embarrassed them. As Mary reached the door, I asked, "Can I have a word with you?" And she said—I will never forget this: "Yes. What do you want to know?" "You don't seem too pleased to be here." That's all I had to say. For the next fifteen minutes Mary unloaded—she was forced to attend; everyone else had a choice of signing up; she didn't want to be here; they were out to get her. I thought, "Well, maybe she has a point." I said, "Okay, let's make a deal. Can we have a truce? You're free to choose. I won't ask you to do anything other than be here since you're required to. Can you do that?" And she said, "Okay." When class reconvened, I didn't call on Mary. I didn't request her to read anything or do anything. She just had to be quiet.

An hour later, we had another case study. When I divided people into groups, I ignored Mary. Within a few minutes, she rolled back her chair and listened in on a group nearby. She even threw in a comment or two. The third time we broke into groups, I asked, "Would you care to join a group this time?" She said, "Okay." This continued for the rest of the afternoon. By the end of the four hours, everything had gone back to normal.

On her post-workshop evaluation Mary wrote, "This was one of the best workshops that I have ever been to." Under general comments she remarked, "No one should be forced to attend a workshop that is for voluntary enrollment." I couldn't agree with her more.

At the end of the three days, the manager of the entire group asked me to write up a disciplinary incident, as he called it. I said, "There was no incident. Mary was very cooperative in the class and she did everything she was asked to do." Boy, was he shocked. It was then that I learned that he wanted me to help him build a case to fire her. In return, he quickly learned there was no way I was going to be a part of that.

I clearly understood that having a choice was at the heart of Mary's continued involvement. I respected her rights and made it clear that she was "free to choose." And, just like Mary, in your life you're also free to choose.

Debrief Questions

- What was your first reaction to the student's disruptive behavior? How did your viewpoint about this woman shift by the end of the story?
- Why did the student become disruptive?
- How would you evaluate the supervisor's and the manager's performance management skills?
- If you were the trainer, what would you have done to handle this disruptive participant?
- If you were the manager of this disruptive employee, how might you have worked with her performance prior to attending training?
- What might cause an employee to become disruptive and non-participative—and display what others might call a "bad attitude?"
- What can organizations do to ensure that participants value the training experience?

Key Point Options

1. One of the things Jean learned from this situation and reinforces in every training program is that adults like to be valued and respected for their opinions. They like to make choices. In every workshop she conducts Jean ensures that trainees are given choices in her classroom. This concept is a key adult learning principle.
2. Training is not a solution for "fixing people." It provides awareness, information, skill practice, and the opportunity to interact with others who have similar roles in an organization. Training cannot *make* someone act differently than the way they choose. Using training as a way to build a case against employees is unethical and can undermine both their confidence in an organization and their interest in self-development.
3. For training to be a positive experience, the organization's leaders need to collaborate with the facilitator by sharing goals and relevant information, supporting trainees' in using the skills back on the job, and in providing clear feedback.
4. Author and educator Edgar Schein developed a process consultation model, adapted here, describing four steps that we go through in responding to events.

It can be used to explain Jean's reactions to this situation. The first step is *observation*: what have you heard, seen, or sensed in your gut. Jean saw a participant who clearly said she did not want to be there. The second step is *reaction*: the emotional response you notice in yourself. Jean's response was to notice how her wonderful mood was being destroyed. The third step is *assessment*: your interpretation or evaluation of a situation. What you might infer is under the surface. Jean's assessment was that she had a problem and needed to deal with it. The fourth step is *intervention*: what you do about the situation. Jean went into the hallway to find someone to talk with and to gather more information (Schein, 1987, pp. 63–69). This cycle repeats several times throughout the story.

Follow-up Activity

Step 1—Small-Group Discussion: Ask the participants to describe when they have been in a group setting in which one of the members (or they, themselves) did not wish to be there. What was that like for them? What impact did that have on the entire group? What did the group do to handle the situation?

Step 2—Large-Group Discussion: Ask for several examples from the small groups. Lead a discussion on what a group can do to work with employees who do not seem motivated or interested in participating. Ask what the employee's supervisor can do to work with this behavior.

IN PURSUIT OF A GOAL (51)

Contributor

Paula Bartholome, principal and corporate jester, Parallax

Type and Purpose(s)

Vignette; engage and explore

Background

Paula teaches a course on storytelling in business at De Paul University in Chicago, Illinois.

Presentation Tips

Use different locations in the room when talking about each student. Also have a specific spot for the narrator (university instructor) from which to speak.

Set-up

Option 1—What is learning really all about?

Option 2—We get out of learning what we are willing to put into it.

In Pursuit of a Goal

Once upon a time I had two very different adult students in a university class on organizational storytelling. Both had jobs and also had family and school responsibilities. Both were very bright. Both wanted to do things correctly. Both wanted to make an A and meet the expectations of the class. But that's where the similarities end.

The first student and I talked frequently as she progressed through the course. She expressed concerns that she wasn't learning, that her personal goals were getting in the way, and that perhaps she was approaching the course with the wrong intent. She would reflect on teachings, often asking for feedback on her work, and then she would revise it and ask for feedback again. The class was a struggle, as though her brain, she said, "was a rusty screw being twisted back and forth in an effort to loosen it and let the learning in." This student struggled with *learning how to learn.* In the end, she gave her all. She learned about storytelling in organizations and collaborative learning and how organizations work.

In the same course, a second student asked me again and again for explicit boundaries and instructions for the assignments. She focused time and energy trying to get ahead, even doing her team's work for them, meeting the letter of the expectations, and planning for next quarter's classes. She asked many times, "If I do 'this and this and this,' that will be OK, won't it?" Her focus was on structure, not content. "The class was a struggle," she said, as if she didn't understand how to do what she was being asked to do. This student struggled with *finding ways to meet expectations.* In the end, she gave enough to get through it. She didn't learn nearly as much about storytelling in organizations or collaborative learning or how organizations work.

Both students had goals. Both had motivation, and both asked for feedback. Yet only one learned! In learning, and in life, you "get what you give."

Debrief Questions

- What goal did each learner have?
- How did their goals differ from each other?
- How did their differing goals impact their ability to learn?
- What do you think is the moral of this story?
- Which student did you most identify with regarding your own learning goals?
- In what situations in your life or work is it appropriate to focus more on "learning how to learn" versus "finding ways to meet expectations"?

Key Point Options

1. Learning is a process—not a list of things to accomplish. Focusing only on the outcome or *product* causes you to miss the *process.* True learning enables a person to understand the process so that he or she can transfer it to new situations.
2. In each training or learning situation you have a choice—doing enough to meet the minimum expectations or working thoroughly, paying attention to the entire inner and outer process. There are benefits and consequences to each approach. What is important is knowing the decision you are making, communicating it to those who are involved, and taking ownership for the consequences of the decision.
3. Learning is not a function of the time you spend or the amount of feedback you ask for and receive. It is a willingness to explore ideas, self-reflect on your own internal process, and notice the resulting changes.

Follow-up Activities

Activity 1

Step 1—Small-Group Discussion: What are your learning goals for this class? How will you know you have achieved them?

Step 2—Large-Group Discussion: Have several participants share their learning goals and measures for achieving them. Ask: How will you transfer this learning to your work? Your life?

Activity 2

Step 1—Small-Group Discussion: Ask half of the participants to identify when it makes sense to focus more on meeting the minimum requirements (doing enough to get by). Ask the other half to identify when it makes sense to be thorough and focus on the learning process throughout a task. Have each group also identify the benefits and consequences of each approach.

Step 2—Large-Group Discussion: Ask each group to present their findings.

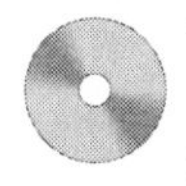

TEACHING A DOG TO WHISTLE (52)

Contributor

Sharon L. Bowman, director, The Lake Tahoe Trainers Group

Type and Purpose(s)

Vignette; entertain and engage

Background

About twenty years ago, Sharon saw a cartoon in a local newspaper that showed two boys and a dog in front of a house. It gave her the idea to typify the difference between teaching and learning through this story. Sharon often uses this story at the beginning of a training program to introduce the concept of shared responsibility for learning.

Presentation Tips

Use different voices for the two boys. Engage in boy-like gestures and body posture throughout the story.

Set-up

Option 1—Learning is not a spectator sport.

Option 2—When do we know for certain that learning has taken place?

Teaching a Dog to Whistle

An older boy named Joey, his dog, Buster, and his younger buddy, Brian, are standing on the lawn in front of Joey's house. Joey turns to Brian and says boastfully, "I taught Buster how to whistle." Brian looks at the dog for what seems like an eternity, then looks at his friend, and says, "Show me." So they both look at the dog. The dog just stands there wagging his tail with his tongue hanging out. "Okay, Buster, go to it, boy. Whistle!" Once again, the dog does nothing. This goes on for several minutes. Each time Buster, the dog, is commanded to whistle, he looks at the boys, wags his tail, and sits there.

Finally, Brian turns to Joey in disgust and says "Hey! You said your dog could whistle. Well, we've been here ten minutes and he hasn't whistled once!" Joey looks at his younger buddy, Brian, with a grin on his face and says, "Of course he can't whistle. I told you I *taught* him how to whistle. I didn't say he *learned* it."

Just because we teach—a concept, an idea, a skill—it doesn't mean that someone learns it. Learners are in the driver's seat. "Learners drive the learning." What about you? You also choose the road to your own learning.

Debrief Questions

- What meaning does this story hold for you?
- What does it demonstrate about the difference between teaching and learning?
- When have you been taught something without really learning it? Why do you think this was the case?
- How does the distinction between teaching and learning impact the way you teach others in your work? How can you ensure that those you have taught have actually learned something?

Key Point Options

1. Learning is not a spectator sport. It makes sense to participate fully in your own learning and team up with others to ensure that you get the most out of the experience. Learning is a mutual commitment that takes the full participation of both the instructor and the participant.
2. To paraphrase speaker and trainer Bob Pike, learning has not taken place until behavior has changed. Upon leaving a training program, there is no assurance that learning has taken place until you actually apply the information in your own life.
3. Often the goal of a training program is not to create a complete behavior change but to fine tune what you are already doing well or to provide the opportunity to practice and add to your current skills.
4. It is useful to have participants establish a learning goal at the beginning of a training session to guide their focus throughout the program. It shapes the way they participate and helps them assess the value of the experience.

Follow-up Activity

Step 1—Paired Discussion: Introduce yourself to a partner and tell the person what you want to learn during the training session (set a learning goal).

Step 2—Large-Group Discussion: Go around the room and have each participant report on their learning goal. If appropriate, list the goals and participant names on paper so that everyone can see them.

Step 3—Large-Group Discussion: Near the end of the program, check in with participants to see if their learning goals were met.

PREPARING YOURSELF FOR THE UNEXPECTED (53)

Contributor

Larry P. English, president, INFORMATION IMPACT International, Inc.

Type and Purpose(s)

Crucible; encourage and explore

Background

Like all of us, Larry was unprepared for what happened on September 11 and the impact it would have on his work. His early religious calling in life was a strength he drew on this day.

Presentation Tips

Even thought this is a somber story it is best told with great strength and boldness.

Set-up

Option 1—How do we prepare ourselves to help those who are experiencing adversity?

Option 2—In a crisis, what prompts us to think about others' needs as well as our own?

Preparing Yourself for the Unexpected

Tuesday, September 11, 2001, was the second day of a three-day seminar that I was teaching for a large insurance company at its eighty-room training facility in the midwest. Ten minutes after we began at 8:00 A.M. central time, one student rushed in and announced a plane had crashed into the World Trade Center. We were dumbstruck. A few minutes later another student left. Choking back tears upon his return, he described the unexpected tragedy that was unfolding minute by minute.

We took a twenty-minute break and moved to another classroom to watch CNN unfold the horror. When we reconvened, we had to wrestle with the decision about whether we should continue. My sponsor wanted us to keep going. And yet I knew that the tragedy was going to be foremost on people's minds. So I suggested we break until one o'clock that afternoon.

My first order of business was to call my wife, my parents, and my kids. My second task was to prepare to lead the group upon its return. I decided to take a walk around the neighborhood—to reflect on what was happening. As I strolled, I observed all the small things that I normally wouldn't have observed. After lunch at a pizza joint, I came back and put some thoughts on paper to focus myself.

When the group reconvened, I shared my observations. I saw people mowing their lawns, a utility crew moving electrical wires, a pair of grasshoppers mating in an open field. I *saw* the message we needed to embrace. "Life goes on and life will go on. While we may want to do something to help, there is nothing we can do physically because we are so removed from the tragedy. We can offer our prayers. This evening, we can give blood. We can donate. We can do other things. As an insurance company, your business is all about providing help to people who have tragic needs and need recovery from them." I shared the prayer of Reinhold Niebuhr: God grant me the Serenity to accept the things I cannot change, the Courage to change the things I can, and the Wisdom to know the difference. I ended with, "Probably the best thing for you to do is to continue doing what you do because that's helping other people who have tragedy."

The group unanimously voted to continue the class. So we proceeded that day, certainly in a more somber mood than we might have otherwise. But we made it through.

In readying myself to address the group on the afternoon of that fateful day, I realized that I needed to work through the unexpected event and prepare myself to help them. I'm reminded of the words that flight attendants tell passengers on the plane: "If we lose cabin pressure, oxygen masks will fall out of the compartments above you. Put your oxygen mask on first. Then assist a child or an elderly person." I think this is true of life. We first have to "*prepare ourselves* for the unexpected" before we are in a position to truly help others. So I ask you, how are you preparing for the unexpected in your life?

Debrief Questions

- What allowed Larry to continue working with his training group?
- How did the crisis and Larry's response change the experience of the group?
- What was the group's response to his support?
- When have you experienced a crisis during a training session? What was that like for you?

- What common themes emerge for you about groups supporting each other during crisis? What does this show us about unity and being connected?
- How can you encourage unity and connectedness in your training when there is not a crisis?

Key Point Options

1. As a trainer, crisis is always a possibility during your time with participants. Being prepared for this possibility helps you establish a comfortable learning environment.
2. Know that people in crisis tend to form deeper bonds and more meaningful connections than during non-crisis times, especially with the thoughtful encouragement of a compassionate leader.
3. In thinking about the needs of others and seeking to meet those needs, we become an *ally* to those individuals. We all need allies in our lives.
4. Often, being reminded of the daily, small events of life helps us come through in times of adversity. As a trainer, helping your participants reconnect to their daily lives allows them to bridge any gaps between people and unite around a common purpose.

Follow-up Activity

Step 1—Paired Discussion: Each partner takes five minutes to respond to the following questions. When have you been helped by others during a training program? What did they do to show support? How did that feel?

Step 2—Paired Discussion: With the same partner, each take another five minutes to respond to these questions: When have you helped someone else through a difficult time during a training session? What did you do to show support? How did that feel for you? What was the other person's response?

Step 3—Individual Activity: Write about what stands out for you from these conversations. Also reflect on the implications these reflections have for you in your life.

HOW MY SONS LEARNED TO DIVE (54)

Contributor

Suzann Gardner, associate professor, Alverno College

Type and Purpose(s)

Pattern; educate and engage

Background

This at times frustrating example of her sons' difference in performance caused Suzann to notice how learning styles impact every new situation.

Presentation Tips

Make a slapping sound by slapping a tabletop or by clapping your hands together each time you say "belly flop." Depict the many changes in Suzann's emotions through vocal changes and gestures.

Set-up

Option 1—One of our challenges is to figure out how to accommodate all styles of learning.

Option 2—Each of us has a preference for how to pick up a new skill.

How My Sons Learned to Dive

My two oldest sons, then aged ten and eleven, wanted to take diving lessons. The lessons were at the public pool—too far for them to ride their bikes. It was only a half-hour lesson so I wouldn't be able to go home after dropping them off. I said, "No, I don't want to take you to diving lessons. Ask someone else to teach you how to dive. It's not hard." "No, Mom, we really want to take diving lessons." I said, "No, no, no, no." After a week of begging, I actually caved in. "All right—you can take lessons under two conditions: that you're ready when it's time to go and that you stick with it and not quit." They said, "Oh, we promise, we promise." I said, "Yeah, just like taking care of the dog."

The first day of diving lessons, I joined all the other moms that were waiting and watching. Donny, the oldest, was in and out of the changing room in a flash. He was standing ready at the diving board. Eventually the teacher came out. He was a college kid. Tom was about ten steps behind him, walking very slowly.

The teacher started the lesson. Donny got on the board and Tom stood over at the fence. Donny dove off the board and did a belly flop, swam quickly back to the side of the pool, got out and got right back in line. Tom stayed at the fence through the whole first lesson. Don would do a belly flop, get right back into line, belly flop and get right back in line again. Each time he would swim a little more slowly to the side of the pool. Tom was still at the fence.

On the way home from the first diving lesson, I said, "Donny, you did a wonderful job. You really tried. Tom, I know you like to listen and watch to learn so tomorrow you can do a good job diving because you paid attention."

On the second day of diving lessons, Donny plunged right in again and does belly flop, belly flop, belly flop. Tom is still at the fence. Donny was swimming back to the ladder more slowly every time he did a belly flop. His stomach was totally red. Tom is still dry as a bone. Driving home from diving lessons, I say, "Good job, boys. Donny, you're giving it a real effort. I'm so proud of you. Tom, you really need to get into the water. I know you like to watch but you've had your chance, so tomorrow I want you in the water. You need to practice."

On the third day of diving lessons, Donny does belly flop, belly flop, belly flop. Tom is *still* at the fence. Donny is now bright red. Driving home from diving lessons, I say, "Donny, you are really, really giving it an effort. I'm so proud of you. Tom, you said you wanted to take diving lessons but you aren't even getting into the water. What's the matter?" Tom says to Donny, "How much does it hurt?" Donny says, "Oh, it hurts a lot." Tom says, "Does it hurt your head, too?" Donny says, "It hurts my head, too." I say, "Tom, this is how everybody learns to dive. You do some belly flops and you figure out how to correct it. So tomorrow, I want you to get into the water." The fourth and fifth days were just the same, belly flops and fence standing.

At the beginning of the second week of diving lessons, it's belly flop, belly flop, belly flop for Donny. Not one improvement. Mothers are starting to think that this is child abuse and they're saying, "That child shouldn't being doing this anymore. He will have brain damage." Tom has now adopted a new attitude. Instead of standing at the fence, he's leaning against it tapping his toe. I yell down to him, "Tom Gardner, get in the pool."

No movement. "I'll take you to Dairy Queen. Get in the pool." No movement. The child does not get in the pool. My other child is belly flopping away.

We are now on the third day of diving lessons of the second week. Tom has adopted a new little kink in his walk—like an "I'm cool" walk—behind the teacher. He walks right to the fence. Now Donny gets in line to do his dive, and does a funny little dive. Kind of a splashy dive but a dive and *it's not a belly flop.* He gets out of pool, goes over to the side and he's just beaming! Donny has only one good dive out of that whole day. Tom still hasn't touched the water.

On the second to last day of diving lessons, Donny is first in line. Again, belly flop. Tom is still at the fence. Donny gets back in line: belly flop, but gets back in line and finally does a fine little dive. Gets back in line, a couple more belly flops, and then another fine little dive. Tom is still at the fence. I am sitting with the mothers, and then I pull out the big bribe: "Tom Gardner, get into the pool." Nothing. "Dairy Queen *and* baseball cards! Now get into the pool." Nothing. About one minute before the end of the second to last diving lesson, Tom leans over so that I can see his face and he holds up his index finger and he mouths to me, "One dive." I put my thumb up and point to the water and say, "Get in there." Tom gets in line behind all the kids. When it's his turn, he plunges in and does a fine dive, a perfect little no-splash dive off the diving board.

Driving home from diving lessons on the second to last day of the second week, I say, "Oh, my boys, you did a fabulous job. See, Tom, if you had tried earlier, you could have been diving the whole time. Donny, those dives were wonderful for you. Tomorrow, I can watch you both dive. I'm so excited. It will be so much fun." Tom says, "I'm not diving tomorrow." I ask, "Why not? You did a great job today." Tom says, "Well, now I know how."

Tom and Donny both learned to dive. They both took the plunge. Donny did it by repeated belly flops. Tom did it by watching and studying. But they both took the plunge. Where is fear of failing or your desire to watch and plan keeping you from diving in? "Take the plunge."

Debrief Questions

- How did Suzann encourage her sons in learning to dive? What might you have done in her situation? Would you have let Donny continue to do belly flops?
- What learning style did each boy have? How did each demonstrate his particular learning style?
- What stood out for you in this story about the two boys learning to dive? What does this story mean to you?
- What is your preferred learning style? How might you have approached learning to dive?
- What differences in learning have you noticed with co-workers? With friends and family?
- What can organizations do to adapt to and accommodate various learning styles?

Key Point Options

1. In this example, Tom demonstrates that he is a reflective thinker. He has to be introduced to something. He has to stand back and watch. Donny has to learn by making mistakes. He has to get a whole bunch of things wrong before he starts catching on. He learns by doing it the hard way. Neither of these learning styles is appreciated in academic or business settings today because teachers and facilitators want to move learners quickly through the material.

2. Our organizational expectations of learning are frequently formed in our early academic experiences. Often managers are not patient with variation in employee learning styles. They may quickly label a new employee and become inflexible in approach to on-the-job training.
3. People learn in different ways. Sometimes we are not patient enough for learning to take place. It means adapting our own style to accommodate the style of another. Organizations will be more successful with employee retention and morale if they accommodate a variety of learning styles and approaches to accomplishing work.

Follow-up Activity

Step 1—Paired Discussion: With a partner, take five minutes each to talk about the following questions: When have you had to change your learning style in order to accommodate a work or life situation? How did that work out? What did that feel like? Why did you need to make a change in the way you went about the work?

Step 2—Large-Group Discussion: Ask several participants to tell their stories about their own situations. Ask the group: What can we do to accommodate different learning styles in the workplace? How can we develop patience with those who learn differently from ourselves?

THE JOCK AND HIS WIFE GO WATER SKIING (55)

Contributor

John Renesch, business futurist, www.renesch.com

Type and Purpose(s)

Vignette; evaluate and engage

Background

This particular couple stood out for John from all his other students because of the significant difference in how they approached learning how to water ski and the impact it had on the husband.

Presentation Tips

When describing the husband and wife and their actions, "act" like them.

Set-up

Option 1—What's the difference between knowing and learning?

Option 2—The mindset you bring to a situation can either facilitate or hinder your learning.

The Jock and His Wife Go Water Skiing

I had a boat on a big lake in northern California where a lot of people came for water skiing. Including me. When I found myself too old to do the sort of hot dog skiing that I enjoy, I became an instructor—teaching other people how to water ski.

One day, a couple came to the lake for lessons. The husband, who was an attorney, was a self-proclaimed jock. He was muscular, he had a kayak, and he played basketball. His wife, on the other hand, was very demure and quiet. She was willing to be taught, valued learning, and had less ego invested. While neither of them had ever water skied before, the husband was very used to the water. He even showed us how to roll a kayak and come back up the other side.

Since they had come to learn to water ski, I gave them my instructions. "Let the boat pull you up. Do not fight it." In one day his wife was up and skiing on two skis. The next day she was able to do it on one! The husband? He never got up on his skis. He kept trying to force it—as though he *alone* could do it. Because of his self-image—that of being a jock—he wouldn't allow the boat to pull him up.

This incident brought home a lesson—the difference between knowing and learning. When you think you know something, it can often be very difficult to learn it. The husband thought he knew how to water ski but showed us that he couldn't. It was very damaging to his ego. His wife, on the other hand, allowed the boat to pull her up without any problems at all. She was very open to instruction and being taught.

What about you? In your own life when you need to gain a new skill, do you "let the boat pull you up"?

Debrief Questions

- What impressions do you have of the jock and his wife?
- What were their learning styles? How did they differ? What results did each style yield?
- What implications does this story have for improving your own ability to learn?
- How do you like to learn something new? What steps do you go through? What makes it stick? What enables you to actually perform the new skill?
- What implications does this story have for teaching others?
- What gets in the way of learning taking place in your work setting?

Key Point Options

1. Learning theory states that adults learn by doing. However, the mindset and attitude that we bring to a learning situation is even more important than practice in determining our success.
2. Two Chinese characters represent the word *learning*. The first character means *to study* and is made up of a symbol that means, "to acquire knowledge" and another symbol representing a child in a doorway. The second character means *to practice constantly*. In this story, the jock practiced constantly but had not actually acquired the knowledge of how to let the boat pull him up. His own preconceptions got in the way of taking in information and applying it to his practice. His wife learned the skill of water skiing fairly easily because she could both acquire new knowledge as well as practice.
3. Training is a specific learning event that can result not just in skill development but in increased awareness and a willingness to view situations in a new way.

Follow-up Activity

Step 1—Small-Group Activity: As a group, identify as many different ways to learn a new skill as possible. If helpful, define a specific skill such as learning a new software package on your computer. Post these methods on a sheet of paper that everyone can read.

Step 2—Large-Group Discussion: Ask each small group to present their learning styles. Ask the whole group: How many different approaches did we identify? Which ones were most frequently listed? Which ones do we think work best in learning a new skill? Why? How can we use this information in our own learning and in teaching others? *Note:* As a follow-up activity, you may want to administer a learning assessment such as the *Learning Style Inventory* (1981) by David Kolb.

THERE ARE MORE STORIES TO TELL

Have we convinced you to use more stories in your one-on-one and group training efforts? There are millions to choose from, for all types of programs and educational purposes. Their power and simplicity are unmatched by almost any other training intervention. Stories touch our minds, hearts, souls, and physical beings. As one of the earliest forms of communication between individuals and cultures, stories hark back to an ancient tradition. They connect you to the past, present, and future, as well as to each of your training participants. Telling a story is a way of coming home.

We hope these stories have captured your heart as well as provided support to the trainer in you. Tell us about your experiences using the stories in this book and your feedback on working with the story framework. Visit our website at www.storiestrainerstell.com to learn more about our storytelling ventures and to download the story frameworks that accompany the stories in Section One of this book.

We would also enjoy hearing your stories. How do you touch your participants' minds, hearts, souls, and physical beings? What stories have you told in a training setting? What made them powerful vehicles for learning? What were the events, feelings, a-ha's, and outcomes? How did your participants react? What debrief questions led to a great discussion? What key points and follow-up activities did you incorporate into the lesson? We would love to hear about the stories that make *your* training stick. Contribute your feedback and your stories by visiting www.storiestrainerstell.com. You can also contact Mary Wacker directly by calling (414) 875-9876 or by emailing her at mary@mbwacker.com. You can contact Lori Silverman at either (800) 253-6398 or lori@partnersforprogress.com.

APPENDIX: INTERVIEW QUESTIONS

Stories

1. Where do you use stories in your work?
2. For what purpose(s) do you use them?
3. What types of stories do you use in your work?
4. What makes you use a story rather than another type of intervention?
5. What are the elements of an effective story?
6. What makes a story poor or ineffective?

Storytelling

7. What are the qualities of a good storyteller?
8. What makes a storyteller ineffective?
9. How did you learn to become a storyteller?
10. How do you set up or lead into a story?
11. What do you do to deliver the story in an effective manner?
12. How do you debrief and/or discuss a story?
13. How do your stories change depending on the audience?
14. Give an example of a worst-case storytelling experience (yours or other's).
15. What words of wisdom do you have for others who use stories in their training and speaking engagements?

Creating Your Own Stories

16. What is the process you use to create your own stories?
17. How do you a) organize and b) remember these stories?
18. What makes you choose to use your own stories versus those from other sources?

Using Stories from Other Sources

19. Where do your stories come from?
20. How do you a) organize and b) remember these stories?
21. How do you change these stories to make them your "own"?

ABOUT THE CONTRIBUTORS

Merrill Anderson, Ph.D., CEO, MetrixGlobal, LLC
9083 NW 73rd Street
Johnston, IA 50131
Phone: (515) 278-0051
Fax: (515) 727-4222
merrilland@metrixglobal.net

Merrill is the chief executive officer of MetrixGlobal, LLC, a professional services firm offering clients performance measurement solutions. He has worked with more than 100 companies throughout North America and Europe to effectively manage strategic organization change. Merrill has more than thirty professional publications and speeches to his credit, including the books *Strategic Change: Fast Cycle Organization Development* (2000) and *Building Learning Capability Through Outsourcing* (2000). His new book, *Bottom-Line Organization Development* (2003), breaks new ground in applying powerful measurement methodology to increase bottom-line value from strategic change initiatives. Merrill is currently clinical professor in education at Drake University. He earned his doctorate at New York University.

Jean Barbazette, president, The Training Clinic
645 Seabreeze Drive
Seal Beach, CA 90740-5746
Phone: (562) 430-2484 or (800) 937-4698
Fax: (562) 430-9603
jean@thetrainingclinic.com
www.thetrainingclinic.com

Jean is president of The Training Clinic, a training consulting firm she founded in 1977. The Training Clinic is the leading "Train-the-Trainer" company in the United States. Her company conducts needs assessments, designs training programs, develops lesson plans and self-paced learning packages, and presents seminars on more than thirty different topics. Jean holds a master's degree from Stanford University and is the author of *Successful New Employee Orientation,* 2nd ed. (Jossey-Bass/Pfeiffer, 2001) and *The Trainer's Support Handbook* (McGraw-Hill, 2001).

Joe Barnes, managing partner, Communications Success
27204 SE 26th Place
Sammamish, WA 98075
Phone: (425) 894-4399
twowaytvjoe@aol.com or joe@communicationsuccess.com

Joe has been a trainer since 1985 and is a consultant with Communications Success in Seattle, Wash., and Pacific Grove, Calif. His workshops focus on creating powerful presentations, techniques to "capture" the attention of your audience, on-camera media coaching, and achieving proactive positive media coverage. He has consulted with more than seventy-five major companies nationwide; has managed major market newsrooms; and has coached hundreds of television performers and leaders on presentation skills. He has studied Ph.D. level leadership and has a master's degree in speech.

Paula Bartholome, principal and corporate jester, Parallax
828 Michigan, Suite C3
Evanston, IL 60202-2541
Phone: (847) 491-0632
Fax: (847) 491-1558
paula@parallax-perspectives.com
www.parallax-perspectives.com

Paula works with organizations of all kinds who seek to provide an environment where hard fun—productive, meaningful, purposeful work—occurs. Functioning as a combined corporate jester and consultant, she helps organizations and the people in them hear what they need to know to work together toward shared goals. Through Parallax, her consulting firm, she has worked with groups in Fortune 500 corporations to small not-for-profit organizations. Paula is an adjunct faculty member in DePaul University's nationally recognized School for New Learning, teaching courses on storytelling in the workplace, collaborative learning, and organizational learning.

Chip Bell, senior partner, Performance Research Associates, Inc.
25 Highland Park #100
Dallas, TX 75205
Phone: (214) 522-5777
Fax: (214) 691-7591
chip@chipbell.com
www.chipbell.com

Chip Bell is a senior partner with Performance Research Associates, Inc., in Dallas, Texas. His consulting practice focuses on helping organizations build a culture that supports customer devotion. Prior to starting a consulting firm in the 1970s, Chip was director of management development for NCNB, now Bank of America. A renowned keynote speaker, he is the author of several best-selling books including *Customer Love* (2000), *Customers As Partners* (1994), and *Managers As Mentors* (1996). His work has been featured on CNBC, CNN, Bloomberg TV, and NPR, as well as in *The Wall Street Journal, Fortune, USA Today, Entrepreneur, Inc.*, and *Business Week.*

Geoff Bellman, consultant, GMB Associates
1444 NW Woodbine Way
Seattle, WA 98177
Phone/Fax: (206) 365-3212
geoffbellman@yahoo.com

Geoff's work as a consultant and speaker has taken him to five continents. He has written a number of books: *The Consultant's Calling,* 2nd ed. (Jossey-Bass, 2002), *Getting Things Done When You Are Not in Charge,* 2nd ed. (Berrett-Koehler, 2001), *The Beauty of the Beast* (Berrett-Koehler, 2000), *Your Signature Path* (Berrett-Koehler, 1996), and *The Quest for Staff Leadership* (Scott-Foresman, 1986). Geoff is a charter member of the Woodlands Group, which has been exploring individual, organizational, and societal change for twenty-five years. He also helped found The Community Consulting Project, a group of Seattle area consultants and learners who give their time to the not-for-profit community.

William Austin Boone, senior associate, MARTIN, BOONE ASSOCIATES
1829 Bissell
Chicago, IL 60614
Phone: (312) 751-9052
Fax: (312) 751-9046
wboone1829@aol.com

Bill has been a management and organization development consultant since 1971, with a wide range of organizations. He is principal and senior associate of MARTIN, BOONE ASSOCIATES, a national, full-service consulting firm with headquarters in Chicago, Illinois. Bill's specialties include the design and facilitation of climate surveys, team building, planning and problem-solving sessions, interdepartmental interfacing, and interactive training interventions in such areas as consulting skills, delegation, conflict management, and managing diversity. He has conducted numerous workshops and behavior-based projects for increasing awareness of the impact and use of diversity in the workplace.

Sharon L. Bowman, director, The Lake Tahoe Trainers Group
P.O. Box 564
Glenbrook, NV 89413
Phone: (775) 749-5247
Fax: (775) 749-1891
SBowperson@aol.com
www.Bowperson.com

Sharon has been an author, teacher, trainer, and consultant for thirty years. She works with people and companies who want to fine tune their information-delivery skills. She is a trainer for corporate human resource programs, national workforce development organizations, and educational institutions across the United States. A member of the National Speakers Association and director of The Lake Tahoe Trainers Group, Sharon is also the author of five popular teaching and training books, including her newest, *Preventing Death by Lecture!* (2001).

Karen D. L. Bryson, manager, Individual Leader Development, Center for Creative Leadership
8910 University Center Lane, Suite 1000
San Diego, CA 92122
Phone: (858) 638-8032
Fax: (850) 638-8008
brysonk@leaders.ccl.org

Karen manages and facilitates the Leadership Development Program (LDP) at the Center for Creative Leadership, San Diego Campus. In addition, she is a member of the Emerging Leaders research team focused on generational similarities and differences. She also volunteers her time to present at local colleges and universities. Karen holds a B.S. in business management from San Diego State University and an M.A. in leadership studies from the University of San Diego. She is currently pursuing a Ph.D. in human and organizational development through The Fielding Graduate Institute with an emphasis in emotional intelligence and leadership.

Chris Clarke-Epstein, CSP, owner, SPEAKING!
P.O. Box 37
Wausau, WI 54402-0037
Phone: (715) 842-2467
Fax: (715) 848-9463
Chris@CreativeLearningTools.com
www.CreativeLearningTools.com
www.ChrisClarke-Epstein.com

Chris has successfully managed a $7-million sales territory, raised a family, and since 1984, built a thriving speaking, training, and consulting business. She has earned a reputation for energizing audiences with her powerful blend of sound research, practical experience, and infectious enthusiasm. Chris is former president of both the National Speakers Association and the Northeast Wisconsin Chapter of the American Society for Training & Development. In 1993, Chris earned the Certified Speaking Professional designation. She is the co-author of *The Instant Trainer* (1997) and author of *Silence Isn't Golden: How to Unleash the Real Power of Feedback* (1996) and *78 Important Questions Leaders Need to Ask and Answer* (2002).

Hortencia Delgadillo, attorney-at-law
3132 W. Calle Toronja
Tucson, AZ 85741-2917
Phone: (520) 575-8864
hdelgadi@yahoo.com

Hortencia is an attorney in Arizona and is currently in private practice after serving as an assistant attorney general in the Office of the Arizona Attorney General for many years. Hortencia has litigated cases, facilitated no-fault agreements to resolve administrative discrimination complaints, and supervised numerous administrative investigations of discrimination in the areas of employment, housing, and pubic accommodations. She is a contributor to the *Arizona Employment Law Handbook* and has conducted numerous presentations on discrimination issues. In addition to holding a J.D. degree, Hortencia has a bachelor's degree in psychology and Spanish and an M.S. degree in guidance and counseling.

Larry P. English, president, INFORMATION IMPACT International, Inc.
871 Nialta Lane, Suite 100
Brentwood, TN 37027
Phone: (615) 837-1211
Fax: (615) 837-8804
Larry.English@infoimpact.com

Larry, the president and principal of INFORMATION IMPACT International, Inc., is an internationally recognized authority in information management and information quality improvement. He has provided consulting and education in twenty-eight countries on five continents. He was featured as one of the "21 Voices for the 21st Century" in *Quality Progress* in January 2000. Larry received the Individual Achievement Award for his contributions in information management from DAMA, an international professional association. He writes the "Plain English About Information Quality" column in *DM Review.* Larry's widely acclaimed book, *Improving Data Warehouse and Business Information Quality* (1999), is also available in Japanese.

Marcy Fisher, former vice president, Organization Development and Human Resources, Shell Technology Ventures, Inc.
Phone: (317) 228-1649
marcylfisher@yahoo.com

Marcy has more than twenty-eight years of industry experience with leading firms: Procter and Gamble, Royal Dutch Shell, and Sapient. Most recently, Marcy's experience has centered on the design and development of new technical joint ventures. She is now working with eLilly. Marcy possesses strong functional and technical knowledge in organization design and development, corporate and business strategy, self-managed and virtual work teams, change management, joint venture partner selection, globalization, leadership development, coaching, and manufacturing management. She holds a B.S. degree in industrial management and computer science from Purdue University and an M.S. degree in human resource and organization development from the University of San Francisco.

Suzann Gardner, associate professor, Alverno College
2165 LeChateau Drive
Brookfield, WI 53045
Phone: (262) 782-2472
dgarder@aol.com

Suzann employs storytelling in her teaching. A seminar leader for twenty years, she has conducted extensive communications workshops and has taught thousands of students how to build bridges between theory and practice. Through storytelling, she teaches students to scaffold context so they may better understand theoretical constructs. Suzann holds a B.A. from Mount Mary College in English, sociology, and secondary education, and an M.S. from the University of Wisconsin, Milwaukee in curriculum and instruction with an emphasis in English and linguistics. She is also completing Ph.D. work in urban studies.

Joan Gillman, director, Special Industry Programs, University of Wisconsin-Madison, School of Business
3260 Grainger Hall
975 University Avenue
Madison, WI 53706-1323
Phone: (608) 262-9982
Fax: (608) 263-0818
jgillman@facstaff.wisc.edu

Joan's office acts as a conduit between university resources and the business community. Her duties span small-business consulting to teaching managers and executives. She is the executive director of the United States Association for Small Business and Entrepreneurship, a comprehensive organization of 790 researchers, scholars, teachers, administrators, and policy makers. Joan travels extensively in the Balkans, training and developing entrepreneurship centers. The second woman to publicly address men in Saudi Arabia, she is active in many organizations and a frequent speaker. Joan received her B.S. from Indiana University and her M.A. in business from the University of Wisconsin-Madison.

Steve Hanamura, president, Hanamura Consulting, Inc.
6070 SW Chestnut Avenue
Beaverton, OR 97005
Phone: (503) 297-8658
Fax: (503) 297-8012
hanamura@integrity.com

Steve, co-owner of Hanamura Consulting, Inc., offers consulting, training, and speaking in the areas of leadership development, managing diversity initiatives, building effective teams, and managing and leading personal and organizational change. Steve received his master's degree from the University of Oregon and his bachelor's degree from Linfield College. He is the author of *In Search of Vision* (Global Insights, 2000). Steve is a member of the Diversity Collegium (a think tank of diversity professionals) and chaired the board for the Oregon Commission for the Blind. Steve has received the American Society for Training & Development (ASTD) Multicultural Network Trainer of the Year award and was one of the torchbearers for the 1996 Olympics.

Lunell Haught, Ph.D., owner, Haught Strategies
7802 S. Cheney Spokane Road
Spokane, WA 99224-8223
Phone/Fax: (509) 443-1319
lunellh@aol.com

Lunell aligns individual and organizational purpose in the public and private sectors. She evaluates programs and initiatives, provides training in management and communication-related topics, and facilitates planning, implementation, and conflict resolution sessions. She has published articles in national periodicals. Her work is included in ASTD's *In Action: Building Learning Capability Through Outsourcing* (2000). Lunell has presented at Hawaii's Conference on Performance Excellence, Washington State's Public Quality Conference, the National Association for Community Leadership, the Association for Quality and Participation (AQP), and the American Planning Association (APA).

Sandra Hoskins, ISP, PMP, president, The Kellan Group
364 St. Anne's Road
Winnipeg, MB, R2M 3B7 Canada
Phone: (204) 253-1896 or (800) MENTORS
Fax: (204) 254-6913
Sandra.Hoskins@thekellangroup.com

Sandra is a speaker, mentor, trainer, consultant, freelance author, and the owner of The Kellan Group of Companies, which includes a management consulting firm and a private college. The Kellan Group has a track record of helping organizations implement a project management discipline that is sustainable and reusable. Sandra believes and promotes the vision that the discipline of project management is a fundamental life skill. She is the author of several articles and professional development workshops and has developed a complete project management curriculum, which customers implement to support a disciplined approach to the subject.

Katherine M. Hudson, president and CEO, Brady Corporation
P.O. Box 571
Milwaukee, WI 53201-0571
Phone: (414) 358-6600
Fax: (438) 438-6957
kathy_hudson@bradycorp.com
www.Bradycorp.com

Katherine has been president and CEO of Brady Corporation since 1994. The company employs 3,000 people worldwide and has annual sales of $546 million. Katherine moved to Brady following a successful twenty-four-year career with Eastman Kodak Company, where she held numerous management positions. With a degree in business management and graduate work in economics at Cornell University, she has received numerous awards. She was named one of the twelve most influential CIO's of the decade (1997), as well as Wisconsin Business Leader of the Year by Harvard Business School Alumni Association (1995). Katherine resides in Mequon, Wisconsin, with her husband and son.

David Hutchens, principal, iconoclast communications
413 Brookhaven Trail
Smyrna, TN 37167
Phone/Fax: (615) 220-0282
hutchens@mindspring.com
www.DavidHutchens.com

David is an author, speaker, and instructional designer who has developed interactive learning solutions for The Coca-Cola Company, IBM, NationsBank, and more. A former advertising copywriter, David is author of the popular Learning Fables books (Pegasus Communications), a growing series that introduces concepts of organizational learning theory in a fun, allegorical format. Titles such as *Outlearning the Wolves, Shadows of the Neanderthal,* and *The Lemming Dilemma* delightfully illustrate concepts of mental models, systems theory, organizational learning, and more. Learners from many cultures are drawn to the offbeat narratives, and the books have been translated into more than a dozen languages.

Joan Lloyd, Joan Lloyd & Associates, Inc.
10701 W. North Avenue, Suite 203
Milwaukee, WI 53226
Phone: (414) 476-8853 or (800) 348-1944
Fax: (414) 476-3212
comments@joanlloyd.com
www.joanlloyd.com

Joan owns a management consulting and training firm, Joan Lloyd & Associates, Inc. She designs and facilitates customized leadership and career development programs for companies such as S. C. Johnson, Kohler Corporation, and Quaker Oats. Her consulting projects include organizational assessments, executive coaching, and 360-degree feedback processes. Her weekly column, "Joan Lloyd at Work," has been syndicated since 1982 in newspapers across America and on the Web. Her weekly television feature, "Joan Lloyd at Work," was syndicated in twelve markets. She is the author of *The Career Decisions Planner: When to Move, When to Stay, When to Go Out on Your Own* (John Wiley & Sons, 1992).

Kate Lutz, MBA, storyteller
130 S. Washington Street
Denver, CO 80209
Phone: (303) 744-8055
katelutz@mindspring.com

Kate is a professional storyteller, speaker, story teacher, coach, and workshop presenter. She enlivens speeches, worldwide folktales, mountain adventures, and personal stories with her warmth, humor, and vitality. She performs at storytelling festivals, national conferences, businesses, schools, and libraries. She chaired the design stage of the 2002 National Storytelling Conference, co-chairs the Rocky Mountain Storytellers' Guild, and is a Toastmaster, Colorado Speakers' Association affiliate, and hospice storyteller. Prior to storytelling, she worked for private industry and the State of Colorado in training, planning, and program management for social service and health care programs serving populations "from womb to tomb."

Robert McIlree
16055 SW Walker Road #406
Beaverton, OR 97006
Phone: (414) 305-1159
robert.mcilree@rjmtech.com

Bob is the principal of RJM Technologies, Inc., a firm specializing in enterprise system architecture, data warehousing and business intelligence, information system valuation methodologies and models, and data modeling and administration, as well as project management services in these areas. His work is widely known in the financial services, insurance, consumer products, telecommunications, and transportation industries. Bob has written articles for software development and software methodology journals. He is also an adjunct faculty member at the University of Wisconsin-Milwaukee in the Project Management Certificate program.

Maureen G. Mulvaney (MGM), MGM & Associates
16026 S. 36th Street
Phoenix, AZ 84048-7322
Phone: (800) 485-0065 or (480) 759-6251
Fax: (480) 759-6257
mgm@mgmsuperstar.com
www.mgmsuperstar.com

MGM is a mother, motivational speaker, and author of *Any Kid Can Be a Superstar* (1999) and contributor to *Chicken Soup for the Teachers' Soul* (2002). She is a certified speaking professional (CSP), with twenty-plus years of experience as a professional speaker. MGM is widely known for her keynotes, training sessions, and customized seminars for audiences from five to 5,000. MGM has an Ed.M. in counseling psychology from Boston University and a B.A. with a dual major in special education and elementary education from Troy State University.

Kathy A. Nielsen, president, Nielsen Associates, Inc.
614 Cherbourg Drive
Buffalo Grove, IL 60089
Phone: (847) 913-8668
Fax: (847) 913-8698
kn@nielsenassociates.com
www.nielsenassociates.com

Kathy is CEO of Nielsen Associates, Inc., a leading training and consulting firm in the Chicago area. She has trained thousands of individuals and has been a course developer for such topics as relationship management, sales and negotiation skills, management, communications, sexual harassment, and diversity. Her interest in golf has led her to create unique programs on *The Seven Habits of Highly Effective Golfers,* providing instruction to the Ladies' PGA's teaching division. Kathy's articles entitled "Stress and Wellness for Women" have appeared in *The Executive Letter.* She is co-author of *Strategies for Better Thinking* (Quorum Press, 1999) and a founding partner of CivilityWorks.

Clare Novak, president, Novak and Associates
782 Springdale Drive, Suite 110
Exton, PA 19341
Phone: (610) 423-4572
Fax: (484) 875-0990
Novakc@earthlink.net
www.novakassoc.com

Clare is president of Novak and Associates. She is also an international performance consultant, with extensive experience in the Middle East. She has significant experience in assessing needs and facilitating the most effective interventions for the business, performance, work environment, and training levels. Recently, Clare was selected to become a chairman with TEC Worldwide, and she facilitates forums of CEOs dedicated to increasing their effectiveness and enhancing their lives. She has spoken for international, national, and regional conferences, as well as numerous professional organization chapters. Clare has also authored articles for several professional journals.

Julie O'Mara, president, O'Mara and Associates
5979 Greenridge Road
Castro Valley, CA 94552
Phone: (510) 582-7744
Fax: (510) 582-4826
OmaraAssoc@aol.com

Julie is president of O'Mara and Associates, an organizational development consulting firm specializing in leadership and managing diversity. A former national president of the American Society for Training & Development (ASTD), Julie is a partner with Performance Champions and field manager with Inscape Publishing. She is co-author of the best-selling *Managing Workforce 2000: Gaining the Diversity Advantage* (Jossey-Bass, 1991), and author of *Diversity Activities and Training Designs* (Pfeiffer and Company, 1995), a manual of activities, lecturettes, and guidelines for effective diversity training. In 2001, PrimeLearning developed five e-learning diversity modules based on her work.

Laura V. Page, managing principal, Page Consulting
P.O. Box 5283
Madison, WI 53705
Phone: (608) 231-1979
Fax: (608) 231-9995
lvpage@execpc.com
www.lauravpage.com

Laura is a management consultant focusing on areas of interpersonal communications, leadership development, team-building, conflict resolution, and strategic planning. She is a frequent public speaker, seminar instructor, and retreat facilitator. Laura was the manager of business counseling for the University of Wisconsin-Madison Small Business Development Center and a management consultant with Arthur Young in Chicago. In addition to client consulting, Laura teaches continuing education programs for UW-Milwaukee, UW-Madison, and Marquette University. She holds master's degrees in management development and marketing. She has received three service awards from the South Central Wisconsin Chapter of the American Society for Training & Development.

Jonathan M. Preston, senior manager of a major pharmaceutical firm
1950 Lake Sherwood Drive
Westlake Village, CA 91361
Phone: (805) 373-0029
Fax: (805) 373-8829

Jon is currently the senior district manager (master level) with a major pharmaceuticals company and is responsible for sales in the greater Los Angeles area. Jon's former positions included assistant to the regional manager, district manager, and senior district manager. He earned a bachelor's degree in chemistry from the University of Wisconsin-Madison and upon graduation was commissioned a second lieutenant in the U.S. Army. Jon spent three years as a field artillery special weapons officer serving in Turkey, Italy, Greece, and Germany, and he left the Army with the rank of captain. Jon resides with his wife, Carol, in West Lake Village, CA.

John Renesch, business futurist
P.O. Box 472379
San Francisco, CA 94147-2379
Phone: (415) 437-6974
john@renesch.com
www.renesch.com

John is a globally renowned business futurist, advisor, and commentator on matters affecting human consciousness and business. With more than thirty years' experience as a chief executive, principal, and entrepreneur, he is also the creator and editor of a series of books on progressive business, including *Learning Organizations* (1995) and *New Traditions in Business* (1992). Global leadership expert Warren Bennis calls John "a wise elder who shines with wisdom." The Stanford School of Business' Dr. Michael Ray calls him "a beacon lighting the way to a new paradigm." *The Futurist* magazine calls him a "business visionary." Renesch's latest book is *Getting to the Better Future: A Matter of Conscious Choosing* (2000).

Shelley R. Robbins, Ph.D.
12 Charles Lake Road
North Oaks, MN 55127
Phone: (651) 486-3815
shelleyrobbins@worldnet.att.net

Shelley is currently the executive director of the School of Business of Capella University, and has been a faculty member at Northwestern University, the University of Wisconsin-Milwaukee, the University of St. Thomas, and the University of Minnesota. Shelley is president of Critical Aspects Consulting, helping organizations align strategy, leadership, learning, and technology, and is co-founder of the Personal Side of Leadership workshops. Shelley holds a Ph.D. in organizational behavior from Northwestern University, and an MBA from the University of Chicago. She lives with her daughter, Isabel, husband, John, and two Irish Wolfhounds, Ginger and Audrey.

Marcia Ruben, principal, Ruben Consulting Group
520 Pacheco Street
San Francisco, CA 94116
Phone: (415) 564-7135
Fax: (415) 564-4998
marcia@rubenconsulting.com
www.rubenconsulting.com

Marcia is the principal of Ruben Consulting Group, a management-consulting firm launched in 1998 and based in San Francisco. Her firm works with mid-market and Fortune 500 companies that must improve individual, team, and organizational performance. Specific services include leadership development and coaching, team process improvement, and organizational change management. In addition, her firm provides services in design and facilitation of meetings and programs for women leaders. Ruben Consulting Group is known for flexibility in creating custom solutions that get results. Marcia is a Phi Beta Kappa graduate of U.C. Berkeley and holds a master's degree in counseling.

Sheriene Saadati, organization consultant
123 Stanford Avenue
Menlo Park, CA 94025
Phone/Fax: (650) 854-0878
sherienes@yahoo.com

Sheriene is a systems thinker with a consultative approach. She has more than nine years of organization development experience in both the entertainment and oil industries. During a recent project at The Walt Disney Company, she led a team in developing the first self-service résumé and job search site. Her service mission is to help others develop their maximum potential through integration of their life and career goals with the goals of the organization. Sheriene has a master of arts in human resources from Azusa Pacific University and a bachelor of arts in psychology and communication from Point Loma Nazarene University.

Edward E. Scannell, CMP, CSP, director, Center for Professional Development & Training

963 E. Driftwood Drive
Tempe, AZ 85283
Phone: (480) 970-0101
Fax: (480) 423-0526
EESAZ@aol.com

Ed has written or co-authored fifteen books and more than 100 articles. His *Games Trainers Play* series (McGraw-Hill) is used by speakers, trainers, and meeting planners across the globe. Ed has taught at the University of Northern Iowa and at Arizona State University. Active in civic and professional organizations, he has served on several boards of directors and as the national president of American Society for Training & Development, Meeting Professionals International, and the National Speakers Association.

LG Shanklin-Flowers, president, InReach

3103 W. McKinley Boulevard
Milwaukee, WI 53208
Phone: (414) 931-8724
Fax: (800) 878-9849
LGInreach@aol.com

President of InReach, LG has been involved in training, leadership development, and human resource management for thirty years. She has worked both nationally and internationally, most recently as an NGO delegate to the World Conference Against Racism, Xenophobia and Other Intolerances in Durban, South Africa. Known for her pioneering efforts within the field of cultural diversity, she has led hundreds of groups in intercultural understanding. In May 1994, she was recognized for her diligent and courageous promotion of racial justice and demonstrated commitment to eliminating racism when she became the fifth recipient of the YWCA of Greater Milwaukee's Racial Justice Award.

Bob Shaver, director of the Basic Management Certificate Series, University of Wisconsin-Madison, School of Business, Fluno Center for Executive Education
601 University Avenue, Room 334
Madison, WI 53715-1035
Phone: (608) 441-7334
Fax: (608) 441-7325
bshaver@bus.wisc.edu

Bob is a faculty associate with the University of Wisconsin-Madison School of Business and program director of the Basic Management Certificate Series. He develops and delivers training in leadership topics including coaching, creativity, instructional skills, change, motivation, performance, problem-solving, and survey design. Bob also delivers in-house training programs for companies such as Aqua-Chem, CUNA Mutual Group, Freeport Memorial Hospital, and Wausau Papers. His experience includes management positions in industry, business, and the military. Bob earned his bachelor's degree in communication, economics, and business administration from the University of Wisconsin-Stevens Point and his MBA from the University of Wisconsin-Madison.

Doug Stevenson, president, Story Theater Academy
2104 Sussex Lane
Colorado Springs, CO 80909
Phone: (800) 773-0265 or (719) 573-6195
Fax: (719) 574-2065
doug@dougstevenson.com
www.storytheater.net

Doug is the creator of the Story Theater Method for storytelling in business and is a professional speaker, trainer, author, and speaking coach. He has authored numerous articles on public speaking and storytelling in business and writes a monthly column for the *Denver Business Journal* entitled "Walk Your Talk." He has coached more than 750 speakers, trainers, politicians, celebrities, athletes, executives, and business professionals in his Story Theater Retreats, Talk Your Walk seminars, and private coaching. His diverse international client base spans corporate, association, and government clients such as Aetna, GTE, the Department of Defense, Maytag, Century 21, Pharmacia, UPS, the American Medical Association, the National Education Association, and many more.

Ed Tate, CEO, Ed Tate & Associates
5753 S. Jebel Way
Centennial, CO 80015
Phone: (888) 607-1642
edtate@att.net
www.edtate.com

Ed is a trainer, author, and among the best speakers in the world. Out of 175,000 members from seventy countries, Ed won the coveted Toastmasters International 2000 World Championship of Public Speaking. He has spoken both nationally and internationally. Ed has earned a reputation as the "speaker who energizes, educates, and entertains." Ed is an "attitude-improvement specialist" who works with organizations in transition. His clients include Dell Computer, Verizon Communication, AT&T Broadband, State Farm Insurance, the Internal Revenue Service, United Artist, General Electric, and Johnson & Johnson. Ed also is an author who co-wrote *Motivational Selling* (2002).

Sivasailam "Thiagi" Thiagarajan, resident mad scientist, QB International
4423 E. Trailridge Road
Bloomington, IN 47408-9633
Phone: (812) 332-1478
Fax: (812) 332-5701
thiagi@thiagi.com
www.thiagi.com

When he was seven years old, Thiagi discovered the art of lying for fun and profit. Since then he has been making up stories as an important element of his job. Thiagi justifies his voracious reading of stories as literature research, his dysfunctional daydreaming as task analysis, and his prolific storywriting as creating case materials. Thiagi encourages participants to come up with their own stories as a part of conducting needs analysis and collecting evaluation data. Currently, as the resident mad scientist (otherwise known as the Director of R&D) at QB International, Thiagi creates interactive stories for use in online and face-to-face training events.

David Zach, futurist

544 E. Ogden Avenue, #700-396
Milwaukee, WI 53202
Phone: (414) 278-0414
dave@davidzach.com
www.davidzach.com

Dave is one of the few professionally trained futurists in the United States, with a master's degree in future studies from the University of Houston-Clear Lake. Dave has worked with more than 1,000 corporations, schools, and associations offering practical and entertaining insights on the personal and professional impact of strategic trends. He taught future studies in the School of Education at the University of Wisconsin-Milwaukee. He is a board member for the American Institute of Architects—Wisconsin, Future Milwaukee, and eInnovate.

ABOUT THE AUTHORS

Mary B. Wacker is the president of M. B. Wacker Associates, a firm specializing in leadership development, team performance coaching, customer service strategies, and organizational change consulting. Since 1988, her firm has worked with health care, finance, legal, insurance, publishing, distribution, and utility industries; education; government; and community-based agencies.

She is an accomplished national conference seminar leader and has written numerous training manuals, kits, and programs in the areas of management, finance, and employee engagement, most recently a manual entitled "Virtual Teams: A Guide for Leaders." Her work on team building has been cited in Milwaukee's *Business Journal* and in the *Milwaukee Journal Sentinel.*

Mary has served as an adjunct faculty member for Marquette University in its Certificate in Management Program and the University of Wisconsin-Milwaukee's MBA program. She directs Leadership Milwaukee, a program focusing on diversity in community leadership. Mary also serves on the non-profit boards of Friendship Center, a reading camp in Dodgeville, Wis., and The Women's Center in Waukesha.

She was the 1995 president of the American Society for Training & Development, Southeastern Wisconsin Chapter, and has received a Professional Practice Award from the American Heart Association. Mary has a B.S. degree in psychology and an M.S. degree in educational psychology, both from the University of Wisconsin-Milwaukee.

Mary B. Wacker, president, M. B. Wacker Associates
3175 N. 79th Street
Milwaukee, WI 53222-3930
Phone: (414) 875-9876
Fax: (414) 875-9874
mary@mbwacker.com
www.mbwacker.com
www.storiestrainerstell.com

Lori L. Silverman is the owner of Partners for Progress, a management consulting firm dedicated to helping organizations achieve and maintain a sustainable competitive advantage. Her expertise spans work in the areas of strategic management, enterprise-wide change, and performance improvement. Industries she has consulted with include petroleum, continuous process, chemical distribution, high technology, retail, paper, insurance, financial services, health care, airline, higher education, manufacturing, communications, association management, and consumer, business, and engineering services. She has also worked with state and federal government agencies and military units.

Having positively impacted the lives of thousands of conference and meeting participants, Lori is sought after as a keynote speaker. She was a major contributor to the book *Planning for Quality, Productivity, & Competitive Position* (1990) and the co-author of *Critical SHIFT: The Future of Quality in Organizational Performance* (1999). Since 1987 she has published more than fifty articles and workbooks on strategic planning, self-managed teams, consumer obsession, performance improvement, free agents, social responsibility, coaching, and enterprise-wide change.

Lori holds a B.S. degree in psychology and an M.S. degree in counseling and guidance, both from the University of Wisconsin-Madison, and an MBA from Edgewood College, Madison, Wisconsin. She serves as adjunct faculty at the Fluno Center for Executive Education, University of Wisconsin-Madison and the School of Continuing Education, University of Wisconsin-Milwaukee.

Lori L. Silverman, owner, Partners for Progress
1218 Carpenter Street
Madison, WI 53704-4304
Phone: (800) 253-6398
Fax: (608) 241-8092
lori@partnersforprogress.com
www.partnersforprogress.com
www.storiestrainerstell.com

BIBLIOGRAPHY

Allen, R. (1997). *Fast fiction: Creating fiction in five minutes.* Cincinnati: F. & W. Publications.

Argyris, C. (1990). *Overcoming organizational defenses.* Needham, Mass.: Allyn & Bacon, pp. 88–89.

Bell, C. (1996). *Managers as mentors: Building partnerships for learning.* San Francisco: Berrett-Koehler Publishers, pp. 115–120.

Boone, W. A. (1972). "A world without blacks." Unpublished story, Chicago, Ill. Used with permission.

Cialdini, R. B. (2001). *Influence: Science and practice.* Boston: Allyn & Bacon.

Clarke-Epstein, C. (1996). "Lie #3: If you're not asked, keep your mouth shut." *Silence isn't golden: How to unleash the real power of feedback.* Wausau, Wis.: Another Pair of Shoes Press, p. 15. Used with permission.

Clarke-Epstein, C. (2002). "What makes you proud of working as a part of our organization?" *78 important questions leaders should ask and answer.* New York: AMACOM, pp. 36–37. Used with permission.

Covey, S. (1989). *The 7 habits of highly effective people.* New York: Simon & Schuster, p. 83.

"Doing the Packarena." (July/August 2001). Reprinted by permission of *Harvard Business Review,* p. 8. Taken from "Transforming a Conservative Company—One Laugh at a Time" by Katherine M. Hudson.

"Employee engagement: Creating a highly engaged and creative workplace culture." Available at www.gallup.com/management/Q12_system.asp. Last visited December 2002.

English, L. (1999). *Improving data warehouse and business information quality.* New York: John Wiley & Sons, p. 251.

Gibran, K. (1968). *The Prophet.* New York: Random House.

Graham, E. (2002, June 12). Southern pastor works to deliver his flock from credit card debt. *The Wall Street Journal.* Taken from www.wsj.com. Last visited October 2002.

Harvey, J. B. (1988). *The Abilene Paradox and Other Meditations on Management.* New York: Lexington Books.

Herman, R., & Gioia, J. (2002, June 12). A corporation of the future—here today. *Herman Trend Alert.* Available at www.hermangroup.com/archive.html. Last visited July 2002.

Holt, D., & Mooney, B., Eds. (1994). *Ready-to-tell tales.* Little Rock, AR: August House.

Hudson, K. M. (2001). Let me tell you a story. *Brady Corporation 2001 Annual Report.* Milwaukee, Wis.: Brady Corporation, p. 3. Adapted based on presentation given by Katherine M. Hudson, "Fireside chat," Future Milwaukee, March 20, 2002. Used with permission.

Jones, M. (2002, June 21). Bun's rush: Wienermobile finds route near Pentagon no picnic. *Milwaukee Journal Sentinel,* 1B. Taken from www.jsonline.com/news/state/jun02/52849.asp. Last visited January 2003. Used with permission.

Kolb, D. (1981). *Learning style inventory.* Boston: McBer and Company.

Lutz, K. (2000, Nov. 29). "Cappuccino, chocolate, chemotherapy." Unpublished story, Denver, CO. Adapted and used with permission.

Lutz, K. (2000, Oct. 18). "A Fable: The dirty window." Unpublished story, Denver, CO. Used with permission.

Mackenzie, R. A. (1972). *The Time Trap.* New York: AMACOM, pp. 38–39. Reproduced with permission of AMA/AMACOM (B) in the format Other Books via Copyright Clearance Center.

Mulvaney, M. G. (2002). Presentation entitled "The secret . . . success lessons for life."

Pennington, B. (2002, June 10). How the Open came to the people. *New York Times.* Taken from www.nytimes/2002/06/10/sports/golf/10open.html?ex=1024713727&ei=1&en=24dd48a3a2e17289. Last visited January 2003.

Quade, K., & Brown, R. M. (2002). *The conscious consultant.* San Francisco: Jossey-Bass/Pfeiffer, pp. 57–58. Used with permission. Adaptations based on an interview with Geoff Bellman, April 5, 2002.

Renesch, J. E. (2000). *Getting to the better future.* San Francisco: New Business Books, p. 91. Used with permission.

Rhoads, K. (2002). Welcome to working psychology's introduction to influence. Available at www.workingpsychology.com. Last visited October 2002.

Roosevelt, E. *Catholic Digest.* St. Paul, Minn, Oct. 1960. Quote 46933 taken from www.bartleby.com/66/33/46933.html. Last visited February 2003.

Scannell, E. E. (1997, July/August). A look at some "myth" information. *Professional Speaker,* p. 20.

Scannell, E. E., & Newstrom, J. W. (1994). *The complete games trainers play.* New York: McGraw-Hill.

Schein, E. (1987). *Process consultation* (vol. II). Boston: Addison-Wesley, pp. 63–69.

Silverman, L. L., & Wacker, M. B. (2003). Getting the most from a good story. *The 2003 Annual: Volume 1: Training.* San Francisco: John Wiley & Sons, Inc., pp. 243–253.

Stevenson, D. (2000, July 27). Story structure. *Story Theater Newsletter,* pp. 2–3. Available at www.storytheater.net. Last visited December 2002.

Stevenson, D. (2001). Story Types. Excerpted from Story Theater: The Science and Art of Storytelling and Humor in Business. (Self-produced audiotape series.) Made in USA.

Stewart, J. (2002, June 26). *The publicity hound's tips of the week.* Issue 90. Available at www.publicityhound.com. Last visited December 2002.

Technical Assistance Research Programs, Inc. (TARP). (1980). *Consumer complaint-handling in America: Final report.* (NTIS PB-263-082). Washington, D.C.: White House Office of Consumer Affairs.

Wineke, W. (2002, June 22). The original cheesehead has aged well. *Wisconsin State Journal:* Daybreak, p. F1.

SUGGESTED READING

Allen, R. (1997). *Fast fiction: Creating fiction in five minutes.* Cincinnati, OH: F. & W. Publications.

Armstrong, D. M. (1999). *Managing by storying around.* New York: Doubleday.

Bell, C. (1996). *Managers as mentors: Building partnerships for learning.* San Francisco: Berrett-Koehler.

Collins, R., & Cooper, P. J. (1997). *The power of story: Teaching through storytelling.* Boston: Allyn & Bacon.

Davis, D. (1993). *Telling your own stories.* Little Rock, AR: August House.

Denning, S. (2001). *The springboard: How storytelling ignites action in knowledge-era organizations.* Wolburn, MA: Butterworth-Heinemann.

Finlayson, A. (2001). *Questions that work: How to ask questions that will help you succeed in any business situation.* New York: AMACOM.

Fulford, R. (1999). *The triumph of narrative.* New York: Broadway Books.

Gabriel, Y. (2000). *Storytelling in organizations: Facts, fictions, and fantasies.* New York: Oxford University Press.

Holt, D., & Mooney, B., Eds. (1994). *Ready-to-tell tales.* Little Rock, AR: August House.

Holt, D., & Mooney, B., Eds. (2000). *More ready-to-tell tales from around the world.* Little Rock, AR: August House.

Lipman, D. (1995). *Improving your storytelling.* Little Rock, AR: August House.

Lipman, D. (1999). *The storytelling coach.* Little Rock, AR: August House.

MacDonald, M. R. (1993). *The storyteller's start-up book.* Little Rock, AR: August House.

Maguire, J. (1998). *The power of personal storytelling.* New York: Jeremy P. Tarcher/Putnam.

McFarlane, E., & Saywell, J. (1995). *If . . . (Questions for the game of life).* New York: Villard Books.

Mooney, B., & Holt, D. (1996). *The storyteller's guide.* Little Rock, AR: August House.

Mulvaney, M. G. (1999). *Any kid can be a superstar.* Phoenix: MGM and Associates, Inc.

Neuhauser, P. C. (1993). *Corporate legends & lore: The power of storytelling as a management tool.* Austin, TX: PCN Associates.

Sawyer, R. (1970). *The way of the storyteller.* New Year: Penguin Putnam.

Simmons, A. (2001). *The story factor.* Cambridge, MA: Perseus.

Slan, J. (1998). *Using stories and humor: Grab your audience.* Needham, MA: Allyn & Bacon.

Stevenson, D. (2000, July 27). Story structure. *Story Theater Newsletter.* Available: http://www.storytheater.net. Last visited December 2002.

Stevenson, D. (2001). Story Theater: The Science and Art of Storytelling and Humor in Business. (Self-produced audiotape series.) Made in USA.

Strachan, D. (2001). *Questions that work: A resource for facilitators.* Ottawa: ST Press.

INDEX

D

E

F

M

N

O

P

Q

R

S

T

U

V

W

Z

CD-ROM STORIES LIST AND CREDITS

The audio CD version of fifty-four stories contained in the book has been created to help foster your storytelling skills at work, especially when you are training others. Many of the stories in the book are written using first-person voice. Since most of you will feel more comfortable telling them in the third-person, we have modified six stories in this manner so you can hear how they sound and gain some ideas on how to adapt other first person stories presented here. The modified stories are: "I Never Noticed You Were Black," "The Houseguest," "Ladies and Gentlemen Serving Ladies and Gentlemen," "You Don't Qualify for the Senior Discount," "The Taxi Driver" and "Upstaged By a Rookie." In addition to these stories, several others in the accompanying text are written as third-person narratives. We encourage you to listen to the CD, practice telling the stories out loud yourself, and adapt them to your training in a way that supports your learning objectives. Enjoy the stories.

—Mary Wacker and Lori Silverman

Stories Featured on the CD

1. A World Without Blacks
2. Look at Me
3. When in Egypt, Do What?
4. Catching an Unconscious Bias
5. I Never Noticed You Were Black
6. The Scratch-and-Sniff Test
7. Are You Listening?
8. If You're Not Asked, Keep Your Mouth Shut?
9. The House Guest
10. How Far is Far?
11. A Fish Tale
12. It's the Little Things That Count
13. Ladies and Gentleman Serving Ladies and Gentlemen
14. I Was Aching for a Fight
15. The Customer Strikes Back
16. You Don't Qualify for the Senior Discount
17. Sorry, We Can't Do It
18. The Taxi Driver
19. The Cobbler's Children
20. I Haven't Worn My Hat in a Long Time
21. The Volunteer Job
22. Missing a Golden Opportunity
23. Upstaged by a Rookie
24. Who Called This Meeting?
25. A Culture Rooted in Gunpowder
26. Expecting Too Little
28. The Worth of a Contribution
29. Fostering Full Potential
30. A Legacy of Generosity
31. Time Brings Perspective
32. In Search of Cappuccino. . . With a Little Chocolate on the Side
33. Values Aren't Accidental
34. A Nation's Values Connect Us
35. The Case of the Magician's Assistant
36. The Roll of the Dice
37. Isolate, Exaggerate and Integrate
38. Thanks, I'll Do It Myself
39. The Forest for the Trees
40. Is He Qualified?
41. For Lack of a System
42. The Porcupine and the Snake
43. Viewing the Problem Through a Different Lens
44. The Disapproving Neighbor
45. The Road to Peoria
46. Doing the Packerena
47. The Slingshot
48. A Family United
49. The Contest
50. I Didn't Ask to Be Here
51. In Pursuit of a Goal
52. Teaching a Dog to Whistle
53. Preparing Yourself for the Unexpected
54. How My Sons Learned to Dive
55. The Jock and His Wife Go Water Skiing

Actors' Bios

Jill Tracy is an award-winning musical artist, writer, storyteller and voice talent. Her diverse endeavors have taken her from the theatrical stage and film houses to recording studios, magic parlors and rock music venues. She lives in San Francisco. www.jilltracy.com

Walt Anthony has over thirty-years of practical experience and formal training as a professional entertainer. He has both an acting and directing background, as well as extensive experience in communications, education and training. Walt has presented programs nationwide for media, organizations, and industry. He is a member of the Actor's Equity Association, and the Society of American Magicians. He also facilitates master-workshops for magicians, to help promote magic as an art form; strengthening performance techniques, and stagecraft skills. www.SpellbinderEntertainment.com.

Actors' Coaching Provided by Doug Stevenson

Doug Stevenson is a professional speaker, trainer, author and speaking coach. He is an internationally recognized expert on strategic storytelling for business presentations. As the creator of the Story Theater Method for making content come alive, he helps individuals and organizations get their point across more effectively using stories. He conducts train the trainer programs and Story Theater Retreats worldwide and has coached over 600 individuals. More information can be found on his website at www.storytheater.net.

HOW TO USE THE CD-ROM

The enclosed CD-ROM features audio dramatizations of the stories included in the book. The recordings are in MP3 format, which is playable in most computers. Some older CD or DVD players do not recognize MP3 files. We apologize for any inconvenience this may cause.

The Autorun Program on this CD-ROM should start the CD automatically in any Microsoft® Windows®-based computer which features an updated version of Microsoft® Windows Media Player or any Macintosh computer which features Apple QuickTime. The Autorun Program will not work on the Mac OSX operating system.

If you have Windows Media Player and the CD does not start automatically, go to www.microsoft.com/windows/windowsmedia/download/default.asp and download the appropriate update for your version of Windows (i.e, Windows ME, Windows 2000). Follow the instructions on how to install your new improved Windows Media Player.

If you have neither of these on your computer, and you wish to use this CD-ROM, you can download the free RealOne player from www.real.com.

Copyright and Use Restrictions

Published by Pfeiffer.
An Imprint of John Wiley & Sons, Inc.
989 Market Street, San Francisco, CA 94103-1741 www.pfeiffer.com

PART # 0-9990-0066-7 packaged with

ISBN: 0-7879-6436-0

Contains dramatized versions of the stories from *Stories Trainers Tell* by Mary B. Wacker and Lori L. Silverman, as well as printable text versions of some material from the same volume, with permission of the publisher.

The materials contained on this CD, including the software and all content and, where applicable, associated online electronic documentation, forms, and content, are protected by United States and international copyright laws. Your rights to use them are governed by the terms of this license agreement. BY INSTALLING THE CD-ROM, YOU ARE AGREEING TO ALL OF THE TERMS BELOW.

The content contained on this CD-ROM (except for those stories for which permission must be obtained from the original source—which are generally, but not always, indicated in this document) may be played by you for personal use and for educational/training activities for up to an aggregate maximum of 100 participants over any 12-month period (regardless of how many sessions this comprises). You may not modify any story on this CD-ROM for any purpose whatsoever.

You may not copy this CD-ROM or any of its contents onto another CD-ROM or a computer. You may not include any material from this disk in any product to be offered for sale. Any such uses are subject to approval, additional fees, and a supplemental written license signed by Pfeiffer. Requests to the Publisher for permission should be addressed to the Permissions Department, John Wiley & Sons, Inc., 111 River Street, Hoboken, NJ 07030, (201) 748-6011, fax to (201) 748-7008, or email permcoordinator@wiley.com.

THE MATERIAL ON THIS CD-ROM IS PROVIDED "AS IS." NEITHER THE AUTHORS OF THE MATERIAL NOR PFEIFFER MAKE ANY WARRANTIES OF ANY KIND, EXPRESS OR IMPLIED, REGARDING EITHER THE FUNCTIONALITY OR THE CONTENTS. NEITHER THE AUTHORS NOR PFEIFFER ASSUME ANY RESPONSIBILITY FOR ERRORS OR OMISSIONS OR DAMAGES, INCLUDING ANY INCIDENTAL, SPECIAL, OR CONSEQUENTIAL DAMAGES TO THE FULLEST EXTENT PERMISSIBLE BY LAW, PFEIFFER DISCLAIMS ALL WARRANTIES OF MERCHANTABILITY AND FITNESS FOR A PARTICULAR PURPOSE.

The following stories may not be played for an audience under any circumstances.

"In Search of Cappuccino . . . with a Little Chocolate on the Side" by Kate Lutz
"The Disapproving Neighbor" by Kate Lutz

If you do not agree to these conditions, do not proceed to install the product and contact Pfeiffer to arrange for return before any use.